YOU'RE NOT ALONE!

Andy Childs

Cover Design by One Fine Day Reading at
www.onefinedayreading.co.uk

Published 26th April 2011

Printed and bound by Page Bros (Norwich) Ltd., Mile Cross Lane, Norwich NR6 6SA

CONTENTS

The contents of this book are largely of a serious nature. The author has through the circumstances faced by the family tried to portray the lighter side of life as it affected the subjects involved even if the principal character Philip was not directly implicated.

Dedications

Helen - A loyal mother par excellence.

Alice - A remarkably supportive sister to Philip, whatever the circumstances.

Philip - Despite his problems, he has achieved feats which are inspirational to others.

Edward of One Fine Day Reading - Gave me the encouragement to continue writing this story which had lain dormant for 18 months.

Jennie – For painstakingly correcting my grammatical indiscretions and unravelling some of the complexities of my jumbled up sentences!!!!!

Griff - A busy person who found the time to contribute a most sincere foreword.

Stephen - Without his computer expertise in recovering and transferring the information stored on the floppy disc of a 20 year old word processor this book would have foundered.

The Home Farm Trust - A charity with the highest ideals and integrity. Whilst there has been no input to this book from the charity or its current staff, without them would Helen and I even be here today?

Bucks County Council - Thanks for their long standing support of Philip by way of their sponsorship of his care.

YOU'RE NOT ALONE!

Foreword
By Griff Rhys Jones

It is difficult for the vast majority of us to imagine how it must feel to have a child born with a learning disability (or what was previously known as a mental handicap). We can think of the sadness and the shock. We can try to imagine the difficulty and the dashed expectations. We can sympathise and we empathise. But I submit that most of us can barely imagine what it really demands: day after day, week after week, year after year – a lifetime of commitment. Yes, an entire life. Because this is not just a new life for a child. It is a new life for a parent. It is a clash of lives, a mix of lives, an alteration of lives, an interaction of lives that will continue not just through childhood and adolescence but long into adulthood too.

The achievement of this book is to show that such an experience can be a triumph for everybody. There is no shortage of pain and sadness here, of disappointment, sheer hard slog and remorseless dedication. But, my goodness, this is also a story of achievement, victory and joy. Philip has autism. He may be stubborn and prone to outbursts of violence. The chronicle of the diagnosis and development is sometimes difficult to read. But Philip is a great person with his own take on the world, and a tremendous personality that shines through the pages. I feel privileged to have been able to meet him myself. Philip became a dedicated and persevering cyclist who with the support of his family raised huge amounts for charity. I mean huge. He twice wins major philanthropic prizes. He becomes lauded and feted by famous people. And his father and mother set aside all their personal ambitions to help him do so much for others and, in a way, for himself. Most of this book is a record of unstinting love.

I have children. They have grown up. I watched them take their first steps as infants and now I watch them take their first steps as adults, steps which, all along the way have carried them into maturity and self determination. Meeting and working with parents and now reading this wonderful book it is the long term commitment that makes the difference. Could you cope? Could I? Andy Childs writes candidly and directly about his son. This is a story of faith. Faith in another human being and his potential. Faith that love will be rewarded. Faith that the rewards of love and support are waiting for anybody who makes the effort. It was an effort, make no mistake. There were difficult times and harsh, unforgiving conclusions to be drawn but with what a result. Philip is a great person. He has tremendous potential and a huge appetite for achievement. In this book we do not see the disability, we see the ability. We do not witness the handicap, we witness the achievement.

I am so proud, as patron of HFT, that our great charity played its part. Amongst the most harrowing passages in this book are the ones where Andy worries that his son may not be accepted by HFT, or at a later stage may have to leave, but the Trust takes up the challenge and finds a place for him and a way of supporting his needs. That is what the Trust is there for. To step in and help people like Philip achieve what they are truly capable of in adult life. When you read this story you will discover that those possibilities are limitless.

Griff Rhys Jones

YOU'RE NOT ALONE!

YOU'RE NOT ALONE!

Chapter 1 - In the Beginning

Who rubs shoulders with H.R.H. The Princess Royal? Who has upstaged Richard Baker on stage at The Bristol Hippodrome? Who won a trophy previously held by Ian Botham, not once but is the only person to have won it twice? Who has been invited to tea with Griff Rhys Jones and, so as not to be outdone, by H.M. The Queen a few months later? Who was congratulated by Brian Johnston for his great courage? Who was greeted like a long lost friend by Helen Worth (Gail) of Coronation Street? Who was featured on ITV London? Who was commended by Terry Wogan on his Breakfast Show? Who has been listed within the Birthdays column of The Times? Who in his early days had nursery tea with James and Marina Ogilvie and lastly but by no means least, who holds an Honours Award from the British Heart Foundation?

This hasn't all happened by accident. It is the c.v. of a very special young man named Philip. As Mary Poppins says. "Let's start at the very beginning; it's a very good place to start."

The moment I had waited for these past few months had arrived. As the snow fell heavily outside the telephone rang. It must have been urgent as I was not normally interrupted when interviewing a customer for a loan or overdraft at the office of Lloyds Bank, which I managed in Luton. Pam, my rather rotund office junior clerk and receptionist, who was a rather meek and mild young lady and who was probably expecting a rebuke, said "I am so sorry to interrupt Mr. Childs but the caller insisted she speak to you."

I took the call. "Is that Mr. Childs?" the caller asked. I was immediately alerted by the urgency in the tone of voice. "Yes", I replied. "This is the maternity sister at the Luton & Dunstable, can you come quickly as your son has been born? Your wife is very distressed as we have had complications with the delivery."

"Yes, I'll be there in ten minutes." I spluttered, and immediately excused myself by handing over the interview to my assistant.

As I ran to the car park within the Vauxhall Motors factory my mind was running riot. Is my son going to live? What were the complications? What will we do if we lose him? How do we break the news to awaiting grandparents? My mind was in an absolute whirl with no answers.

I often wonder how I got safely to the hospital as I have no recollection of the three mile journey through the congested heart of Luton, Bury Park and Leagrave. I had been in a similar turmoil only two nights previously when Helen discovered she was losing blood and a placenta previa was suspected. Some forty years on, I recall that evening vividly, with the doctor urgently calling an ambulance. A mini drama then commenced as, having loaded us on board, the ambulance would not start. After much cranking and whirring it eventually got going and, to save further embarrassment, the journey took place with the blue light flashing to ensure it did not have to stop and risk the vehicle stalling.

There was an initial reprieve at the hospital as it was decided a caesarean was not necessary, but Helen would be kept in hospital for the baby to be born naturally. Panic over, I walked pensively home.

Knowing my way from two days earlier, I rushed up the stairs to the ward. As I entered I was met by a nurse who was probably on the look out for me. She quickly briefed me before going to see Helen. "Your son was strangled at birth by the umbilical cord and could not breathe for twelve minutes, and we are afraid he may be seriously damaged." My face had horror written all over it. "He is in an incubator and comfortable," she added.

Helen was not in the ward where I had left her with the other mums and their babies. I was escorted to the doorway of a single bedded room. She looked bewildered, trying desperately to greet me but immediately becoming distraught as she tried to coherently relate the nightmare. With the nurse's words ringing in my ears I already felt inadequate and even more so on seeing Helen. Anxious to console and reassure her, I was unable to put on a brave face and to counter the feeling of helpless inability to do any such thing. It was an experience I never wish to encounter again.

Helen had lived through the traumatic period of delivery not really knowing what was going on except that there was a state of urgency and that she sensed there were big problems. She did her best to relate what had happened, having been reassured by the comment that our son, now known as Philip, had kept a good colour and the oxygen had not left his brain. All we could do was sob into each others arms and pray that Philip would be O.K.

After a short while I was taken to see him. There he lay, along with other babies, so small and pink and helpless as he slept peacefully in his incubator, adorned in just a nappy. He looked just so perfect, what had he done to deserve this start to life? "Will he be alright?" I asked the nurse.

"We are doing all we can for him." What else could she say? The earlier words 'difficult birth' and 'seriously damaged' would not go away. What did they mean? What would be damaged? These were thoughts I dared not repeat to Helen before I left for home. There was no sleep that night as the horror options kept boomeranging around my head. The early hours are certainly the low time for those sorts of nightmares as I had already experienced. As a bank manager, if one woke in the night worrying over a particular bad debt, another dozen could well be in the frame before one dozed off again but in the morning it never seemed so bad as the necessary action could be taken. With Philip however the easing of the pain was not possible as everything was beyond my control. I could do nothing except support Helen and pray for our son.

Trying to keep my emotions under control, calls were made to grandparents and family, simply to report that Philip had arrived but it had been a difficult birth. Why say more, as it would only prompt questions to which there were no answers? Subsequently it transpired they gathered from my creaking voice that something was sadly amiss.

Thankfully however, shafts of light started to come through the pitch-black tunnel. Philip was feeding from Helen which was a good sign. After four nerve-wracking days he was removed from the incubator and we were told he was progressing O.K. and that as far as nursing staff were aware, despite the twelve minutes of strangulation, the air had not left his brain. It was seven days before Mum and Philip came home with the caveat that in view of the difficulties at birth, we should watch his development very carefully, which we did along with the medics. All was well after all. Or was it?

Chapter 2 - Hope turns to Disaster

Over the following six months, taking us to October, our anxieties decreased. Philip was a happy, contented baby. He matched the other babies around him, progressing both physically and mentally.

The time came for his injections, including one for whooping cough. Within days of these injections, Philip was not his usual happy self. Gone were the chuckles and excitement as his early bottle of milk, along with our first cup of tea, ascended the stairs. The change was such that we referred him to our doctor who put the change down to indigestion and teething.

Philip's strange new disposition both continued and intensified but a more worrying pattern was emerging. We were naive and could only explain to the medics when the attacks came that Philip drew his legs up and winced in discomfort. Pathetically, he would then cry to a state of virtual exhaustion but could still not relax and sleep peacefully. The original diagnosis continued, with deluxe gripe water prescribed. This seemed to help in that the distress after an attack diminished and he could get to sleep.

After the difficult birth, these were worrying times and we became more anxious as the attacks became more frequent. Sometimes there would be as many as four attacks in a day. At last, and not before time in view of his difficult birth, Philip was referred to Dr. Fagg, a paediatrician attached to the Luton & Dunstable Hospital.

As we sat anxiously waiting for our turn to see Dr. Fagg in a crowded waiting room, Philip had an attack. Without ceremony, and against all etiquette and to the utter surprise of the nurse, we raced into Dr. Fagg's surgery.

The problem was soon diagnosed as a convulsion. In other words Philip had been fitting for some weeks and this had not been suspected. In hindsight would anything be different today had there been an earlier diagnosis? Probably not, but we will never know.
Tests were undertaken, all of which were negative. Medication was changed twice, with Predlesline prescribed just before Christmas.

Our first Christmas with Philip should have been a very special one but instead it was like a roller-coaster ride. On Christmas morning a large red paper parcel caught his eye. When it was ceremoniously split open he shrieked with joy, smiled and had a fit as if his body could not cope with the excitement and had to shut down. Boxing Day morning was a happy time though not without a fit, but this did not deter his endearing smile.

In the afternoon Philip awoke from his sleep in some distress, having cut his third tooth. We hoped this may have changed things for the better but it was a short lived false hope as, soon after this, he had a severe fit which changed his ongoing disposition completely.

The cumulative strain for both of us, from fearing the worst every time Philip cried was enormous. How we, and in particular Helen, coped with the fits one does not know, but cope we had to, and to pass through short anxious periods until the next one. Life was a constant see-saw with no answers and therefore with little in the way of comfort we could give each other.

Dr. Fagg referred Philip to Professor Tizard, a consultant paediatrician based at Hammersmith Hospital. He was admitted to hospital in early January for assessment, spending a long six weeks in their care.

Reassuring comments were made by all and sundry.
'He is in the best place.'
'It is marvellous what modern medicine can do.'
'We know what you must be going through'.
Did they hell, I thought. They had no idea unless they had been through a similar experience themselves. They could have had no inkling how we were being pulled to and fro, trying to hold a job down and support each other. We felt absolutely helpless. To a lesser degree, forty years on, we still get the same third party comments. As each crisis arises we can only pray that it will gradually subside again, but with advancing age coping becomes ever more difficult.

The time Philip was in Hammersmith Hospital relieved us of the day-to-day strain and responsibility but it brought other problems. Luton to Hammersmith was not an easy journey. Hardly a day passed without Helen visiting or staying at the hospital. There was no alternative. Emotionally, we could not abandon Philip even for a single day. We would get back late at night, not be able to sleep and then have to be off to work the next morning. Thankfully, we had the fortitude to survive, but not without the odd hiccup.

A doctor on his rounds came into Philip's ward room one morning and said "Good morning" to Helen, who was staying at the hospital. At this, she burst into tears and was immediately sent home by the sister to have a break from her daily vigil. The pent-up emotions in this sort of situation are unrelenting and indescribable. When the to-ing and fro-ing was over and Philip was home again we wondered in retrospect how we had coped. There was no place for exhaustion or feeling sorry for ourselves; life had to go on and we had to support our son.

Philip was monitored day and night at the hospital, having endless tests and X-rays, but nothing very conclusive transpired. Helen helped the nurses where she could and as she was judged to be a sensible, reliable mum she was even asked to take Philip off down the long corridors within the hospital for his EEG's.

Time at the hospital created relationships and time to talk to 'mums' similarly affected, as all of the resident children were in serious trouble with one problem or another. There were also lighter moments during the time at Hammersmith Hospital as Helen became involved for two days in a BBC T.V. documentary entitled "Children in Hospital!" It very much epitomised our plight, but despite the anticipation of a starring role and the considerable film footage being used, she was limited to a few seconds feeding Philip his bottle - what a let down. Looking back, at least it passed a couple of days in a harmless and interesting way!

The hospital had a fairly relaxed attitude to taking Philip off the premises for excursions. One hastily arranged outing was to Thatched House Lodge in Richmond Park, the home of Princess Alexandra. My step aunt, Miss Rattle, known as Aunt Olive, was the long term nanny to the princess's children James & Marina.

Security clearance was not a problem as Sir Angus and The Princess were away on an overseas tour. Nevertheless, we rather nervously approached the front gates of this imposing house in our modest, green, wooden-battened Mini Traveller. We were welcomed rather excitedly by James and Marina and shown upstairs to their nursery. They showed great interest in Philip as he lay on their hearth-rug.

Philip enjoyed these trips out, especially where a ride in the car was involved. We also enjoyed being able to take him out and to have him to ourselves for a few precious hours, away from the hospital environment.

Some thirty years after our initial visit to Thatched House Lodge, Nanny Rattle held a 90th birthday party, which I arranged at a hotel in Richmond, for her and her ageing nanny friends, many of whom had also looked after members of the Royal Family and who were featured in a Sunday Times article concerning the then institution, the British Nanny.

The lunch was followed by the most informal and charming afternoon tea in the company of Sir Angus and The Princess at their home. We walked the gardens, laughed and joked and took group photographs just like any other family occasion. It was our privilege to be there.

During his stay at Hammersmith, Philip had numerous tests and X-rays. The final X-ray was to be of his brain. We were petrified by the thought of this and I was particularly fearful Helen would get to know the results without my presence. Such was my concern I telephoned the house doctor, on a Friday, who said "I am relieved you have phoned as the news on Philip is, as we feared, far from good and I did not know how to break it to you." Rapidly collecting my thoughts I asked if we could meet on Monday as this would give me the weekend to work on Helen, preparing her for a "what if" scenario should we be faced with the dreaded bad news.

Helen was at the hospital as we spoke and I later met her off the train when she came back. We were to go to a dinner dance at Dunstable in the evening. Despite our anxieties life had to go on. We had to meet others and keep sane. It was also awkward for our friends; they knew we had a big problem and, whilst they wished to know the latest news they did not want to bring up the subject of Philip when we were trying to relax in their company. On this particular Friday evening we were not good company, either to our friends or to each other. I knew, and Helen knew, or suspected, that something was seriously amiss.

Helen was aware the X-ray results had not been revealed, having asked the question during the day at Hammersmith. With the house doctor not available she was told by the ward sister that she would arrange for a meeting on Monday. Our conversations over the following two days were all on the fearful and pessimistic side.

Whatever the results, we were full of resolve to stand by Philip but little did we really understand what this would amount to.

Despite trying to prepare ourselves for the worst scenario, actually hearing the results and the ongoing prognosis was a devastating experience. In hindsight nothing could have prepared us for this news. Philip's brain was damaged and he was likely to be severely mentally handicapped. How do you cope with a statement of fact like that? For a start you just go numb, and try to get comfort from cuddling the little bundle and reproaching yourselves for his likely life-long predicament. Words could not begin to describe the repeated feeling of helplessness and bewilderment as we looked down on this tiny mite who had had the chance of a normal life snuffed out before it had begun, through no fault of his own. Life can be oh so cruel and it does make one wonder if there really is a God in heaven.   If there were, I thought to myself, why would he let such things happen?

When giving talks on the aspects of Philip's life, I always start with the statistic that the chances of being mentally handicapped (now referred to as having a learning disability) are 100 - 1 and the difference between an illness and mental handicap is that with the former, however serious the condition, one has a chance of making a full or partial recovery whereas with the latter the brain has been damaged and the person involved will never recover from that disability - this statistic and the finality of the problem can be guaranteed to grab the attention of the audience.

Despite his problems, Philip was still eating well and from a low point of lying in his cot virtually motionless he had started to take notice and to react to us again. He had formed a bond with a Panda his godfather, Uncle Ed had brought into the hospital, probably because of the contrasting black and white colours. This toy was to become his inseparable companion through subsequent operations and numerous recoveries. Perhaps predictably, the panda became known as 'Pa Pa'.

A week after the shattering news of the brain damage was broken to us we were summoned to see Professor Tizard, as Philip was to be discharged from hospital. It was not that he was better, or improving, but rather that it was the end of the road as an in-patient as far as the hospital was concerned.

Carrying Philip, we walked slowly down the seemingly endless corridors and ascended the narrow spiral staircase to the professor's office. He knew we were desperately caring parents from observing the unstinting support Helen had given Philip whilst in the hospital's care. This made the initial comments from him even more difficult as he thumbed through his papers searching for an opening and not meeting our eyes in the process. The opening words suddenly blurted from his mouth "You know we are about to discharge Philip. His future is not bright." He paused and then continued "There is little comfort or hope I can offer. What can be made of Philip is up to you both."

Whilst we were not expecting too many words of positive reassurance or comfort, this was even more stark and dramatic than we expected. The shock of hearing these ominous words was even more devastating than anything previously experienced - they were numbing. Helen asked whether it could have been the whooping cough injection that had caused the dramatic change in Philip, as within a matter of days of having it he had changed from a happy, progressive baby to what was now being described as a virtual cabbage with no future. This very obviously took the professor aback. He said after due pause that he could not rule it out but neither could it be conclusively proved to have been the case, bearing in mind the difficult birth Philip had experienced. This could also have been a contributory factor.

Even forty years on, the controversy still rages about the effect of some drugs on children and whether the triple vaccine is safe. We will never be other than convinced that Philip's problems stemmed from the whooping cough injection. After all, he was 'normal' for six months and started to fit immediately after his injections. What else can one think given the circumstances of his sad decline?

In my opinion with controversial medicine it is sad, that where it suits them, politicians who should be showing the way appear to hide behind privacy which to me exudes the message 'don't do as I do, do as I tell you!' It doesn't give those similarly affected too much confidence in the only option open to them.

Chapter 3 - A Guardian Angel Appears

Having been handed our precious ten month old human bundle along with the devastating comment from an eminent paediatrician, that Philip had little future and that what we made of him was up to us, we were utterly shattered as we returned to the ward. Sister put her hand on Helen's shoulder and said in very quiet tones to her "I know the news you have received this morning is not what you, or any of us, would have wished but we have admired your fortitude these past weeks. Philip will, with parents like yourselves, get every chance in life to reach his full potential." These were emotional words from a person who had seen it all before. She then turned her face away quickly and returned to her office. We said our crestfallen thank yous and good-byes to the other nurses, many of whom we had come to know too well, but try as they may, they could not be fully detached from their long term patients, especially where a child was concerned. Philip's belongings were slowly gathered up and we left the ward in an emotional state, not daring to look back, to return home with our charge. It was the first time for six weeks we had been solely responsible for his care.

It was a long, lonely journey back to Luton with hardly a word spoken. We were still in a state of shocked stupor from the prognosis handed out a few minutes earlier. Philip slept the thirty miles back and Helen held him tightly in her arms on the back seat of the Mini Traveller. Us, why us, why Philip when he had appeared to be doing so well, were our recurring thoughts? What will we be able to do for this little bundle of such brief joy if his future is predicted to be so bleak? Many moments of despair, heart searching and self recrimination, with the occasional ray of hope, were always around as we tried to come to terms with our lot.

We asked ourselves what had changed during the past three months? Philip, who earlier splashed and reacted so happily in his bath, was now largely passive, and gone was his infectious chuckle. Now he had little interest in things around him. He was making little use of his hands and, for long periods, stared at them as though they were foreign to his body. Those baby noises and shrieks of joy were things of the past and had been replaced by lots of one tone droning.

In amongst the gloom we also tried to look on the plus side - he was growing well, was a good looking lad and was forming a strong bond with his new friend Pa Pa, whom he placed over his nose and mouth when he went to sleep. The effects of the cortisone drugs were also making him look chubby in the face.

Sleep was important to us both in coping with Philip's problems and with each other's times of feeling down in the dumps. In these circumstances it was difficult to stay positive but we had to remain so. Every little grizzle or snuffle made by Philip during the night alerted the ever light-sleeping Helen, as a fit would be suspected. It was impossible to totally relax. On numerous occasions our fears would be confirmed, and so it was another disturbed night until we settled him down again. This was exhausting for Helen as she was on duty day and night. This could not go on so we agreed we would attend to Philip on alternate nights but Helen, on duty or not, was always switched on to the problem first and she would wake me so that I did the running about and supervision until after the fit and Philip had settled back to sleep. This was not always immediate and neither was it immediate with ourselves. These were long, tortuous nights.

To this day Helen's light sleeping continues but it is now me who creates the disturbance. I get no comforting words however, in fact just the contrary, plus for good measure a hefty unceremonious dig in the ribs!

As the days and weeks passed the mist of shock and uncertainty gradually lessened and we started to come to terms with our predicament, if you ever really can. At least we started to think more positively as, after all, Philip was not the 'cabbage' we had been led to expect he would be. With our love and stimulation he was showing positive signs of progress, albeit slowly, by way of movement and interest. The single tone droning with the occasional high pitched interlude still went on with Pa Pa. He was so obviously very much part of Philip's world and comfort.

Despite what we saw as progress, times of dark despair still occurred, particularly when Philip was having a fit. On one such evening the telephone rang and, as if by magic, our prayers were answered. A Leslie Barker of Martlesham in Suffolk, (Douglas Bader country, if ever one was looking for inspiration), and who knew of Philip and his problems through Helen's parents, had said he would like to see Philip when he came out of hospital. True to his word he had regularly asked about the ongoing welfare of Philip and now wished to see him.

Mr. Barker was an osteopath, an occupation then seen as quack medicine and largely frowned upon by the medical profession. To our great sadness we only learnt on his death that not only was he a much respected osteopath but he was also an acknowledged world authority on cranial treatment, regularly making trips to America to lecture students. While we were desperate for Philip to receive help, that our hopes should be raised, as they were, by someone we had never met or even previously spoken to was quite incredible – but what a Guardian Angel he turned out to be!

With nothing to lose and no idea of his likely fees we travelled what were in those days the torturous 120 miles to East Anglia. Fortunately this was the area of our origins and as our parents still lived there we had a base to stay for the weekend after seeing Mr. Barker. As we neared Martlesham for the first appointment we became increasingly nervous as we feared we may be about to have the words of Professor Tizard repeated and our hopes dashed before they even had a chance to bear fruit. As we approached the bungalow set amongst the trees our fears seemed to evaporate and the atmosphere as we waited on a Saturday afternoon in his reception area, with no other patients around, was one of peace and tranquillity. Mrs. Barker, who had a warm, caring disposition, welcomed us and chatted as if we had known her all our lives - not once did she mention Philip or his problems. Quietly, an inner door opened and Mr. Barker entered the room. He had a kindly face with a welcoming smile and an air of someone who went quietly about his business without too much fuss. We were all quickly at ease in his company. These relaxed vibes, without doubt, would also have been transmitted to Philip.

We went through to his treatment room. He asked a few questions to ascertain a brief history of Philip's short life. He gently ran his hands over Philip and carefully lifted him on to a raised couch. Not a word was spoken and then with the back of Philip's head cupped in his hands he closed his eyes and we can only assume, with our subsequent knowledge, gently worked on the cranial area of his head. Philip didn't move or protest. All of this was carried on in such a quiet, yet positively relaxed manner, without a word being spoken. Through Mr. Barker's quietly and gently performed actions, confidence flooded through to us that our Guardian Angel seemed to know exactly what he was trying to achieve.

What a relief at the end of the first treatment to hear Mr. Barker saying, "I think I can help Philip overcome SOME of his problems. His skull needs to be straightened but our biggest battle will be to get the level of Philip's drugs reduced as they are feeding the condition." What a staggering statement the latter comment was. It would have been like a 'red rag to a bull' if this information was passed on to Hammersmith Hospital, or had they known we were consulting an osteopath. We would surely have been shown the door, such would have been their indignation.

Philip continued to fit but on a reduced basis shortly after the first and subsequent treatments, though sometimes a major fit took place before the improvement. This was always extremely worrying and disturbing to us, but Mr. Barker was always reassuring in his telephone comments, adding that we had to be patient. In answer to our question of payment for his services he simply gave one of his reserved smiles and quietly said, "We'll see."

Our first follow up appointment was due at Hammersmith. We did not see Professor Tizard, but his team were very obviously surprised to see the progress of this bundle we had been handed only a few weeks earlier. Against what they called their 'better judgement' the drug level was rather reluctantly reduced. Cortisone, which was Philip's medication, is a drug which can only be reduced gradually and in any event, we said, it could always be increased again if we had made a mistake in asking for a reduced dosage.

Being now totally reliant on the expertise of Mr. Barker for our guidance and support, we gleefully passed on the news that the hospital had agreed to reduce Philip's dosage. He was surprised, pleased and encouraged with our success, continuing to see Philip on a monthly basis.

With roads as they were in the late 60's and with me trying to hold down a responsible job at Lloyds Bank, the burden of regular travel fell to Helen. Bob, our brother-in-law, offered to meet us half way and would then transport Helen and Philip to Martlesham. We would all do the reverse journey a day or two later.

As Philip had become so relaxed in the company of Mr. Barker during his treatments he would often fall asleep, particularly whilst those healing hands worked on his neck and head. Everything that Mr. Barker did was so serenely performed.   It was an incredible boost to our confidence in him. No extravagant claims, just quiet professionalism.

After each visit to Mr. Barker, Philip's mobility noticeably improved and the hospital agreed, based on our verbal up-date, to reduce the drug intake still further. Whilst Mr. Barker's period of treatment was going on it was not all smooth going by any means, but if Philip's condition gave us cause for concern, which it still did, a phone call would bring reassuring words, which without fail, would come to pass. Through this confidence we were certainly given the determination, strength and not a little hope to carry on, particularly as it was clear Philip was physically doing so well.

Progress was such that, between being handed a helpless bundle in March 1967, until the next time we met Professor Tizard, a year after Philip's discharge, he had learned to sit up, crawl and walk. Even his spastic tendencies had lessened considerably by this time.

Every new milestone achieved by Philip was oh so sweet and a cause for relieved and thankful celebration. Helen was in tears when she telephoned me at work to exclaim, "He's sitting up and he's so pleased with himself." Shortly afterwards he was rolling around and suddenly started to project himself about on the floor which very quickly turned into a crawl. He really was 'feeling his feet' as he started trying to pull himself up on chairs. It wasn't long before he succeeded.

To help this sudden burst of progress we bought a Baby Walker which had a soft material crotch support and four wheels on casters. Once placed inside, Philip could freely use his legs and most importantly we would not have the fear of him falling and hurting his very fragile head. The Baby Walker was like a magic potion to us all. Philip soon found, as his legs strengthened, that he could propel himself along in any direction, even on carpet, never knocking into furniture or scarring doors or their frames. Philip suddenly had the run of the ground floor of the house. This was wonderful. He was tiring naturally from his own physical endeavours without increasing his level or intensity of fits. He never tired of sitting in his walker or watching the traffic speeding along the slightly elevated nearby M1 from our conveniently placed front window with its low sill. A motorway was a novelty in those days, not only to Philip but to everyone who visited us. As he sat in his Baby Walker observing the traffic one could watch his eyelids drooping which soon transferred into peaceful sleep, such was his fascination with the nearby movement.

This was a time of great excitement with the Baby Walker soon redundant as Philip progressed to unaided walking. Every development in this way brought joy and renewed hope to us both.

Whilst these exciting developments were going on we had noticed Philip was becoming habitual in his behaviour in that whatever else was on offer for tea he always wanted soup with toast dropped into it and a piece of Mum's home made sponge - the latter was a wise choice! When playing with cars he always arranged them in straight lines and he got upset if an interfering father placed them otherwise. This did not bother us; there was so much progress elsewhere, as a happy and inquisitive child became reborn moving on at last with his own recreation.

Further months passed and it was our time to visit Hammersmith again. On this occasion we were to see Professor Tizard. We were thrilled and proud of Philip's achievements since the previous appointment. The professor, who was already on the ward, had a look of utter disbelief on his face as Philip literally ran into the room and straight up to the ward sister, who for a second time had problems controlling her immediate emotions as she excitedly exclaimed "Is this our Philip?" The professor was obviously pleased and amazed at Philip's progress. He added, "I congratulate you both on what you have achieved with Philip but please do not get too optimistic about his future as he will still face serious problems during his development."

Physically, Philip was doing fine, but we were only too aware that mentally he was only making slow, spiky progress. Compared with the darkest days only a few months earlier we could accept where we were today, but we could not ignore the professor's caveats, which were still ringing in our ears as we left the ward.

We still did not feel able to reveal to the professor, Mr. Barker's presence or the treatment Philip was receiving from him. Today we have moved on and there is a limited place for alternative medicine, but I seriously doubt whether if our circumstances were repeated in 2010, much encouragement would even yet be given to seeking outside help from an osteopath.

We finally got the all clear to stop the medication completely. Unbelievably, the day the medication stopped so did the fits. Mr. Barker's initial words uttered only a few months previously had been borne out but we still kept this information a secret, at least for the time being. What caused the fits to start we will never know, but we will always suspect the whooping cough inoculations.

What is certain is that Mr. Barker's hands certainly helped Philip physically for all to see after his treatment started. There were no before and after X-rays as he quietly showed us how he had changed the shape of Philip's forehead and in turn, had straightened his skull. To us it was an incredible gift of perception coupled with the divine ability, used without fuss, to be able to help Philip in the way he had. To our untrained eyes, and those of the doctors, not too much had ever looked amiss in the first place. If it had been spotted, Professor Tizard admitted later, there would have been little they could or would have tried to do about it.

Thank you, thank you Mr. Barker for your perception and expertise; where would we have been without it? Philip without you would have had a slightly misshapen head, probably not walked too well and not developed into the able bodied six foot, well built, agile young man he is today.

Chapter 4 - On the Move

It was some weeks before we could believe the fits had stopped and that every little noise coming from Philip's bedroom was quite normal. Gradually we were able to relax and return to some semblance of a normal life.

Whilst we had stayed with parents during the visits to Mr. Barker, family members had not visited us for months. We were too busy flying hither and thither to make commitments. Now, telephone conversations were less guarded as we could report progress without trying to sound more reassured than we felt; not an easy task when the future is so uncertain and you yourselves feel low and emotional.

From time to time, the emotions boiled over, but only with each other. Somehow, Helen, when it mattered most, kept the lid on things with incredible dignity. I went to work, which gave me a change of scenery and with the excellent understanding camaraderie this temporarily took my mind off our problems. Helen had no such valve, she was always on duty and there was little I could do to change this scenario or, other than taking her shopping, to give her a break.

With grandparents staying and having the confidence to start looking after Philip again we were able to go out for a couple of hours, usually to the Sugar Loaf in Dunstable. It was bliss just to sit down, be waited upon and have a quiet, undisturbed drink with our meal. There were no mobile phones in those days so we just hoped there would be no call to the restaurant and everything was going on O.K. at home. Thankfully it always was.

With the fits having ended, Hammersmith Hospital soon bade us farewell and handed Philip's records back to our G.P. and Luton & Dunstable Hospital. His general health was remarkably good, as it has always been, so visits to the doctor were rare.

Shortly after our loss of contact with Hammersmith, Mr. Barker also said he had done all he could for Philip and we bade him too, a sad but eternally grateful farewell. What he had achieved for Philip physically was beyond words to express. This also applied to what he had done psychologically for us. His intervention and reassuring words when things were not going well inspired us to keep going. He had taken us from despair to a world of hope and renewed determination to do all we could for Philip, whatever the future threw at us, with the knowledge he had a damaged brain and that it was an irreparable item. How that damage would affect him in the years to come we still did not know. With all the excitement of the physical progress it had not gone unnoticed by us that Philip's speech was virtually non- existent, and what there was, was very monotone and repetitive in content. Improvement to this element of his limited abilities had, therefore, to be top of the list.

Prior to our departure from Mr. Barker we tried for a final time to get him to take some financial reward for his endeavours on behalf of Philip. His reward was obviously what he had been able to do to help Philip as he just smiled and quietly said, "If I have been able to help that young life in some way it has been my pleasure and privilege to be able to do so." How can one even try to put into context the sincerity and power of those few words?

All of a sudden, from running hither and thither to keep appointments to discuss Philip, we were on our own, but fate soon occupied our minds. The bank offered me the Sub Manager's position at their Sidney Street, Cambridge branch. Without too much deliberation I accepted, as despite our problems I still had to think about a career and our future security.

The promotion would mean a change of house, with Helen being left with Philip until we could move, as daily travel was out of the question. This arrangement worked well, Philip continued his progress and Helen was able to catch up with a few friends. There was always great excitement from Philip prior to Dad arriving home at lunch time on Saturdays. He was pleased to welcome me back and would be standing in the front window awaiting my arrival.

As a family, in addition to the excitement of finding a new house, there was the added welcome news that a new baby was on the way. Incredibly, after much thought, we were ready to cope with those new responsibilities and were looking forward to them. Philip, despite his likely problems in the future had not, up to now, been a difficult child.

A business trip to London was used as an excuse for us all to have a day out, expenses paid. The first highlight for Philip was hailing a taxi and jumping in. His face was a picture. He soon adopted the rear folding seats and looked out of the window in awe at the big red buses going to and fro and the hive of activity around us when we stopped at traffic lights, and as the cab weaved in and out of the hubbub outside.

He was mesmerised by all the activity. He was a very happy little boy.

The second highlight was one of some eye-popping magnitude - a visit to Hamleys, Oxford Street! When we had got over the Aladdin's Cave of toys, (this being our first visit to the store) we settled down amongst the mayhem of the special ground level and aerial displays to start our own wide-eyed viewing. Almost immediately, Philip spotted a big brightly painted red tin with a handle and lid. We guessed what it was. Helen made to gently turn the handle only for the first movement to go POP and up shot a kindly-faced clown. The person playing with this before us obviously had a wicked sense of humour. We were all startled and Helen nearly dropped the box. Philip thought this was hilarious and, far from being frightened, turned the handle to play the nursery rhyme through for the full 'Pop goes the Weasel' treatment to be meted out. Our first purchase of the day was enthusiastically made. What a favourite toy this became over many years, especially when we had unsuspecting visitors who would be subjected by Philip to exactly the same scary treatment we got on that first day at Hamleys!

We did our best to involve Philip in the move. Whilst he could not respond we were sure he was more aware of what was going on than we gave him credit for. With his acute hearing not too much passed him by.

The Luton house sold easily and we moved upmarket to Cottenham on the north side of Cambridge. This took us back into the bank's East Anglian region from which we both hailed and we would, at some sixty miles away, be closer to family. Day visits both ways would now be practical.

Philip was quite happy riding around in the car house-hunting and quite unfazed as we popped in and out of selected houses. The chosen house was the last one we saw at 7 o'clock after a full Sunday afternoon circling around Cambridge. The house was ideal for us all in every respect. We would have the then luxury of warm air central heating together with a large south-facing, enclosed, flat rear garden which backed onto market gardens - an ideal playground environment for Philip.

Cottenham was a long sprawl of a village but it had all the facilities we needed for a good quality of life, especially with Cambridge nearby. This is in contrast to today when we are forever seeing on T.V. the continuing controversy over the blight of alleged illegal traveller's sites in the village.

It was all going too well, the job, the house sale and we had a date for moving. Unexpectedly there was a problem with the purchase at Cottenham. As we did not want to lose the property we had so fallen in love with we opted for a delayed completion. We completed the sale at Luton, our furniture went into store, and Helen moved with Philip to stay with grandparents in Ipswich for a few weeks.

This was not seen as an issue as it would be nice for us to make up lost time by staying with close family for a short period. Travelling at weekends would be the same for me, only easier. We were all very relaxed about the delay and temporary arrangements.

The Cambridge job was demanding but going well, with great staff and management support towards our family circumstances. Then, one afternoon, 'out of the blue', another of those dreaded phone calls from my mother. "Helen is threatening to miscarry, can you come? The doctor is with her."

'Oh no, not again,' I thought to myself as I left immediately, breaking all the speed limits along the way. Sadly, by the time I arrived in Ipswich it was all over, and another disaster presented itself; we had lost our expected baby. Had we not suffered enough already? Who knows, perhaps if all was not well it was for the best. We could not have faced yet more problems.

This was another unexpected blow to get over but, thankfully, Helen was with family and the move to Cottenham suddenly came on stream. This ensured our minds were fully occupied with the future again rather than the past. It was worth the wait to take up occupation.

We soon settled into our new surroundings. To be living in the heart of the fens and backing onto market gardens, with very friendly and generous owners and orchards to the side, gave us such a peaceful and open environment - it was total relaxation and just right for our family life.

With a large lawn area to play on, Philip was in his element, busying himself in his first sand pit in the shade of the beech hedge at the bottom of the garden. When he was outside, he could be unobtrusively observed. He loved copying me, gardening and moving his tools, sand and soil around in his bright red wheelbarrow.

He also marvelled at a small new instant lawn area as turf arrived and was placed on the soil he had helped me to rake flat. 'Helped' is perhaps the wrong word as he insisted on walking on the flattened area as soon as my back was turned and then admiring his little foot prints. 'Oh yes I'm helping Daddy all right!'

The swing arrived, together with a large slide. Whilst Philip could only use these with supervision he would often be seen taking Pa Pa to the top steps of the slide, pushing him down, scampering down the ladder, round to the front to collect him and then repeating the exercise time and again. He would also enjoy and look forward to being gently pushed to and fro on the swing. Pa Pa, who was by this time getting filthy also had to have his turn. We now had a two year old son who was always busy, contented and usually happy and so, for the first time, we decided to take him away for a holiday. It would do us all good to have a few days' break in a new environment with other members of the family and their young children.

We decided on a self-catering holiday at Cromer with my sister and her family. We hired a large house with plenty of recreation space and coupled this with a hired beach hut at Mundesley for use during the day. Philip loved the company and the sandy beaches. He also enjoyed pushing his little net along the sea bed at low water trying to catch shrimps. The shrimps were boiled with the aid of a small Gaz stove complete in its blue tin - a very popular picnic cooking utensil in those days. Philip happily ate the peeled catch with bread and butter. What could be nicer, or fresher than a tea straight from the sea?

With our holiday the next year we were more ambitious, joining friends John and Julie and their children at a hotel in Ventnor on the Isle of Wight. It was again a great success, with Philip enjoying the ferry crossing, sandy beaches and riding on the hissing, puffing steam trains. There was just the one little problem but it could have been a major one. With the children all safely tucked up in bed we were enjoying our dinner when the head waiter came over to our table with some urgency in his stride and said "Will you return to your bedroom as there is a water leak?"

Panic set in as we ran up the stairs. For the first time, as far as we knew, Philip had got out of bed, turned on a tap and water was flowing out of the basin and seeping into the bedroom below. Thankfully the people occupying the bedroom below were in their room so the alarm was raised as soon as the water started to run down their wallpaper. To this day we still monitor taps being fully turned off.

Whilst Philip seemed well aware of what was going on around him his speech was still virtually non-existent. Just the odd word would be uttered more often in desperation to communicate than for the sake of talking. He held his bottle but refused to feed himself, and he continued to study his hands in great detail as if he was mesmerised by the movement of his fingers.

Suddenly, from a stance of non-cooperation with his solid food feeding, just as if something had clicked into place in his brain it was all change. He picked up and mastered the use of his spoon and pusher. Very soon after this most of his food was finishing up in his mouth and very little was ending up in his yellow pelican bib.

Looking back we can only remember the sun shining on the garden at Cottenham, although we do have photographs of Philip thoroughly enjoying a heavy snow fall. We had Ted and Trixie as neighbours. They spoke endlessly to Philip out in the garden. Whilst he could not respond, they were very adept at keeping the one-sided conversation going. This was good stimulation for Philip. Ted, a well built, quietly spoken man in particular reminded us so much of Mr. Barker with whom we were still in touch, but only on a social basis.

In the spring of '69 there was further excitement and joy. Helen was due to have a baby in the following December. This gave new impetus to our second summer at Cottenham. Philip was still making progress and we were all enjoying life. Philip had found that if he rocked his cot hard enough the side bolt would come out so at times it was difficult keeping him in bed if he felt otherwise! Toilet training was going better than we dared hope. Day-time nappies were dispensed with and the pot was adopted quite quickly with only the occasional 'too busy' type of accident. Night training took a little longer but it was a relatively easy process. Not like his sister who subsequently had to be promised she could go into town with daddy to buy a new nightie if she was 'dry!' It did the trick.

When Philip had moved into a bed he would even get up, come into the bedroom and quietly say "Mum, Mum!" until she responded if he wanted to go to the toilet. Progress on the physical side was certainly going well.

Exercise via walks with Philip's new big red pedal-tractor was a much-looked-for highlight. Blocks were put on the pedals so that he could propel them to and fro and thereby move and drive the tractor himself on firm surfaces. Interference was not appreciated and especially so when it was time to turn round to go home. He would have pedalled to Cambridge some six miles away rather than have his obvious enjoyment curtailed by having to retrace his steps. Suddenly, his legs would become listless or, worse still, became rigid on the pedals, which hampered our efforts to pull him along. This reluctance to use his legs for the right purpose made for hard work as the pedals could not be disconnected so we had to ensure his feet were clear of them. To combat this little foible we worked out circular walks and thereby reached an acceptable solution.

Exactly the same happened when he had learnt to ride a bike. As he dawdled along on a path it would take twice as much time to get home as it did to do the outward journey. One had to remember this likely disruption and plan accordingly, as time was often of the essence.

Philip had two nasty incidents during that summer. He was knocked into Auntie Gwen's pond by her boisterous dog Chips. Thankfully we were there to retrieve him, dripping and squawking, back onto dry land. This accident is something he has never got over in that ever since he has disliked and distrusted dogs and always tries to give them a wide berth if he is out walking. Philip is still petrified of dogs from his earlier experience, worried that when they bound up to him they will jump up or knock him flying. I do wish that dog owners would understand that even a 6', 13 stone young man can be petrified by their dog's presence. They make no attempt to call off their pooch, simply saying "He won't hurt you he just wants to be friendly" etc. They just do not seem to appreciate that not everyone likes animals. The one exception, when dogs don't bother him, is when he is out on shoots and beating alongside me, with the gun dogs running to and fro. These dogs are only interested in game and are not concerned with his or anyone else's presence, and are also usually in wide open spaces.

The other potentially very serious incident happened at The Marine, in Tankerton, where we were staying whilst visiting my brother in Whitstable for a short summer break. We had gone down to dinner and on returning during the meal to check if Philip was alright, we found to our horror that the room had been ransacked with Philip still in his cot within the room. The thief would not have known of Philip's inability to communicate and could have set out to quieten him. Thankfully, he was unharmed and probably asleep during the presence of the thief who was only looking for cash. He relieved us of £80 which the hotel owners immediately made good.

Despite all the problems Philip was facing he was a loveable little chap. He had a cheeky grin with a sense of humour and a mind of his own. His play tended to be repetitive and his speech remained very limited. The development of his personality was, at the time, disguising other shortcomings.

The filthy state of Pa Pa was a problem Helen had to combat as he had become a bosom pal to Philip. He had been washed and washed but now had a threadbare front. Helen managed to find similar materials and told Philip that Pa Pa was not very well and needed a new coat. This was not received too enthusiastically but the new coat had to be put on or his stuffing would have fallen out. There was an initial rejection but after a day or so he had acquired the right odours and feel to be acceptable again. Smell, as then, continues to play an important part in Philip's acceptance or rejection of food. We jokingly comment that we could never poison him, as if new food or drink does not pass the smell test it remains on his plate or in the glass!

Two unrelated excitements took place during Helen's pregnancy. First, Les and Phil, who owned the adjoining smallholding, lit a bonfire which they then proceeded to leave unattended. It flared up and set fire to our bottom hedge and the dry grass at its roots. Helen was in no position to do anything about it and had to call the fire brigade. Philip was in his element with all the excitement as the part-time Cottenham crew arrived with bells ringing and blue light flashing. In a matter of seconds the flames were doused and the excitement was over.

Shortly afterwards, not to be outdone, I was clearing an overgrown ditch by the orchard which infested our garden with weeds. I had a small fire going which suddenly decided it wanted to expand its territory. At that precise moment 'her indoors' looked out of the window and could see the potential danger. Before I knew what was happening, neighbours were rushing round just as I had cleared a fire break in the undergrowth and before another 999 call was made! It did, however make me realise how quickly one could get engulfed in an out-of-control fire.

Thankfully, Helen was having a trouble-free pregnancy, with December rapidly approaching. As all appeared well the midwife suggested a home birth. After the problems with the birth of Philip this was worrying as we were living six miles from Addenbrookes Hospital in Cambridge if complications occurred. Despite reassurances I was still apprehensive but Helen was happy and it suited us domestically with Philip being kept fully involved, as he had been all along with the anticipated new arrival, so a home birth it would be.

There was, nevertheless, a feeling of unease as the day drew ever closer. This was only natural after the problems with Philip's birth added to which there had also been the trauma of the miscarriage.

We need not have worried as spot on time our little girl arrived but not before Philip had insisted on sitting on Mum's lap all the afternoon demanding cuddles. The midwife was not present but Helen was happy for him to do this as she awaited the call to 'action stations.' He had obviously got the vibes that his sister or brother was soon to appear.

During the evening Alice duly appeared, with Philip, despite all the frenzied activity, fast asleep in his bedroom. Miraculously it seemed, no sooner had the midwife left, with Alice tucked up in her cot, than Philip was out of his bed, into Mum's bedroom and jumping on top of a squawking but happy Helen. He was beside himself with excitement at the long awaited and much talked about new arrival. Thankfully these were good early signs of Philip's interest.

All was well with Alice and life took on a new impetus. There were many precious moments but none more so than when Philip came into the room where Alice was being bathed. He put one of his hands on each of Alice's knees, looking down at her as if to say, but couldn't, "something's missing."

In Cambridgeshire we had come to know our Social Worker well. He was a practical sort of chap who, to ease the burden on Helen, arranged for Philip, who was by now approaching four years of age to attend the local Histon nursery three mornings a week. It did, however, create more running about as with only one car logistics became a problem. Without a nearby family to share the burden we somehow managed nonetheless. It did Philip good to mix with other children, although he was generally insular in his own play patterns around sand and water. For the first time, Special School education was mentioned by the Social Worker after, no doubt, receiving feed back from the nursery. We were by this time aware that some aspects of Philip's development would need extra help if it was to be brought up to scratch but how to set about this we did not know. After all, he was barely four and had come so far in many ways and still had time on his side. There were not too many local school options available but we were to be kept advised. Was this a way of softening the blow of what was looming round the corner?

Chapter 5 - Reality Rears its Ugly Head

With our new little girl safely in our midst we had a lovely family Christmas with Nana and Grandpa coming to share the workload. Philip responded well to Alice sharing the limelight and all was well with the world, at least for the time being, and so we made the most of it.

The weeks passed. Philip and Alice were both getting on all right, with Philip so obviously enjoying helping with looking after Alice, particularly at bath time. He was very gentle and attentive towards her except that he would, if not watched, get too boisterous when she was strapped into her Baby Relaxer.

In the spring of 1970 Mr. Turner, the senior branch manager at the bank, came to me and said, "The bank wants to promote you to Assistant Manager, at High Wycombe. In view of your personal circumstances I have been asked to make enquiries of Bucks County Council to find out if the county provides good facilities in the areas of education which will be necessary for Philip. I really don't know what he will require. Would you make enquiries and report back to me so that I can at least sound knowledgeable when I give the Staff Manager in London his answer?"

Neither Helen nor I fully understood what Philip's future educational or care needs were likely to be. Out of desperation I rang our Social Worker who for the first time detailed some of Philip's likely ongoing needs. Special Education for the mentally handicapped was mentioned. He said "There are two streams, educationally sub-normal and severely sub-normal. Where Philip will fit in nobody knows as he has not been assessed."

At least I had a flavour of what I required to know of the councils at High Wycombe and Buckinghamshire. A positive conversation ensued and whilst Special Education had a nasty ring to it, it appeared as if the High Wycombe area was geared up for our likely needs.

I went to London for the formal interview and was offered, and accepted, the promotion, but as expected we all had grave misgivings about having to leave Cottenham. We had had a very happy time there, making good, understanding friends in an area full of clean air after Luton's industrial pollution. Coupled with this was the freedom to readily roam around the countryside, including full access to the smallholding over our rear fence. Les and Phil, who had no children and were approaching retirement, were so kind to us and would try to engage Philip in conversation if they were working near his sand pit. On the other hand we had established that, whilst Buckinghamshire was a pretty county, High Wycombe itself was quite industrialised with many of its firms allied to the furniture industry.

We consoled ourselves with the thought that we did not have to live within High Wycombe. A second car with children's seats became a must as Helen was again left 'holding the baby', now babies, as I went off to pastures new. She had to shop, get Philip to nursery school, and run about for two children.

In addition to more money my new position provided the family with its first fringe benefit, in the form of private medical health care. The health cover only excluded Philip's recurrence of fits. As he had been free of them for some time we were quite relaxed in accepting this exclusion.

We found a house in the process of construction overlooking Hughenden Park, in High Wycombe, the former home of Benjamin Disraeli, Prime Minister during the 1860s. The move was going smoothly except for continuing uncertainties with the actual completion and hand over of the finished property. The builders who were part of a national group were impossible to nail down to action and time scales. Nothing too unusual in that I would suggest!

Helen had sold the Luton property in my absence to the first viewer and did the same at Cottenham. Who needs a man around? We made a profit of £1,000 during our two years in occupation. This was good appreciation in the 1970's. The time to leave our Cottenham home arrived only too quickly. After the furniture vans left to put our belongings once more into temporary storage we, as a family unit, walked round the garden picking our last raspberries, desperately sad that an extremely happy two years in those surroundings had come to an end. So much had happened and it was all good. We had, however, realised that life had to move on; such was a career in banking.

It was not all bad news, despite our furniture having gone into storage for two weeks. We had our larger new house to look forward to and in addition, we would be staying at The Windsor Lodge, Great Kingshill, a hotel in the country where we knew the owner Pat Riley would welcome us as a family, as my weekday living and a house-hunting weekend had been spent there. Helen, whilst not free of the responsibility of the children, with Philip and Alice now four years three months and seven months old respectively, at least did not have to worry about meals.

We had a family suite which the children thoroughly enjoyed. The hotel gave Helen freedom to use their kitchen facilities for bottles, washing and drying etc. It was a very relaxed atmosphere, just what we needed and a facility unlikely to be available today.

Graham, my demanding new boss, and Muriel his wife, were close family people and adopted us immediately upon arrival, providing a day time sanctuary from hotel life for Helen if needed. Both Philip and Alice looked forward to Graham coming home at lunch time, sweeping them up in his vast arms and carrying them round the garden on his shoulders.

We took possession of the new house, having stayed on at the hotel for an extra two days to get ourselves and the house organised before the furniture arrived. In those days gardens were not handed over already turfed. Thankfully a customer of the bank, in an early favour, managed to get his rotovator onto the large corner splayed back garden before fences were put up. On moving, we soon had a son who was desperate to get outside onto the bare earth to play. To placate him and to satisfy his immediate needs a large sand pit was quickly built.

As a cleared virgin plot, with its single tree, it looked a formidable sloping area of bare soil. Hundreds of turfs which amounted to a vast heap were quickly delivered and laid at weekends. On a Friday evening, Philip was in his element, helping to fetch and carry a single turf in his wheel barrow. His help, bless him, was largely counter productive as invariably I would find him with his barrow overturned on a corner where the ground fell away. He did not give up however, and by persevering, quickly learnt to control the weight pressures.

Saturday became a day of patience as it was "me help" when it came to levelling, raking and actually laying the large square yard rolls of turf. Philip always seemed to be under my feet, with many a time during the day when our paths collided, but he was not to be deterred.

Thankfully we had an Indian Summer in 1970 and it was not until the fourth and last weekend of September that it rained. Sodden turf was like handling heavy bars of wet soap with tacky soil underfoot which clung to the wellington boots, making freedom of movement difficult. Philip insisted on helping, watched by an envious Alice from the lounge window. He got absolutely plastered in mud. Pa Pa had to be forcibly banned from participating. He had already been re-covered twice and was again getting bare.

Although we tried to make 'no go' areas on the newly laid grass, of course Philip preferred to play on the grass areas before they had bedded down rather than in his sand pit. Thankfully, we were scheduled to go to Swanage for a holiday which gave the lawn ten days of peace from tiny feet scuffing it up on a daily basis. By the time we returned from our holiday, the earlier rain had penetrated and the roots were pulling it down sufficient enough for its first cut. It was absolute bliss, with Philip having complete freedom to roam and play within the garden.

We were blessed with continuing good weather and our hotel holiday was a great success. Alice and Philip busied themselves on the beach with Alice thinking she was Queen Canute in trying to shoo the water away as it encroached up the beach. Philip loved to sit close to the waters edge paddling a raft that we had hired for all he was worth, just like Dad did when we had our gentle trips out in a rowing boat into the sheltered bay. The rope attached to the raft would be at full stretch with the depth of water barely eighteen inches but who cared if he was busy and happy?

For the first time we experienced third parties not knowing what to make of Philip. They did not get the reaction they expected when speaking to this outwardly normal, well mannered, good looking little boy. It was only on our last night at the hotel when we were all gathered in the garden watching a night rescue going on at sea that a fellow resident tactfully raised the subject. We found that we were able to talk quite comfortably to a virtual stranger about what we knew of Philip's problems.

We find it regrettable when hardened and bruising politicians seem to shed crocodile tears during interviews, particularly when they are striving to change their outward persona for what appears to be solely political purposes! To us, and probably everyone else this type of behaviour lacks sincerity and is so unnecessary.

This was a holiday of many more happy memories of those early days in Philip's and Alice's lives. Those memories continue to be priceless, even today, as we look back at happy, smiling, active children in old photographs.

Philip's records were passed to Bucks County Council. What we did not know when sounding out the move to the High Wycombe area was that although, yes, they had a wide range of facilities for the mentally handicapped, these were already full to overflowing.

An assessment was eventually carried out by an educational psychologist. Her findings confirmed the need for Special Education. She also recommended that Philip should urgently see a speech therapist, which we were relieved to hear as we realised progress on this front was proving very difficult and slow. Other than continually chattering to him we had no ability to help this aspect of his development.

Philip worked well with the therapist, who despite her large stature, would crawl around on the floor with him, trying to get closer to his world. A few new words were gained which was a step in the right direction. The therapist confirmed that Philip assimilated much more incoming information than he could respond to - something of which we were well aware.

We had been allocated a rather large, negative, lacklustre lady Social Worker who always seemed to be asking lots of background questions but never came up with any forward looking answers. She was all froth and little substance, in short, a very frustrating person to have to deal with. Rather unkindly we nicknamed her Mrs. Waffle. Sadly, we had little confidence in her at this vital time in Philip's life, having to push her hard to get any action or help for him.

In Cottenham Philip had been used to going to nursery and we were unwilling to allow this discipline to cease. Such was our desperation to find some formal schooling and help for him that we applied to a private nursery in Amersham, only to be met with a snooty interview and subsequent 'awfully sorry' type of rejection letter from the Headmistress.

It took weeks to get some sort of action from the county. After much badgering, Philip was eventually placed at Terriers Nursery in another area of High Wycombe each afternoon. He bawled every time Helen left him at the nursery but she was told this stopped almost before she had left the building. It appeared he just did not want to leave his Mum.

By this time, with money in short supply and having no use for two cars, we sold the second vehicle. This meant I started cycling to the bank. Whilst what Philip did at the nursery was largely repetitive sand and water play, the nursery was good to him and enabled Helen to snatch a few quiet hours with Alice.

In addition to being slow to react, it seemed our unsociable Mrs. Waffle had to belittle any proclaimed progress we thought Philip had made. He had learnt to count and pass the required number of objects to us. "Of course he doesn't understand what he is doing" was her retort, rather than to offer words of encouragement even if he didn't know what he was doing – but we did not hold with her view. Subsequent events have proved he probably knew exactly what he was doing as numbers have always been his interest.

Alice was a live wire. She and Philip had a good bond, which we encouraged. We realised by this time that within a few years she would have overtaken her brother's ability in many things but vowed to keep their bond going for as long as possible. Philip would, without knowing it, stand to learn a great deal from his little sister. This was how it turned out to be.

As there was still no formal commitment to schooling and the position at the bank was very demanding we would use any time off to get away, so that domestic issues did not clutter the day. One such break took us to Waldringfield on the River Deben, where we somehow slept on very sultry nights in a small caravan. We were however, fortunate to be able to use a beach hut on the river during the day. It was an ideal venue for a relaxing few days. There was a small beach which was washed at every high tide. We had the use of a rowing boat, and complete with yellow life jackets Philip and I would anchor a few yards out into the river with our hand lines and nets successfully catching small crabs. They really were voracious eaters of our bacon or fish head baits which we scrounged from local shops.

Alice would join in the fun, counting our catch as we emptied the pail on to the slip-way and letting the crabs charge off back to the water, with their menacing front pincers in the air ready to nip any interfering fingers, no doubt to be caught again another day!

For our main summer break we ventured back to the Isle of Wight with the Leech family with whom we had enjoyed our earlier holiday at Ventnor. This time, rather than a hotel we chose self catering. We stayed in an old, rambling house with a garden to match, just right for a posse of energetic young children all of whom were of an age to enjoy each other's company.

Philip and Alice loved having new playmates for cricket on the firm sand of Seaview beach. Philip was still coping and holding his own with younger company. He had very sharp eyesight and it was a great thrill for him to find cockles in the running river at low water which the older folk had walked over. He did it time and again, simply putting his hand down and popping them into his yellow plastic pail. After the cockles had been cooked and eaten, the shells were made into patterns or figures by the other children but Philip's were always in straight lines, just as with his cars on the carpet at home.

Time passed well into 1972 with Philip, now aged six, still not at full time school. We pushed our useless Mrs. Waffle for some action, she continually coming up with the excuse that there were no places available at the local schools.

In desperation she arranged for us to visit the schools for educationally sub-normal and severely sub-normal children in High Wycombe. We were horrified by the latter. We could not comprehend that our son needed to attend a school with children who looked handicapped, were in wheelchairs because they couldn't walk or hold their heads up properly and many of whom continually made peculiar noises. Words cannot describe how we felt, as it was by far the most upsetting experience of our lives. Despite our years of problems with Philip we had never previously been exposed to anything like this.

We were, in our naivety, regarding Philip's future as being able to concur with what we saw at the ESN School. The children at that school looked more like Philip and had largely behavioural problems. We could accept a place for him there.

Philip had been in Bucks for eighteen months before he was offered a schooling place, not at the ESN School but at the SSN

School, Vinio House. We were distraught with the thought of our Philip having to attend such a school. We consoled ourselves with the expectation that he would soon prove he had been wrongly placed and would gravitate to the ESN School. Little did we appreciate what his ongoing educational needs were going to be.

Mrs. Quartermain, the head of Vinio House School, a lady for whom we later had the utmost respect, asked to see us. She was a quietly but firmly spoken lady and explained from the records she had seen that Philip would be correctly placed at her school. He would be collected and brought home by mini bus. Helen should bring him in on the first morning of the following term and thereafter he would be ferried to and fro by mini coach. No room for negotiation there.

We were absolutely dumbfounded and demoralised by the news that Mrs. Quartermain imparted on how she assessed Philip's schooling needs. Had we been so blinkered in our hopes for him? Yes, we probably had been as his physical progress had been so normal, which coupled with his delightful personality and happy disposition had masked the spiky mental progress. With our rose tinted spectacles we had not seen him as mentally handicapped, just slow. It was so obvious that he understood most of what was being said and going on that we had come to overlook his very limited speech and the tendency towards repetitive ways.

Oh dear, those earlier precautionary words of Professor Tizard were now coming to the fore. What a shock as suddenly we realised that despite there being over a hundred children at Vinio House School, (and this was only one of many such schools), we had never met another parent who had a child classed as mentally handicapped.

From the time of his discharge from Hammersmith Hospital we had with sheer tenacity managed our own emotions and created a life style which suited Philip, but in retrospect he had led a sheltered though up to this point, happy life.

We made no effort to hide our disappointment, making it plain to Mrs. Quartermain that we had nothing against the school but didn't feel that Philip belonged there. She made no comment, just smiling and nodding in a form of acquiescence - she had probably heard it all before, many times. Ultimately, how wrong we were.

After a heart-wrenching and tormented few days when we could still not come to terms with the word 'severely,' we realised we had no alternative but to agree to the proposed format of education. This was the first offer we had had and with no other options arising and Philip well past his sixth birthday we just had to accept that Vinio House would be where he started.

For the first time in Philip's life we felt a deep sense of guilt that his education had come to this. The only consolation we had was the continuing belief that the assessment was wrong, and if it proved to be so we could always fight for a move. It took time, but we slowly came to the conclusion that we were wrong and that the professionals were right. Philip spent twelve long, reasonably happy, but sometimes very difficult years at Vinio House.

Chapter 6 - Life Goes On

After the trauma of being told that Philip was destined for SSN education, coupled with our lack of appreciation of what the future held for him, we began to wish we had not come to Bucks at all. It had taken over eighteen months to get him into formal education by the time autumn came and he started his schooling. It was quite ridiculous that it had taken this long and to make matters worse where Philip had been placed was far from what we expected.

There was no turning back the clock, however, so we had to make the best of what we felt was a bad job. Once again, in the face of adversity we had to increase our resolve, to be positive in our outlook and to do whatever we could within the family environment to make the most of Philip's abilities. We would not look for negatives, for others would certainly do that. We had after all, been doing this for most of his life but the schooling delays and uncertainties over his future created untold strains on his upbringing.

We were however coping, and as he remained a happy little soul this probably contributed to why we were left on our own to get by as best we could by those who should have been providing support and, in particular, Mrs. Waffle our Social Worker. What a waste of time she continued to be, all establishment bluster and no action. Despite being middle-aged and, we assumed, experienced in her work, not once did she make positive suggestions or recommendations. It seemed apparent there was an air of conflict whenever we met, ever more so as the schooling of Philip became continually delayed.

Alice, meanwhile, was growing up fast. She was a lively little girl with an independent but very loveable disposition. Philip and Alice were good for each other. They played happily around the house and garden, but not without incident or argument. What's new in that with two youngsters?

With play in mind we had acquired, through an HP Sauce offer, a large ride-able replica sauce bottle with four fixed wheels which was appropriately named Hot Rod. As arguments over propelling Hot Rod around the house grew without us being able to create a sharing culture, a small orange tractor and trailer were bought which could also be propelled around the house by feet. Alice quickly commandeered the latter and all was well.

The hours of fun, given by those two simple toys was incredible. Inter-connecting doors would be quietly opened which went from the lounge into the hall, to the dining room, to the kitchen and back into the hall. This was their circuit and off they would go round and round. If the action got too boisterous a halt would be called on the premise that petrol was getting low. After a short pause an imaginary petrol filling station would appear and off they would go again. Whilst there were near misses with doorways and many a close shave of ankles getting mutilated their skill and speed of manoeuvres had to be admired. We already knew that Philip, at a more leisurely pace, had those skills from his Baby Walker times at Luton. He still tended to be careful but his sister was full of energetic bravado.

Although the children received a few minutes of quality time with Dad each day at midday as I cycled home for lunch, bedtime stories were still a great conclusion to the day. Two books in particular, The Little Red Hen and The Hungry Caterpillar were the favourites which they never seemed to tire of listening to, or reading.

When they were doing joint reading they took alternate pages. Of course they knew the stories off by heart but it made no difference. To ensure they took it in turn to read the last page where the drama occurred and the hungry caterpillar turned into a 'Beautiful Butterfly', or the hen met her doom through meeting the naughty fox, we had to alternate who read the first page. This was simple, but very rewarding fun as the children sat cosily on the bed in their dressing gowns with their favourite toys, which always included Pa Pa. They lived every word that was uttered and in particular if Dad was doing the reading were eagerly waiting for the deliberate mistake to occur. When it came it would be greeted by both with loud and raucous cries of derision.

From those happy experiences Philip started his reading. He progressed, with our help, through the Ladybird series of books, (which are sadly no longer produced), featuring Janet and John. He could take on board a growing number of words and remember new ones from one evening to another. Reading was kept for bed time when, however busy we may have been, those special fifteen or so minutes were sacrosanct.

Helen and I were able to have a reasonable social life as finding baby sitters was not a problem. Both children once they were in bed, were soon asleep and, seldom woke up. When they did it was not a problem as they were always told if we were going out and knew the person who was looking after them. We could easily have retreated into our shells because of the problems Philip faced but having the good fortune to have a number of similarly aged neighbours, and friendly management colleagues around the area, we could relax in their company. Those friendships have continued for over thirty years.

As it was a family affair, with wives doing teas and the children a welcome part of the day, I joined the Bradenham Cricket Club which gave us a further informal social outlet. Philip loved watching and, given the opportunity, would enthusiastically tinker with the scoreboard. What is still an amusing family anecdote from those cricketing days is Alice running along our landing, observing me with my jock strap on and exclaiming with some glee "Daddy's wearing his titchy pants!" She has always had, and continues to have, the knack of using odd words or phrases to embellish life. Long may it continue!

Various family members came to stay with us and we returned to East Anglia whenever possible. On one such occasion we brought back a large bag of gooseberries. The children, having started, insisted on topping and tailing every one with their little blunt scissors before going to bed. By the time they had finished their little thumbs were raw.

We always made every effort to attend family gatherings in East Anglia to ensure that Philip, who enjoyed the occasions, was part of everything going on. Birthdays were celebrated and reciprocated with family parties, there being three young cousins living in London who were always ready to join in the fun. Grandma was a welcome guest to stay, as on her final night she would always pay for us to go to the Catherine Wheel in Henley for a Berni Inn supper. For £5, three adults and two children could eat well. In those days steak, followed by the infamous black forest gateau, were the fashionable meals. The children loved the occasion of dressing up smartly and being out later than usual. They were always a pleasure to take out, with Grandma, who was a stickler for etiquette, very proud of their behaviour. There was never a murmur of disquiet or grizzling, as sadly one so often experiences today. The 'I want' culture had not arrived, at least not in our family. Alice would regularly put scraps of meat in a serviette to take home for the cat, only to get very cross when she found she had left them behind.

In the garden, which was maturing nicely, Alice was initially quite happy pushing her horse and trolley laden with brightly coloured wooden bricks, both on wheels, around the grassed paths. Before too long she coveted Philip's large red tractor although she could not even reach the blocked pedals. Philip happily pushed her around, with Alice steering but with her little legs in the air with the unattended pedals flailing furiously to and fro below. He seemed pleased to have a change, gravitating from giving Pa Pa rides to Alice, although the former was much less demanding!

When Alice had grown a little more, the tractor rides progressed from getting a push to free wheeling over the grass, down the sloping garden to the flattened out area at the bottom. On one such occasion we were sitting in the garden enjoying a quiet cup of coffee watching, so we thought, the children play, when suddenly 'our little madam' was hurtling down the lawn. Where she got the momentum from we have never known. She just seemed to gather speed and disappeared out of sight, round the raspberry canes to a resounding clump, momentary silence, and then a piercing, aggrieved squawk. Fearing the worst, we raced down the lawn to find her neatly and firmly wedged between the wheelbarrow handles against the compost heap, thankfully unhurt. We laugh about the incident now but, looking back, there could easily have been a horrific outcome. From then on, wheelbarrows were always left standing on end.

We were, given any opportunity, quite active as a family. Sledging in Hughenden Park was a great treat when we had snow, with no complaints about it being cold. One had to be very careful to make sure the children stayed close by as other uncontrolled sledges were whizzing about at speed on the hillside. On one such occasion we were having a great time, all three of us managing to get onto the wooden Davos sledge which my mother brought back from Switzerland in 1947. Once the rust was off the runners it was a very fast, smooth running vehicle which turned out to be our undoing. On one speedy descent another sledge slewed over in front of us. To protect the children I put my legs up only to get a nasty knock under the right knee. After limping home in some discomfort, to a severe bout of chastisement from Helen, the wound needed stitches. My being carted off to hospital and thoughts of 'what might have been,' upset Helen greatly. As a result a neighbour whilst I was away gave her her first (and rather large) tot of whisky. It was found to be quite palatable and she still enjoys it, as a very occasional tipple!

Christmas Common, near Stokenchurch, in The Chilterns, was a regular spot to visit for walks on Saturday mornings. Afterwards, Philip, and to be fair, all of us, loved watching from above as the earth moving equipment went to and fro like ants below with the lorries taking the spoil away. The next few miles of the M40 were being gouged out of the chalk hills.

The walks through the trees of the common, based on Alice's speed, seemed, at the time, long, fulfilling outings. Philip would hold Alice's hand trying to speed her along, much to her annoyance. They enjoyed the freedom to express themselves in that tranquil environment, with a multitude of birds singing and grey squirrels scurrying around in the trees. Occasionally we disturbed the odd timid deer, and often saw no-one-else – it was a peaceful, relaxing haven.

Only recently we all returned to the scene of the childhood walks and in thirty five years it had all grown up to such an extent it was largely unrecognisable, although the footpaths were in the same place. Nothing else had changed but the area seemed so much smaller than the one we remembered. As a family it was nice to be able to turn the clock back for a few precious moments.

For no particular reason Philip, in his younger days, had not possessed a tricycle. Whilst, as far as we were aware, he never coveted anything owned by other children, we noticed he was paying more than a passing interest to a bicycle ridden by his cousin Julia in her garden at Hampton. The movement had obviously taken his fancy but he declined a ride, probably fearing through his cautious nature that he might fall off. In his mind was there an idea for the future?

An already robust and growing six year old could not be given a small two wheeled bike so a larger version was bought for his birthday with stabilisers attached. This meant of course that Philip was quite high off the ground. With the seat at its lowest level he could just about touch the surface but having not ridden even a tricycle before he obviously still felt vulnerable. After a short period of indifference he was suddenly interested in the bike and it was embraced with open arms! Within the grassed sloping garden there was little scope for him to learn the necessary co-ordinated skills of balance, steering, brakes and pedalling. Quite a package for any child to take on board all at once and even more so for Philip, one would think.

As we lived in a quiet area, I could take him out on the footpaths, with my hand lightly holding the back of his saddle on downward slopes as brakes, and their gentle, rather than sudden application were a challenge which had to be mastered. With incredible ease this phase soon passed. It was clear he had both balance and, providing he was left alone, the presence of mind to co-ordinate the use of the bike properly. Whilst he was probably not fully aware of the stabilisers' purpose they were quickly removed and hey presto, again with my hand lightly holding the back of his saddle, he was ready for progressing to the next stage: solo rides. To accommodate this, my next task was to locate a safe flat area.

A brain wave then came to me. If we could use Harrison's (they printed the postage stamps in the '70s) car park, which was a short distance away, the necessary experience could be gained. With the factory closed and not a vehicle on the car park the security man on duty was not at all helpful "Sorry mate, it's more than my jobs worth to let you do that," he retorted to my request.

Not to be put off we trundled along to the next nearby factory, Broom and Wade. What a different attitude to the same request! I introduced Philip to the guard and it soon became apparent he knew of Vinio House School and attended their Christmas Bazaars. When I posed the question he just quietly replied "I shouldn't let you use it but I can't see what harm you would be doing."

Great, I thought, a large tarmac-lined flat surface on which to practice and to let Philip be independent. In very quick time he accepted his new cycling environment and away he rode at just sufficient speed to keep his balance as he was now riding without his stabilisers. Occasionally, a foot went down but there was never any suggestion he would fall off. As his confidence grew I realised he was using the white lines between parking spaces as his roads. This was ideal as I could then introduce points at which to stop and start to make life as realistic as possible. He coped with and enjoyed these extra disciplines, reacting just as he was asked to do.

The guard watched with great interest, congratulating Philip on how well he had done as we left after our first visit. He said he would tell his colleagues about us. This he did and we always got a cheery wave on future arrivals. It was a relaxing and open atmosphere in which to teach Philip his riding skills. This activity went on for some time, with Philip always ready for the 'off' when it was mentioned. Liking the cycling as he so obviously did he was not able to ask for an excursion but the delight in his eyes at the suggestion said it all. Subsequently, of course, Alice on her tricycle insisted on getting in on the act which, thankfully, did not cause any problems with the factory security guards. It probably gave them an interest on a quiet Sunday morning.

The cycling expertise soon developed into wider spheres in that there were footpaths from No. 22 which turned into undulating tracks for some miles beside the park and into Hughenden Valley. Our outings became longer and longer but always with the old problem of Philip being reluctant to turn round to head back home. The second half of the journey always took much longer than the first half. I tried, but could not make the outing into a circular route as there was no safe way, with paths, out of the valley. Initially, when we started these extended jaunts, I accompanied him by walking, but quite quickly had to resort to riding my own bicycle on the road to keep up. The length of paths was over three miles - quite a distance for Philip's little legs but he never complained.

It was not long before Philip coped comfortably with the six mile round trip, and more, as he would cycle round a housing estate on the way back to prolong the outing.

When we look back, Philip's cycling skills were then, and have continued to be, a very satisfying and constructive safety valve for his energies. It also gave him a feeling of independence, as whilst closely supervised he was by himself and therefore in control. He was also doing what others of his age did but without doubt with a superior level of skill and care - his level of concentration was unwavering and not easily deflected.

Life still threw up its quirks, none more so than when Philip made shopping excursions awkward for Helen. He suddenly developed a phobia about passing any shop and most certainly would not enter them if they had a full length hanging blind made of plastic strips or metal chains in the doorway. Both were light and would flutter in the breeze making different noises. They were very much the fashion in those days and they completely spooked him. He knew where every one of them was throughout the central shopping area of High Wycombe and tensions grew as he anticipated passing them. It became an obsession and nothing that we did or said helped to quell his fears. We never knew the reason for this phobia but suspected it was the low rustling or metallic noise they made, or that they moved suddenly and unexpectedly as people threw them aside as they came out of the shops. Shopping became a nightmare as these blinds seemed to be everywhere.

We still enjoyed our family holidays. Salcombe took over from Swanage as our favourite venue. What a delight it was to drive through the Devon countryside in the spring on narrow roads with high hedges and an abundance of flowers in the verges making everywhere a delight to behold. We were fortunate to find a delightful family run small hotel perched high over the town where the children had their own little room adjoining ours which looked out over the water and yachts below. This was picture postcard stuff. The hoteliers, Bob and Pat, originally came from Bucks and quickly got on to Philip's wavelength. They soon offered him the job of banging the brass gong each evening to tell other guests it was dinner time. He had to be dressed early and glowed with satisfaction at the importance of this duty, welcoming guests as best he could into the dining room. Those he welcomed soon caught on and always responded most graciously.

The children's eating habits were first class in this environment and also at home for that matter, which made eating with other guests in the hotel restaurant a pleasure. No pre dinner 'kids' meals were needed to keep them quiet!

The sandy beaches at Salcombe were reached by ferry but we had to watch the children very carefully as there were strong ebb currents. After extensive sand castle activity they both loved playing cricket. Philip had a good eye for a ball and nothing gave him more pleasure than seeing me having to scamper into the water chasing his lusty hit. Alice always wanted to be wicket keeper and, for a tiny tot, threw herself around with great vigour and, like her brother, with no little ball skill.

The walks around Salcombe in early summer were so pretty and the nearby bays to explore seemed endless, just right for Philip's energy. This was quite natural zeal - he was not hyper active, thank goodness.

Whilst Philip has always enjoyed robust general health there was a period when he was regularly getting infections around his private parts. Dr. Hill, who we found to be an excellent and understanding G.P., not just for Philip but for the stresses of his parents, quickly arranged for a circumcision. A further short period of concern followed as this was the first general anaesthetic Philip would have received. Thankfully it passed off without a problem.

Our life, despite Philip's shortcomings, was generally going along fairly smoothly and happily. We were busy with the children, who were developing very well together. Only in quieter moments did misgivings have time to rear their ugly head. What more, in the circumstances, could we have been setting out to do? Not too much we feel - even with the gift of hindsight!

Chapter 7 - Better Late than Never

With our holidays in East Anglia and Salcombe over, the 5th September 1972 duly arrived with a certain amount of relief that Philip was at last to start full time education. There were none of the emotions of 'my little boy is growing up and starting school' as there were to be with Alice's subsequent first day at school. We were already aggrieved as we felt that Philip was, at six, at least some eighteen months late in being catered for - how different it is today!

Having been asked to arrive at Vinio House after the incoming bus transport bringing the handicapped children from the villages around High Wycombe to the school had departed, Helen and Philip were welcomed by Mrs. Quartermain and taken to his class-room where there were ten other children of varying junior ages and wide-ranging abilities. Everywhere was very fresh and new as the school had only been occupied since the start of the previous term. They were introduced to Freda Wheeler, the deputy head, who was looking after the class. She took Philip by the hand and led him to a small table where he sat down looking rather bemused.

Quite quickly, Mrs. Quartermain turned to escort Helen from the room. Before parting she stole up to him to give him a lingering good-bye kiss. Helen was told Philip would start his journey home each day at 3.15 on a Motts mini coach, with Joyce Smith being the usual escort on the coach with the task of supervising the 15 children on board. After dropping off other children on the way to No. 22 Philip should arrive home by 3.45. There must always be someone there, and in evidence, to meet him off the coach. In the morning the scheduled collection time would be 8.20. Philip should always be ready to board the coach at that time otherwise unnecessary delays would occur and other children en route to the school would be inconvenienced. We knew at once what was expected of us.

We were however thankful that we lived within High Wycombe, as the coach started its journey in far flung outlying villages. Had we lived out there the journey would have added up to at least an hour of extra time each day on the coach. Philip may have enjoyed this but it would have meant a very early start to the day for everyone else.

Philip seemed to settle in at school very quickly and was ready to accept his new, more disciplined way of life. For the first few weeks of the term he was very tired by the end of the week but he retained his good health and no reappearance of fits. They were a thing of the past!

It was very obvious that Mrs. Quartermain was a hard but fair task master who was held in some awe by her staff and who, in her quiet but stern manner, also took no nonsense from her pupils. Mentally handicapped they may be but there were still standards to be set. A visit to her office was soon recognised as a chastening experience. She also took on parents who were not pulling their weight as far as their offspring or the school were concerned. For all of this she had the utmost genuine respect from everyone. We all knew where we stood and what she expected from us on behalf of the school.

Freda was impressed with Philip's elementary skills in his number work and his ability to read simple words. He could retain repetitive information but, like his father, he was no budding artist. He knew his colours, however, in this respect being superior to his father who is colour blind. From time to time Philip would be pleased to bring home a certificate for good work. These were not awarded lightly, being presented by Mrs. Quartermain at assembly on Friday afternoon.

From the outset one was very aware that the members of staff were all very dedicated both to their work and any supplementary activity involving the school. It was incredible, with even spouses joining in the support, none more so than Cyril Quartermain who, despite having a full-time job and living in Maidenhead, was always there supporting his wife's school. It was very obvious he was proud, and rightly so, of what she achieved and the standards she set within her school.

Everyone was well-groomed and reflected the lead set by their head. Trousers amongst the female staff and sloppy outfits were taboo. This, in turn, reflected in the children attending the school as Mrs. Quartermain's philosophy was, "They may be mentally handicapped but that is no excuse for them not being properly cared or catered for," Without exception staff, parents and pupils responded positively to her leadership.

Through the school and its Parent Teacher Association we were for the first time coming into contact with other parents who faced similar problems to ourselves. The common theme threading through their experiences, was the need to fight the authorities for facilities for their offspring. Within their domestic environments they felt isolated by lack of understanding and appreciation of how a handicapped child completely dominates your thoughts and the family's life - it is inevitable. Our feelings were much the same with regard to our lack of confidence in our Social Worker. Some of the parents were unfortunate enough to deal with the same Mrs. Waffle!

Whilst family members were generally supportive of our plight they had little real understanding of the daily pressures and stresses we faced. They could only think they did. It was soon apparent that having a handicapped child affected parents from all walks of life with a varied mixture of creeds and problems to contend with. There was however, one common question: what does the future hold? This was a continuing worry. Nobody could give us an answer.

Initially, Helen and I seemed very much to be Parent Teacher Association (PTA) outsiders, never more so than at the first Christmas Bazaar, held some ten weeks after Philip's arrival at the school. It was a sizeable but largely uncoordinated event. Whilst we readily volunteered to help, it was very apparent that despite offering our services to stall-holding parents, they were all very set in their ways. They had run their stalls for years and did not welcome our offers - they knew what they were doing and were too busy doing it to welcome newcomers, however well intentioned they were.

This was our first experience of fundraising and we spent a fairly miserable and largely fruitless first couple of hours drifting around, moving the odd table or desk as requested. It was soon apparent that we needed to be running a stall to become fully involved. Suddenly it was all change. "Mr. Childs, Mrs. Quartermain is urgently looking for you and she is in a bit of a tizzy. Please can you go and find her?" said Kath the school secretary. As I hadn't seen Philip for some time my immediate thought was 'oh dear, where is he and what has he been doing?'

Searching the hall, classrooms and corridors I eventually found Mrs. Quartermain who certainly was in a 'two and eight'. "Mr. Childs," she blustered, her eyes sparkling with indignation, "Can you get into your bank? Mr. Foster, the P.T.A. Treasurer, has just telephoned. He is not well and, to make matters worse, he has forgotten to get the floats. With over twenty stalls needing floats we have a big problem."

As it was Saturday and the office was closed I explained that whilst I could indeed get into the bank, I had no access to cash, as at least two additional key holders would be required to open the safe. Her face dropped and she looked so forlorn. Thankfully resourcefulness came to my rescue. I said "It's 11.15 which gives me forty-five minutes until the Building Societies close. Can I use your office to warn them of our need as this will save time when I get to each society?"

"Certainly," she quickly replied with an air of relief.

As I knew the manager of each society, six telephone calls later Philip and I were rushing into High Wycombe to collect cash, each against my personal cheque, for what amounted to £280 in all sorts of mixed coinage. Philip carried the canvas cash bag until it became too heavy as we raced from one society to another in the Town Centre of High Wycombe. He thought this was great fun without realising the urgency of the exercise.

As it was my money, so to speak, I made up the floats as best I could from what we had collected. My offer to act as Treasurer for the afternoon was gladly accepted. All went well - we got to know more parents and by six o'clock the job was complete and we had arrived within the bosom of the PTA and my thirty-eight years of serious fund raising had started.

At the March 1973 AGM I was elected the PTA Treasurer and two years later Chairman. In 1978 I was invited to become a Parent Governor of the school.

I unashamedly used my contacts within the bank to get celebrities involved in our fund raising activities. It was incredible who knew who locally and who was prepared to help. Wendy Craig (from Butterflies) opened bazaars, Lionel Jefferies (Grandpa Potts in Chitty Chitty Bang Bang) greeted all the children at the end of a sponsored walk, Sylvia and Gerry Anderson of 'Thunderbirds' fame brought 'Lady Penelope' along to a fete. These people all gave their time willingly and never gave the impression they were in a hurry to leave. Just their being there brought the school into local focus and increased the attendance at fund raising events. I encouraged other parents to spread the word to their employers about what was going on at the school in order to further its needs where possible, especially where a product was being manufactured which we could use to raise money.

If they were bashful about doing it I asked that they supplied me with names and I would make the approach simply mentioning their name in the letter - it worked like a charm.

In a very short time we raised enough money to complete the financing of the new Swimming Pool and, later on, an Adventure Playground. To open this we had the charming David Tomlinson (Mr. Banks from Mary Poppins) at our disposal for a whole afternoon - he was such a gent and couldn't believe a parent would collect him and return him home. A round trip of over one hundred miles!

Kath told Mrs. Quartermain she thought my approach to fund-raising was ruthless, which she relayed back to me with a twinkle in her eyes saying "We get things, don't we?" We most certainly did and it was very satisfying to do so, but never for personal gain. My experience of fundraising has always been, folks and firms are most generous when they are asked properly, kept informed, not taken for granted and finally, the act which is so often overlooked - a note of thanks for their contribution, however small. They are then ready to be approached again!

As part of the fundraising for the Swimming Pool we were awarded a Flag Day in High Wycombe. It was another day of great activity and organisation. Graham and Muriel brought their caravan to the Lloyds Bank car park in the centre of the town and used it as the control point. Street collecting is not, for many, a favourite Saturday pastime, but after much cajoling an army of parents and friends took to the streets throughout the day with their collecting tins.

Through Graham's contacts with Ercol Furniture it was arranged that their Brass Band would play during the morning to support us in the central Octagon. Philip was in his element, as were the other children from the school, sitting by a mocked-up model of the pool one of the parents had made, merrily shaking their tins as they sat listening to the music. Whilst it was really taboo to do this, not too many people had the heart to pass them by without making a contribution. Nobody objected to their little fingers placing the adhesive stickers on parts of the anatomy reserved exclusively for ladies - it was all good fun!

During the day, Philip enjoyed opening the collecting tins for Graham to count the proceeds and toured the town with me taking refreshments to collectors and replacing their weighty tins. The Flag

Day raised £1.4k, which was a very large sum in 1973 and, at the time, a record for High Wycombe. Along with others we were working hard for the school. We found this to be a new, indirect and fulfilling way to provide support for Philip.

Within a few months of Philip starting school at Vinio House we had realised, despite our hopes and initial expectations otherwise, that Vinio House was likely to be Philip's long term school, particularly as it was shortly to create a Further Education Group to cater for pupils up to the age of eighteen. What an age range for the staff to cope with both mentally and, more importantly, physically.

The realisation of Philip's limited ability was a mighty hard pill to swallow but the slow acceptance made it much less painful to bear.

Unfortunately and unexpectedly, Philip was soon back at hospital. Playing games he had been hit on the wrist, but seemed all right, so the note from school said. When he got off the mini coach it was obvious something was wrong. When Helen read the note handed over by Joyce the coach escort she was soon alerted and took action. Off to the hospital for X-rays which revealed cracked bones in the wrist. As the next day was Friday we kept him off school until Monday by which time he had accepted the inconvenience and pain and was coping quite well. He became quite proud of and ready to show off the dressing but could not tell enquirers what he had done or how it had happened. The wrist healed just fine with no after effects, and life continued its normal pattern.

Chapter 8 - All Change

With life now seemingly settled at the latter end of 1973 and Alice having enjoyed her 4th birthday we were all looking forward to Christmas, especially as Grandpa and Nana were coming to stay. Alice was full of expectation as her birthday presents had not included a tricycle so she was hoping that Father Christmas would put this right. A big problem for her was "how would he get it on his sleigh and down the chimney?" Philip, whenever asked what he would like, said "Its a secret," probably getting the meaning of his answer the wrong way round, which he still does today.

Life was particularly hectic at the bank, where I was working extremely hard. Graham, the manager, was a hard task master but worked no less diligently than he expected others to do.

Early one afternoon in December, the internal telephone rang. It was Graham. "Andy, can you pop along for a couple of minutes?" I detected an element of urgency in his voice. The news he gave me was, much to his consternation, totally unexpected and therefore caught me completely unawares. The bank wanted me to take a new job, as manager of the Bourne End branch, at the start of the New Year.

My time at High Wycombe branch had been very enjoyable. It was a position that stretched my abilities to the limit. The imminent promotion was obviously a bombshell which I could not disclose to Helen on the telephone. Whilst Bourne End was only seven miles away it was not somewhere we knew too much about, although it encompassed the area with which I was to become involved through my recent induction into Bourne End & Flackwell Heath Round Table. It was on the Thames, between Cookham & Marlow, places we regularly visited with the children for walks, but we never stopped in Bourne End as the village centre was not actually on the river. This was soon to change.

I was home later than usual on that night so by the time I arrived Helen was fairly well spent, soon to be shell-shocked as well. I managed to keep the news until the children were settled and then sat her down with a glass of champagne. The questions came thick and fast. Helen was looking for stability, and rightly so.

Our thoughts over the next few days turned positive and things moved very quickly. The Head Office interview was the next week with a likely start date immediately after Christmas. By the time of the interview, as I needed to know something of the area beforehand, we had occupied ourselves by spending the Saturday touring around Bourne End and its immediate villages. There were excellent first schools for Alice, and Philip could continue at Vinio House, but he would be collected by a different bus. As we lived on the wrong side of High Wycombe for daily travel to Bourne End we began to feel a move would be a good thing, especially as there would be no interim family disruption, just me going to a different nearby place to work. The big question was, could I get an assisted move for such a short distance transfer?

The Head Office interview, whilst nerve-racking, went like a dream. The first General Manager, who formally offers the post and advises the terms of the appointment, also authorises an expenses paid house move, if thought appropriate. Mr. Parish, the Staff General Manager, knew the area reasonably well. This enabled me to bring into the conversation how diverse I thought the communities were and how I felt the business at Bourne End would benefit from me living close by, especially as my Round Table involvement would enhance and consolidate my presence within the community. He agreed whole-heartedly that it would be preferable to move.

In the 1970s great importance was placed on the manager's active involvement within the community he served. How things have changed in thirty years - today nobody knows the bank manager; if you have one and where he or she lives is irrelevant.

The interview was also a chance to discuss Philip and to update the bank's records on his progress and ongoing likely needs. For the first time, whilst life and my career were going along quite smoothly, I asked for it to be placed on record that Philip would always have problems and that whilst my future promotion was important to me I could not ignore the fact that my mobility in future may have to be restricted by his ongoing needs. As career mobility was part and parcel of "getting on" in those days it was some relief when Mr. Parish assured me that the bank would take into account the current circumstances when asking for a decision on any future moves.

The earlier unanticipated bombshell had now so quickly turned to excitement and, yet again, we were looking towards pastures new. Whilst properties were more expensive near the Thames we felt we could cope with this fairly comfortably. Christmas was a splendid occasion with exciting visits to where "Daddy" was going to work.

The children could be very much part of the new job and were both old enough to be a part of the search for a new house as well.

When buying a new property bank employees were treated as cash purchasers, which gave us a certain amount of negotiating clout. Our excitement soon evaporated, however, as we were frustrated in our efforts to find a property locally which met our desires and needs. Despite working in a tight knit community the other locals were not able to uncover any new leads for us.

We could not look further afield than two miles from Bourne End otherwise our ten mile relocation may have started to look like a bit of a mockery! Suddenly I learned of a plot of land at nearby Wooburn Green, in a quiet spot 1½ miles from the branch. We quickly arranged a viewing and liked what we saw. For the children's safety, and in particular Philip's, it was set back off the road with open meadow land to the rear. Although it was ideal we wondered how we were ever going to go about building a house there.

Derek Pink, a builder who was also a customer of the bank, and somebody whose expertise we would need later, agreed to build a chalet bungalow for us which would be ready in six months, just as Alice was due to start school. Philip would continue at Vinio House but be transported to school via a different bus route. It was an ideal way forward.

Philip had by now settled at Vinio House School and readily accepted the regular routines involved. His speech was still frustratingly limited and stilted but this was being helped by both his chatterbox sister and the nightly reading.

The cycling was still going well but the visits to the Broom and Wade factory were no longer solo efforts as 'madam' would not be left behind now that she had her coveted tricycle! Whilst Philip had turned eight and appeared very competent, the progression to cycling on the road was a big step to take and was put off time and again. We realised, however, that moving to Wooburn Green where the roads were busier would be more of a problem than taking the next step forward in Hughenden Valley as this was an area with which Philip was very familiar.

On a quiet Sunday morning in July we all got up early to break the news to Philip that we would have a short ride on the road as far as Hughenden Road and back. Whilst he could not express his feelings, one only had to see his face to realise he was well aware of this big grown-up step forward. I rode behind him slightly to his right to provide protection.

All went well. He was a model of how one should behave on the road. He rode confidently forwards concentrating very hard without apparent nerves, probably not realising the significance of his achievement or the nervous state of his dad bringing up the rear. The progression was a credit to him in that he was careful, fully aware of vehicles around him and he observed traffic signs to the letter. I had to make sure that any bad habits I possessed became a thing of the past and that we only crossed lights when they were green and not amber!

Looking back, as one so often does in our circumstances, it was remarkable that the prospect of moving house again and the uncertainties involved did not faze Philip one little bit. In fact he appeared to be enjoying the experience, perhaps because we talked about it with enthusiasm to both him and Alice. It could also have been that his world was less cluttered with other issues in those days. He was therefore able to digest what was going on and, as far as we were aware, appreciated the time scales and implications of our plans.

Derek turned out to be as good as his word and we soon had a copy of the plans. We were then able to tell the children about the house in more detail and the likely timescales. Most importantly we could discuss with them the various rooms and this would be enhanced as the building progressed. It seemed a natural process to do this and I'm sure it paid dividends, especially with Philip, because as a family unit we were looking forward with great anticipation.

One day we had met Derek on site and were at the rear of the property when who should appear running round the scaffolding at first floor level with a look of bravado and triumph on his face, but Philip, closely followed but somewhat more circumspectly by Alice.

"Don't panic don't panic" as Corporal Jones of Dad's Army would say! It was easier to say than do as Helen and I were thrown into mental turmoil.

Derek, who was no less pole-axed, shouted, "Philip! Stop!" and he thankfully did. From that point onwards we were able to control the mayhem but not before a few anxious moments had passed getting them both safely round the planking and back to the ladder up which they had climbed.

With the danger now over there was no point in issuing a stern rebuke but it was certainly the time for pointing out how dangerous their actions had been and how they could so easily have turned into a disaster. No such attractive adventure opportunities were again left on site when it was unattended.

When we returned to No. 22 we somewhat nervously laughed about the children's escapade with the overtone "what Philip did was just what a 'normal' child would do."

With the speed the building was taking shape it suddenly dawned on us that there were fewer than three months to the proposed completion and we had not even thought about putting No. 22 on the market. There was no need to worry. Helen again came up trumps, selling at the asking price to the first viewer on a Saturday afternoon whilst I was away playing cricket. By the early '70s property inflation was well set and in just over three years No. 22 had more than doubled in value.

On one of our visits to Wooburn Green, finding the staircase fitted created a further wave of excitement as the first floor layout could now be explored. "This is my bedroom" and "This mine" said Alice and Philip respectively. This all happened without hesitation. Thankfully, they had both chosen a different room. Was this already in their minds from seeing the plans? We will never know! At our weekly family visits the children could see the changes taking place in their bedrooms, with Philip particularly intrigued by the big cupboard space via a door in his room into the eaves, an area very soon to be adopted by his toys.

Life as the manager of a bank certainly held more status within the community, even if you only managed a staff of twelve against being the senior assistant with a staff of forty. You were 'the bank manager,' which in those days carried a great deal of respect. You were on a par with the doctor or solicitor.

Bourne End was a delightful community to work for and in. Within a town such as High Wycombe a walk along the high street was like in any other town; you were largely anonymous, but not so in a smaller environment. We quickly came to know a large proportion of those we met or saw, both customers and non-customers. Personal relationships were important in expanding the business and with the area being developed commercially, I was fortunate to have a very personable staff. Pleasingly they worked as a team which suited my way of operation and the business prospered.

Whilst schooling for Philip was settled and we could simulate his new journey to Vinio House for him by making detours and driving over the route on the way home from visits to Wooburn Green, we suddenly realised in July that we must sort out schooling for Alice. In two weeks the schools would be starting their summer holidays and with Alice five in December we needed to get organised for her to attend one of the two Wooburn Green schools catering for infants.

Derek, our builder, and his wife Shirley, with whom we had become good friends, advised that St. Pauls, the Church of England School which had just been relocated, was the one to aim for as their two boys attended it and they were very satisfied with the results. It had an excellent 11+ record and embodied all that a parent could wish for regarding good old fashioned discipline and respect for the teachers, so much so that it was always full to overflowing.

A further instance of the standing of the bank manager within the community was about to unfold. I telephoned Roy Harris, the head master of St. Pauls and explained how we had been recommended to his school and as we would be living in Wooburn Green from September whether it would be possible for Alice to attend his school at the start of the autumn term. I recall expecting this would be a formality, only for Roy to reply, "As you are going to live nearer the Boundary Road School you really should apply there, and in any event this school is already at its capacity."

Thankfully, in a tight corner my brain kicked in to part with the comment, "If you do find you have room for Alice perhaps you would telephone me at Lloyds Bank where I have recently become manager."

"Oh," said Roy and nothing more, and the conversation terminated.

Three days passed until a Mr. and Mrs Harris, who were customers of the bank made an appointment to see me. Who should it be but the Mr. Roy Harris I had spoken to about Alice's schooling and his wife Alma who also taught at St. Pauls School. Small talk over, it soon transpired that the appointment had nothing to do with banking. Roy said, "A few days ago you telephoned about Alice and her schooling. We will be pleased to welcome her to our school. She can start in September and Alma will be her teacher."

"Oh yes, thank you," I blurted out not realising the significance, as the chalet may not have been finished and we would still be living in High Wycombe, ten miles away.

There was no need to have worried. Derek continued to be as good as his word in holding to the original chalet completion. Alice was one of only fourteen in her class for the first term. This would be a superb start to her education and a complete contrast to poor old Philip.

Before moving house we managed to fit in a further holiday at Salcombe. It was its usual success with us all being made very welcome. Bob and Pat would always single out Philip for a special welcome and he would reply by telling them when their birthdays were. This immediately helped to put him at ease, as he always remembered their respective dates along with dozens of others. As a test without any prompting, having not seen or heard of the couple for over thirty years, I recently asked Philip if he remembered Bob and Pat from Salcombe, which he did, followed by when their birthdays were. He reeled them off without a moment's hesitation. I have no way of knowing if he is right but I would bet my worldly wealth he is.

Bob and Pat would continue inviting Philip to be master of ceremonies for dinner, which always pleased him He would bang the little brass gong and stand by the door to welcome the guests as they came into the dining room. Alice for the first time asked why Philip was always allowed to bang the gong for dinner. We just said, "It makes him feel important and he is only allowed to do it as a special favour by Bob and Pat." On the last night we did ask if they could both do it, with Philip being last. They were both happy but, sadly it was likely to be our last visit to this particular hotel as Bob and Pat were retiring and we could not imagine it being the same without them. We have never been back for a holiday.

We generally did the same things around Salcombe. We played on the beach at Hope Cove, exploring the rock pools as the tide ebbed leaving as it did so firm sand which was ideal for the bats and balls to have an airing, along with the buckets and spades. Alice was quite creative in her play but Philip simply filled his pail and made single castles with no particular aim in mind. Alternatively, he would dig a large hole in which to bury me.

We would retrace our steps to Kingsbridge to have an afternoon boat trip along the Dart towards Salcombe or a popular circular tour in the car which would encompass crossing the river on the Dartmouth ferry. Philip loved these excursions and we soon realised he knew better than us where he had previously been. There was a phenomenal memory locked up in his head.

As we always had the same bedroom at the hotel we were suddenly made aware of just how much Philip had grown over two years. He now had to bend down to get into the annexe bedroom area and he could not sit upright on his bunk bed.

He was certainly becoming a good looking lad. This at least masked his problems as far as we were concerned. In other ways however it created awkward times when he did not react as third parties expected, or was spoken to and opted out simply because he could not cope with the one-to-one confrontation with strangers. Alice, in those circumstances, was incredibly protective if she was around. She would simply say "Philip doesn't speak very much," and that said it all; bless her. An old head, on very young shoulders, was already developing and continued to do so in the kindest of ways.

Schooling settled, we visited Dr. Hill, our G.P. As we suspected, by living at Wooburn Green we would be moving out of the area served by his surgery. He confirmed our worst fears that this was the case as we were going to live on the wrong side of The Green. He paused and then thoughtfully added, "I will make a case to my fellow partners for us to make an exception for Philip's sake. If they are agreeable I am more than happy to continue to be your family's doctor." Two days later we received a call of confirmation - what a relief. We liked him as our doctor and another change had been avoided. The one change we were looking forward to was the loss of

Mrs. Waffle our Social Worker, with the hope that a more positive being would be allocated to us.

Right on cue the day of the move came. All went well - out of No. 22 in the morning and into Wooburn Green (Old Stocks) in the afternoon. We had arranged for Philip and Alice to be looked after for the day but ensured they stayed with us until the furniture van arrived so that Philip in particular could see his belongings being prepared for the move as he would not be returning there again.

He was apparently unsettled during the day, with Pa Pa being used liberally as a comfort. He was not however a problem, just obviously very uneasy, although he knew, as far as we were aware, what was going on, but as usual the talking was largely all one way.

Everything turned out fine despite the chaos which greeted the children's arrival at Old Stocks. There were boxes everywhere, furniture being moved both upstairs and down, garden implements in the drive adding up to a disorganised shambles. Thankfully, we had had the forethought to get the carpets fitted throughout the upstairs area so it was relatively easy to establish some semblance of order for them by the time they went to bed.

Chapter 9 - It's All Go

Another hectic phase in our lives was about to commence. Getting Old Stocks organised and Alice ready to start school were the priorities. This was urgently followed, as the weather was set fair, by setting out the virgin garden. Thankfully, unlike in High Wycombe, it was a flat plot. Very quickly it was turfing time again! This time there were two helpers, but the extra pairs of hands were largely counter productive. Philip could just about lift a turf which was invariably dropped, or would miss his wheel barrow and then unroll and break up on the drive. To counter the negative help I moved as much turf as possible from front to back after bed time. An instant lawn soon transforms a garden but it ideally needs two weeks to bed down. Just as with the High Wycombe garden this was a luxury it didn't get.

Philip and Alice soon settled down and enjoyed having a flat garden. The chalet had a short, gated entrance drive with concrete paths all round. The exterior at the rear incorporated an oval shaped patio. These areas soon became race tracks, Philip on the red tractor and Alice on her pride and joy, the blue tricycle. At least it was better than the in-house track at No. 22!

They careered round and round the chalet at great speed, the noise from the tractor's hard plastic tyres probably driving the neighbours mad. They never had an accident or fall but the life of the first drainage down-pipes was very limited. These had been smashed before we even realised they had been introduced to the churning wheels of the tractor.

Emotions ran high with Alice's first day at school. She looked very smart and grown up in her uniform. Having not attended nursery school, although outwardly confident, she was new to the area and was naturally very apprehensive about being left in the classroom. This phase soon passed and she quickly made friends and settled into her small class. Mum, whilst containing herself at the school gate, was quite upset that her 'little girl' was moving on to a new stage in her young life. The level of emotions expressed may well have been a reaction to the subconscious pent-up feelings regarding Philip for the past eight years.

Whilst outwardly life was fairly tranquil, there was great excitement when Philip took noticeable steps forward, but not for one day could one now forget his obvious mental limitations. Any speech he had was very limited and stilted and, whilst there was improvement it was still very slow going. We continued to clutch at straws, being thankful that he looked 100% and could ordinarily cope until when confronted by strangers his lack of confidence made him appear very withdrawn.

In other words, we focused on the better things in life, as we were at this stage having to let tomorrow look after itself. It is often said that 'a family with a handicapped person is a handicapped family'. We preferred to take these words as restricted, as we certainly tried to live our lives to the full, children included.

This approach and attitude could not, however, entirely eliminate subconscious worries about the future. We had to ensure that we kept as busy as possible to stop feelings of despair surfacing too often. We were fortunate in that, for Alice's as well as Philip's sake, we had the strength of character to do this.

After the move, life soon settled into an acceptable pattern. Philip was enjoying his longer journey to school and Alice was starting to make friends with her new class-mates. I was able to get home for lunch, which gave Helen and me a few quiet minutes each day. During the holidays the children loved it when we would all have ten minutes on the settee watching Mr. Benn, Trumpton or Spot the Dog. It became a family joke that I regularly had to be woken at the end of the programme whilst the two little souls were still enjoying their sleepy cuddle.

As the TV began to play an increasingly important part in the lives of the children and they would, if permitted, watch it all day, we introduced a rather sneaky regime in that if it had been switched on for too long it would be announced that it was getting hot and needed to cool down. Some thirty-five years on Alice still reminds us of how, as a child, she was deprived by her parent's harsh regime - poor little soul! How we would have coped with today's TV culture vis-a-vis children and viewing we have no idea.

Soon after the new term started we were made aware that Philip was both enjoying and doing well at the swimming sessions in the newly opened pool at Vinio House. This surprised us as it was not something he had ever done in our company - he had always fought shy of water.

As I was unable to swim I went off to Amersham for a night school session of lessons in the pool. In time we were able to enjoy a new facility being offered by customers of the bank, George and Ann Lock who ran a very successful engineering business. Very soon after we moved into Old Stocks we were asked to their house for a cup of tea followed by a swim. Off we went, the children complete with armbands for what we expected to be an outside garden pool, with heated water. How wrong we were. It was a large purpose-built building nestling on the side of the hill looking over the landscape towards High Wycombe and connected to the house by an enclosed covered way. There were changing rooms and large internal expanses, in addition to the sizeable pool area, in which to relax. Four sets of eyes were out on stalks!

These were very kind, genuine people with whom we became good friends. They had a very caring interest in Philip and his welfare. We were invited to use their pool whenever we wished. As it was always heated this was indeed a privilege. Initially, we would telephone seeking permission to use the pool but it soon became obvious that this was not expected. If however, we planned on taking a guest, whether it be a friend of Alice's or a member of our family, we always asked permission, which was willingly given. These were such generous and caring friends. The use of the pool, which was always unlocked, was a marvellous facility and one which we cherished.

Philip always looked forward to his visits, particularly during the winter when the water would be covered with thousands of ping pong balls to keep the water temperature up and to reduce the levels of condensation. The balls did not inhibit swimming. The children thought this was great fun as they thrashed about, often getting, as we all did, balls suddenly appearing in embarrassing places!

Our new Social Worker, Mrs. McBenefit, called to briefly introduce herself to Helen. As usual, this called for the harrowing experience of going back through Philip's problems rather than taking his history from the file and moving forward. She got off to a poor start as Helen, on saying good bye to her, realised that whilst making her call she had left a young child unattended in her car!

I was becoming increasingly involved in the Vinio House PTA as both Treasurer and Vice Chairman, attending meetings whenever I could. Within our new environment there were other parents who had a child at Vinio House. This helped us considerably, as for the first time there were people around us who understood what life was like with a mentally handicapped child in your midst - not that we were looking for sympathy - far from it.

It was when travelling to a PTA meeting, which we were both attending, that I gave Margaret Chapman a lift as she lived nearby. In conversation she casually referred to her son Paul's Day-time Attendance Allowance being due for review and mentioned how they tried as a family to use the money for everyone's benefit. I had no idea what she was talking about and asked her to enlarge. She was astounded that with Philip now approaching nine years of age we had not even heard of the allowance. She explained, based on her own mentally handicapped son Paul's case, we could have been eligible for the allowance for the past seven years. The allowance was split into two categories, Daytime and Night Time. She concluded by saying "You must be entitled to at least the Daytime allowance with Philip at Vinio House." On enquiry, other parents at the meeting confirmed they too received it and couldn't understand why we did not. When I arrived home the allowance was also news to Helen.

The following morning our telephone was red hot to Mrs. McBenefit asking why we did not receive at least the Daytime Attendance Allowance. Her reply was unbelievable, "You haven't applied for it," she said. My reply to her is not repeatable but it did not seem to register with her that one had to know about these things to be able to apply!

During the many hours we had spent with both social-working 'ladies' it had never been mentioned; they always seemed to be more interested in the past than ensuring we had the allowances we were entitled to. On looking back our first Social Worker in Cottenham should have alerted us to the benefit but to be fair to him no formal assessment had been made of Philip during our time in Cambridgeshire. We were at that time still very much 'paddling our own canoe'. Our High Wycombe Social Worker who for want of better words 'looked after Philip' should most certainly have mentioned it - was 'useless', a word used earlier to describe her, now fully justified? I think so.

State benefits were not as widely advertised and were certainly not thrust down one's throat as they are today. Having nothing to add, Mrs. McBenefit concluded by saying, "I will get an application in the post to you." After a chasing call ten days later the package arrived.

The copious form was completed. This was followed up by a home visit by an assessing doctor. He needed to go through the answers to questions and hear at first-hand about the limitations experienced by Philip and how it affected us. He was also astounded to learn how the personnel within the system had let us down so badly. It took a further three months before the allowance was formally approved. This was back-dated to the date of the initial application.

Whilst its sanction was doubtless welcome, it was not something to celebrate. Using the back-dated allowance at half-term we all took off for a Trust House Forte bargain break at Ventnor. The children thought this was regal living. They enjoyed the long ferry ride from Southampton to the Isle of Wight plus a big family room in a very smart three star hotel. We made sure, as a family unit, that we used the allowance to good effect, which included at least one of these weekends, at a different Trust House Forte hotel each year.

A selection of the children's toys, were always taken with us, including Pa Pa, but the priorities seemed to change for these breaks. The evenings were always the time for playing cards and especially Whot, Speed and Round the World. These were all games with pictures or shapes on them, plus a number where one had to be able to either take one's turn by matching the picture or number, or collect another card from the central pack. The concentration was intense and the fun immense. Philip played his full part and although we thought he did not understand the finer points of the games he never made a mistake and would be the winner as often as anyone. He loved laying his last card and shouting "Out," much to the irritation of his sister, especially if she had only one card left and was anticipating being the winner - it was to us such innocent but rewarding fun.

These games certainly helped, without pressure, the single word development of Philip's speech as he would repeat, without thinking about it, the number on the card or the subject such as 'square' or 'triangle', which he decided without prompting to call 'tringles', or motors or aeroplane as appropriate. Stringing words together was not a skill he had mastered. He would then happily collate the scores and finally do his best to add them up. Without making a fuss we had to ensure Alice had her turn at being in charge and Master of Ceremonies. Oh what a joy these evenings were!

We regularly worked on numbers and word speech through play. For this we used the Ladybird flash cards to supplement the books. It was a regular Saturday morning play session whilst Mum and Dad were still in bed. Tea would be served and they would sit on the bed and single word cards would be produced from the box, supposedly at random, and answered by the children alternately. This was taken as great fun and certainly helped Philip with the more difficult word recognition. He may have seemed slow for his age but he was quick with the words he knew and equally quick with words he didn't know to say, "Alice's turn." The only concession we made was not giving Philip two consecutive words we were aware he didn't know so that he appeared to keep on a par with Alice. These were simple but happy and rewarding sessions with a serious overtone built into the play.

Through age and distance from Bradenham I felt my cricketing days were coming to an end so I severed those connections. As Wooburn Green had a flourishing Tennis Club and my free time was at a premium I turned my attentions to a sport I had not played for many years. The courts were in an enclosed area, within a large playing field. This was just right if I needed to take Philip and Alice along with me.

Although the bank would have happily paid my subscription to a golf club I had purposely never attempted to join. I received numerous customer requests to play but always declined. Initially, some were not able to understand my reasoning for not participating. I decided that if one wants to play well, or even not so well, it is a very time consuming game which I did not think was fair on Helen, and in any event as a largely weekend game it was not family friendly. We all enjoyed our free time together - golf would have impinged on this.

My activities with Round Table increased but in 1977 I would have to leave, having had my fortieth birthday. Helen was invited, and joined the ladies side of the organisation, named Ladies Circle. She enjoyed it but soon found that with a young family and with the additional commitment towards Philip, she was putting herself under constant pressure to give more time to the club than she could afford. Having given it a good try she resigned. As with my golf non-participation, most fellow- members could understand the reasoning but some of the more selfish people amongst their numbers could not. Rightly or wrongly we always put the family first in anything we did.

The Wooburn Green area was good for walking, with woods and plenty of footpaths to explore nearby. Cycling with Philip was more of a problem as the roads were busier and the use of pedestrian footpaths was difficult as they were virtually all within built up areas. To one side we had steep wooded hills and, on the other the conurbation leading back towards High Wycombe or Bourne End.

We did gradually manage to expand our horizons as we explored local lanes where the traffic levels were lower. Sadly, however we found the motorists always seemed to be in more of a hurry and less considerate the nearer we got towards London, always seeming to be driving at excessive speed and all too ready to meet their Maker. It took us some time to get used to this hectic way of life.

With these limitations it inevitably became a pastime in which we could no longer involve Alice. Whilst not pleased, she accepted this without too much fuss. Our most fruitful area to explore was towards South Bucks and Slough. This encompassed the very large wooded area of Burnham Beeches which was looked after by the Greater London Council. When Philip and I were off cycling it gave Helen quality one-to-one time with Alice. Despite trying to do otherwise, it was very difficult when Philip was around for him not to be the centre of attention.

As life moved on a nasty shock was awaiting me during what I thought was a routine visit to a chiropodist to sort out my poorly toe. "You will need an operation as you have a spur of bone growing under your big toe," he said. Just the thought of this made me feel queasy and led to a further bout of excitement!

I was duly admitted to a hospital in Beaconsfield where the nursing staff consisted largely of nuns. As my time for the operation approached a nun in white robes entered the room. The purpose of her visit was to administer the pre-med. She suggested I should sit on the bed to receive the injection and then sit out in a chair, and after some thirty minutes get into bed and await being taken to the operating theatre.   Without further ado she inserted the needle into my arm and the next thing I recall was thinking I had been called to 'another world' earlier than expected as I came round from fainting to find the nun/nurse clad in her 'shroud' standing over me telling me to relax and to take deep breathes.   Take deep breathes; I felt I was already gasping for air!   She then suggested I should stay in bed and await a further call.   What a whimp I am!

Alice continued to be incredibly supportive of Philip and unwittingly helped him a great deal.   She was a model of a little sister in such circumstances.   She had known nothing else and the old head on young shoulders continued to mature very confidently, but without, at any time, becoming precocious.   This 110% support for Philip could not go on without Alice obviously, at times, thinking quite deeply about her lot regarding herself and her brother.   Suddenly, one day she said very quietly, and as near to being upset as we had ever seen her about her elder brother, "Why does Daddy do so much for Philip's school?"   We explained it was a way of supporting him and over a hundred others like him at Vinio House in the best way he could.   It was also a way of showing our appreciation for the work Mrs. Quartermain and her staff did for Philip and the other children at the school.

Her comment certainly took us aback and made us realise that here was a little girl who, whilst not craving for more home support, nonetheless was wishing to see her Mum and Dad giving time to her school.   Thankfully, by way of positive response we could tell her how Helen had already been asked to serve on the very active PTA committee at St. Paul's.   She quickly made her mark there by organising a tombola stall at the Christmas Dance rather than running a dreary raffle.   It certainly raised lots more money, and was a very popular attraction   As with the Vinio House parents, the St. Paul's parents were asked to canvas their firms for prizes, which worked well.   The large stall was compulsive to some parents and would last most of the evening.

Roy had also asked Helen if she would help with the school library. This certainly pleased Alice as she, like other children, then had her Mum popping in and out of school.   If she was passing the library she would cheekily pop her head round the door with a "Hello Mum" and disappear to a lesson before Mum could reply.   A problem solved!

After holidays at Salcombe our attention for a two-week break turned to Wales where a friend had bought a cedar-wood chalet in Happy Valley near Towyn eighteen months earlier. In 1976 we made our first visit and the weather could not have been kinder - cloudless skies, warm sunshine with a little rain on one afternoon. This was also the home of the Talyllyn Miniature Railway. It was quite a trek to mid West Wales, with the roads as they were in the '70s. Up early in the morning and off on a new adventure, we planned to stop at the Green Dragon, a three star Trust House Forte hotel in the centre of Hereford for breakfast. Within the hotel foyer stood a single one-armed-bandit. Alice, in particular, had eyed this upon entry into the hotel and after it was explained to her how it worked she was desperate to have a go. With some agitation, this was deferred until after breakfast when, to keep the peace, and as a treat, we gave them both a few coins with permission to leave the table with the promise they would return to the dining room as soon as the money had been lost. In those days there were no banks of flashing lights, numerous wheels and nudges to contend with. Any winnings were simply paid out immediately into a little tray at the front of the machine.

With no second bidding necessary, off they both ran clutching their coins. Before we even had time to be concerned about what they were doing there was a loud shriek and a continuous clunking noise. We both rushed from the table thinking something nasty had happened only to find them both standing, mouths wide open, transfixed to the spot. They had hit the jackpot and silver looking tokens were spewing out all over the floor! The tokens were rapidly and gleefully gathered up, and exchanged for £10 in cash - and we continued on our way!

The excitement of the earlier events was immense and ensured there was plenty of chatter along the way, added to which it was such a pretty journey with plenty to see.

The area we were visiting was perfect for the children with so many things to see and do. The River Dovey passed Aberdovey as it emptied its fast flowing water into the Irish Sea. It was, at low water, an area of vast sandy shores with areas of dunes backing the wide sandy beaches which were fully washed at every high tide. One had to be wary of the strong currents near the river estuary on the ebb tide. The pools left in the sand by the tide eddies were also very interesting for the children to explore, but they could also be unexpectedly deep and therefore dangerous. There were also mountains and big open spaces for walking together, with an array of 'little trains' nearby.

We were fortunate with the chalet we rented, as the previous occupants had been encouraged to enter in a book any walks or excursions they had been on, together with their star rating This made it very easy, in a strange area with so much to do, to prioritise how we would spend our time. With the sun on our backs, whatever we decided to do was great fun.

As the 27" Talyllyn Narrow Gauge Railway was nearby at Towyn this was soon singled out for a priority trip. Ahead of this, Philip was intrigued by the smoke and hissing as he watched from the bridge above the line the shunting of the engines to-ing and fro-ing in the sidings. They all had a name and this really was Thomas the Tank Engine stuff!

We were soon off on the seven mile trip from Towyn to Abergynolwyn, having to stop as the train was 'thirsty' and needed to take on water, at Dolgoch Falls. It took almost an hour to chug along the seven miles of rising track. One wonders how long it took when it was a slate train.

There was another narrow gauge line (only 15 inch) on the riverside at Fairbourn which was not too far away. Both of the 'Little Trains' were a great hit, one with its small enclosed carriages and the other more open. To see the excitement and expectation on the children's faces as the huffing and puffing train with smoke billowing out of its funnel approached was a great joy to us both. As if to say "I've arrived" as it pulled into the station it always gave a shrill toot!

We bought a rake and again tried our skill at cockling on the opposite side of the river to Aberdovey at Borth. The children loved doing this, not in the running water as on The Isle of Wight, but in the muddy wet sand. As soon as they heard the rake hit an object in the mud they pounced. Muddy we all got, but who cared when we just paddled in the sunlit water and cleaned ourselves? I coveted a fishing trip out to sea with Charlie the boatman at Aberdovey, but leaving Helen with two young children all day was not an option. It was something to look forward to another day.

The walks in and around the tops of the mountains were endless but not without their frights. On The Precipice or Panoramic walks R.A.F. jets would scream through the valleys below, having gone before we knew they had arrived, such was their speed. Despite, at times, the narrow paths the children were fleet of foot and never gave us cause for concern. Along with them we could enjoy the freedom and beauty of our surroundings as we glimpsed sight of Barmouth and the river Mawddach below.

We climbed Bird Rock which dominated the lower Dysynni Valley and, from its time of being in the sea, still housed colonies of Cormorants and Guillemots. At the top we met a bird enthusiast who pointed out the Red Kites floating in the bright sun on the thermals above. Sitting quietly what a spectacular sight it was to also view them from above when they occasionally dropped below us. They moved around with such effortless ease, looking for an inviting carcass below.

The 2,957 foot Cader Idris, was conquered, on a clear sunny day, with effortless ease by the children. What splendid views at the summit of the surrounding area. On returning to the chalet, Helen and I rested our weary limbs and enjoyed a quiet cup of tea, but not so young sir and young madam who were outside thumping the Swing Ball for all they were worth, as if they hadn't been anywhere! It was great to see them enjoying life together.

From this holiday we were amazed at how Philip was able to pronounce place names such as Abergynolwyn and Dolgellau correctly and without the slightest hesitation – singularly they just rolled off his tongue - there must be a bit of Welsh blood in him somewhere!

Those two weeks are remembered so fondly, it must have been our best family holiday, but there are other close contenders. We still remember our final picnic on the way home, sitting on the large boulders mid-stream in the River Wye, wistfully lamenting now our holiday was over. We had all had such a wonderful time, so full of fun and freedom we vowed to return, and so we did.

Chapter 10 - The Truth Revealed

Despite the overriding problems in looking after Philip these were happy and fun times with progress being made, but Alice was now developing her life-skills at such a rate that she was very obviously starting to leave Philip behind.

We had accepted that Philip was correctly placed at Vinio House. With this came more guilt and a realisation that he would need support for the rest of his days, added to which was the knowledge we would not be here forever to give him the necessary back up and support – a frightening prospect!.

One hopes that this problem is many years away but it cannot be ignored and is a situation that most certainly will not go away but will become more acute as the years pass by. Whilst we would hope Alice would be in the background, we could not, and would not, expect her to be saddled with responsibility for Philip for her lifetime.

At about this time, we saw that Professor Tizard (from our Hammersmith Hospital days with Philip) had been appointed the First Professor of Paediatrics at Oxford. He was based locally in Oxford at the John Radcliffe Hospital. We made contact with him as we thought he may be interested to see Philip some eight years on. He remembered Philip and was delighted to hear from us and an appointment to renew acquaintance was soon arranged.

When the appointed day came, for no good reason we felt very nervous. What would he say? What would he think of Philip? We need not have worried. Here we were, with a very eminent paediatrician, being greeted like long lost friends with an apology that he had not kept in touch and that we were simply jettisoned at Hammersmith in the manner we were. He could not have been more charming.

Philip was on top form. The professor looked at him in apparent amazement. "Well," he said, "I can only congratulate you on what you have achieved with that little bundle I left you with, it is wonderful to see him in such fine fettle. Sadly though," he continued, "You do realise that whilst it will improve slowly, Philip's speech will never be anything like 100% and that he will need support throughout his life." We had to admit we had already reluctantly reached those conclusions ourselves, but to date, we had done nothing about it.

The professor then proceeded to make some notes. Suddenly he looked up and turned to me somewhat quizzically and asked, "Mr. Childs, could I ask a big favour of you? I know what parents such as yourselves go through with a mentally handicapped child but my students don't, and I think they should. It would do them good to hear it at first hand. Would you be prepared to return to the hospital and talk to my students on this subject?"

Completely taken aback I said "Yes."

"Good," he said. "I will get my secretary to give you some suggested dates."

Oh my goodness, I thought, what have I let myself in for? Me, without an 'O' level, addressing an audience, complete with professor, of some of the brightest young medical academics around? What could I say and how could I say it?

I decided my 'A level' in common sense would just have to do. There would be nothing elaborate, I would cover the mental anguish, the constant reminders, family and social implications and the constant uncertainties of life coupled with the ongoing feelings of isolation in trying to cope with ones problems. Finally I would make a plea to them to at least make some pretence on a first appointment of having read the file of the patient as it is very upsetting to have to keep repeating the 'nuts and bolts' from the beginning to everybody one meets for the first time.

With our slow realisation, and Professor Tizard's words ringing in her ears, Helen took up an invitation by Christine Locke of Marlow to join a party of similarly affected parents to visit a village type environment to the West of Oxford. This was for parents to get a feel of the facilities such a community could offer for the future of our children.

Whilst we, unlike some other parents, had no immediate need, Helen went along to see for herself what was available. She came back rather disillusioned, with an overriding view that the staff of this particular set-up seemed to get more out of the care and accommodation than the cared-for residents.

The house and its complex were isolated at the end of a long drive and, specifically, she could not accept that residents appeared to be denied everyday comforts and entertainment such as television which our children took for granted. This was not how she saw Philip's ongoing needs being catered for. She was not alone in those thoughts but one can only make long term goals from what one sees.

With the future still in mind, shortly afterwards, Christine arranged for an Eric Gibson to talk to virtually the same group of anxious parents. Eric was the Chairman of the High Wycombe Group of Friends of The Home Farm Trust (HFT), a charity at that time providing lifelong residential care for the mentally handicapped. He had a career in timber and was a volunteer to the charity's cause with no 'axe to grind', through a vested interest in a handicapped child or relation. He was a unique and good-hearted soul. Helen found Eric's talk like a breath of fresh air in comparison to the earlier visit. It was an enlightening insight into the charity with the aid of slides, showing large houses, smiling residents apparently enjoying respect and a lifestyle as normal as possible. There appeared to be an open door policy with no high fences or locked doors. In other words, the residents being cared for seemed to have their dignity intact, and it showed.

After Eric's insight we found out more about the charity, and the more we delved the more we liked what we saw. HFT was based in Bristol, being largely controlled by the parents of resident offspring who were in the care of the charity, through a board of governors. Additionally it was steadily expanding its residential numbers through the energetic fundraising of forward-looking parents who wished to find a settled environment for their son or daughter. The charity also appeared to have the stability and ideals we would wish for Philip.

The Trust, which was formed in 1962, had a good track record and was blessed with a number of well-known patrons who seemed not to be just names on a letter-head but very supportive, active people. All in all it was a set up we both felt we could identify with, and we were most certainly prepared to work, along with others, to enhance their ideals, irrespective of whether we would need, or ultimately be offered, their services at some time in the future.

Within our enquiries, day-to-day placement funding costs for the first time reared their ugly head - these had to be borne by committed sponsorship from the applicant's local authority before a residential place could be finalised.

Whilst our needs were some way off, an application form was filled in for Philip's admission to HFT after he reached the age of eighteen - the earliest age placements were made. This was a heartrending but necessary early decision to make - our feelings of guilt towards Philip came flooding back by the bucket-load. The completion of the application form was carried out with the same reluctant frame of mind as Philip's initial introduction to schooling and Vinio House. We comforted ourselves with the thought that if we subsequently found long term support was not needed his name could be removed.

Hard as it was, we had to think positively, to try to ensure, as far as possible, that long term security for Philip was being put in place. HFT seemed as good a solution as we were likely to find. We repeated our earlier poignant thoughts that we wouldn't be around forever, but hopefully the charity would, and whatever the future held we could not expect Alice to be obligated to make all the decisions on the care element of Philip's later life.

Learning county sponsorship would be required, as a minimum, if Philip was to ultimately go into care with HFT or another such charity, focused our minds regarding my career in the bank. For a county to take on a commitment of this magnitude one needed residential stability to be even considered for financial support. No county would take on this liability for a new arrival in their midst. As we had already lived in Bucks for seven years it was paramount we must stay living within the county.

As it was such a vital issue I immediately asked to see my Regional Manager, wishing to be specific in limiting my career moves as I needed to continue living in Bucks. Thankfully the bank was both understanding and positive. As there were a number of branches in and around Bucks and as London (heaven forbid) was also easily accessible, convenient career movement would not be a problem. What a relief and, all credit to them, they never wavered from this helpful and considerate stance.

The appointed day duly arrived for my talk to Professor Tizard's medical students. I had been allocated forty-five minutes. It won't take that long, I thought. The professor ushered me into a spartanly furnished compact room full of fresh and expectant-looking faces. The sight of this obvious expectation from the students created a momentary mental panic. The professor introduced me, along with Helen, as two of the most incredible parents it had been his pleasure, in extremely difficult circumstances, to have encountered during his professional life. Where do you go from there?

Rising with my notes quivering in my hand and without pre planning, but probably unwittingly playing for time, I wandered round to the front of the small table and rested myself on it. This worked like a charm. What I thought would be an emotional and personal sort of talk immediately turned into an intimate chat.

After twenty minutes I stopped talking, having said all I had to say, making it appear I thought questions from the students may be of more help than me continuing to ramble on. Probably to break the ensuing silence and to get things going, the professor asked "Did you have strong religious beliefs or in hindsight where did you draw the strength to tackle everything head on in the way you did after my original devastating prognosis?" Half turning to the professor I disclosed the influence of Mr. Barker and how, as a friend and osteopath, we came to rely on him and how we thought he was responsible for Philip's physical changes. In layman's terms as best I could I told them what he had set out to do for Philip, including reducing the drug intake and how I understood he had achieved it. I added for good measure, "The day the drugs stopped so did the fits." I then asked "What did this tell us?"

The professor's mouth dropped open. He was speechless, being so obviously nonplussed with this revelation - he couldn't believe what he was hearing. He was rescued by his students who found this information revealing and fascinating. From that point their questions came thick and fast and the talk took on a completely unexpected and different emphasis.

At the conclusion, in summing up the professor said he had, despite his years of experience, got just as much out of my talk as had the students. Without doubt Mr. Barker was very much caught up somewhere within those words.

As we prepared to depart the professor, still obviously very much taken aback by the news about Mr. Barker said "I wish you had told me at the time what was going on."

I replied "If we had you would have protested and washed your hands of us."

"Yes," he said wistfully, "I suppose I would. Well done anyway."

We kept in touch with him for a while but there was little he could do or add to the words of caution issued earlier when we met again. He did, however, endorse as very appropriate the avenues we were pursuing for Philip's future.

Chapter 11 - Simple Pleasures and New Friends

Visits to the Catherine Wheel at Henley were still looked forward to, especially during the holidays and when Grandparents were with us. We were still of the opinion they did not understand Philip's problems but at least they were happy in his company and he in theirs. Our horizons had been widened to now include Windsor, where Philip loved to watch the sentries marching about with their gleaming boots and spotless uniforms, especially when the guards on duty changed over.

Family visits to us were quite frequent but our visits to East Anglia were usually for something specific. With the roads as they were it was still quite a trek for a weekend visit. On one of our visits we arranged for it to coincide with the Suffolk Show. It would be a chance for Helen to bump into friends of yesteryear and Philip and Alice could fulfil their dreams and fantasies by jumping on and off the gleaming show equipment. They reserved their most enthusiastic attention for the biggest tractors they had ever seen. Anything with a steering wheel was fair game! The 'Brmm Brmm's,' in their worlds of fantasy, were a joy to see and hear. After an exhausting, but happy day, the children said they would like a walk by the sea at nearby Felixstowe. Helen thought a meal at The Regal restaurant along with other show goers would be a nice way to round off the day. Not too much persuasion was required for a unanimous 'Yes' vote to that suggestion and a good hearty meal was enjoyed by all.

Sitting at an adjoining table a rosy cheeked, well proportioned jovial farmer and wife had observed the obvious relish with which Philip had tucked into his meal. Gently leaning over towards us, much to the embarrassment of his wife he jokingly said, "I'd rather keep 'im for a week than a fortnight." We still smile when we relate this story some thirty years on. It was said with such a typically Suffolk dry sense of humour.

During one of our visits to Grandma we realised what a mimic Philip had become. There he was banging away at the piano twisting and turning to his audience of Helen, Alice, Grandma and myself, just as Joan Howell, a teacher at Vinio House would do, ensuring the music class were paying attention. Neither Philip nor Alice could play the piano but they would fight for a turn to create what can only be called a din! In comparison, Les Dawson was a musical maestro! Philip was also getting into his own world of make-believe in giving us names from his Rupert Bear annuals.

Alice was enjoying and doing well at St. Paul's School. After her earlier comments regarding my apparent allegiance to Philip and Vinio House she was pleased by our efforts to help her school, in that I subsequently joined the PTA committee, followed by two years as Chairman. We worked hard to raise money for her school and she loved seeing either of us around the buildings. We always got a happy acknowledgement of our presence.

Philip enjoyed robust health but he did seem to manage frequent visits to hospital for one thing or another. A call came from school that he was far from well and it appeared the problem was his tummy. Thankfully, as we were again back to one car I was free to leave work, collect Helen, and rush up to the school. He was certainly in some distress.

We managed to trace Dr. Hill who was taking a surgery at Beaconsfield. He agreed to see Philip immediately if we brought him to the surgery. Philip was very obviously in considerable pain and a very tense period elapsed which was probably only minutes but seemed like hours before the doctor saw him. A quick diagnosis by Dr. Hill confirmed that it was appendicitis and Philip needed an urgent operation. After a call by Dr. Hill to High Wycombe Hospital we were told to take him there immediately as this would be quicker than calling for an ambulance.

Off we went but the important ingredient in Philip's life was missing, Pa Pa. As it was only a small detour on our way to the hospital we quickly called to collect him. At least this gave Philip some temporary comfort, as he really was in a bad way. By the time we got to the hospital he was screwed up with pain.

Dr. Hill must have communicated more urgency to the hospital than we were aware of as Philip was expected and seen virtually immediately by a doctor, who turned out to be a surgeon, dutifully followed by a posse of students. The sight of so many white coats and peering faces alarmed Philip. Thankfully the surgeon soon realised this and turning to his students said, "I think I can do this one on my own."

With Philip in safe hands and Helen in attendance I left to collect Alice from school. She was somewhat distressed by the sudden and unexpected news that her brother had been rushed into hospital and needed an urgent operation.

For Philip, hospital etiquette, even in those days was surely broken. Thankfully, in his case common sense prevailed. Helen went as far as the operating theatre doors with him and observed a rather scruffy Pa Pa still being clutched as he disappeared.

After the successful operation Helen was called into the recovery room. There she saw a sight to gladden her eyes, an unconscious Philip peacefully sleeping with Pa Pa safely tucked cosily into the sheets with him. Philip coped remarkably well during his period of recovery with no after effects. Another trauma in his young life had been safely negotiated.

Whilst Alice's progress at school was good, as she grew older it became apparent that visits for tea by friends had lessened. It was obvious she felt other children of her age would not necessarily understand some of the unexpected quirks of Philip's behaviour. We as a family took no notice as it was part of our way of life but with her peers Alice became more perceptive. She would happily have her birthday parties at home, however, with Philip opting out of the noise created by a group of excited young girls.

Helen and I had to be aware of these issues but to be careful not to make an incident of them. After all, in every other way Alice was a model little sister to Philip. To widen her horizons she became involved with Brownies and also started playing netball. She was an athletic, competitive little girl who experienced success at sport with, and on behalf of, her school.

Philip's lack of speech was a frustration to us all but none more so than to him. If on the odd occasion he did say something co-ordinated and we did not understand what he said he would not repeat himself. Some thirty years on his attitude is still very much the same. 'You've missed it, tough' so to speak.

The cycling was developing well with Alice able to join in the fun around the Suffolk roads and villages as Grandpa bought them both old, but quite serviceable bikes. To escort them I borrowed his 'sit up and beg' vintage type machine. None of us had three speed gears but without large hills we all coped and thoroughly enjoyed our excursions. For Philip, in particular, he could relax and lead the way on the quieter, more open roads. It was nice to be able to include Alice in our Suffolk jaunts as she was not now able to participate in those from Wooburn Green as the rides were getting longer and on busy roads.

Schooling for Philip was going as well as could be expected with the routine that, if the morning collection coach was held up for any reason, he and Mum would have a cup of coffee. His behaviour at school was sometimes prickly but generally acceptable.

On one occasion, when he had been 'kicking over the traces' it was some time afterwards that Helen found out. On leaving the mini coach he was handed a letter from school by Joyce, the escort, and in the short distance from the coach to the front door, the letter had been pocketed and was quietly dumped in the waste paper basket in his bedroom. When his slight of hand was discovered it was too late for retribution but it caused amusement at both school and home when Mrs. Quartermain confirmed Philip knew the contents of the note. The little devil, we thought - there is a cunning little brain which functions when needed!

We took this as a process of growing up which was further evidenced by the sudden and unexpected rejection of his previous soul-mate Pa Pa. One evening when Helen went into the bedroom to say a final goodnight, Philip passed him to her and said, "No more Pa Pa." Although it was time for this to happen, it was a sad moment consigning his long standing friend to the attic. He had been such a comfort to him for so long. It was the end of an era!

After the 1976 holiday in Wales our enthusiasm for the area continued for many years but the heights of the first holiday could never be surpassed as it all seemed so special for so many varying reasons.

In 1977 we made our usual early start for our two-week break, with the children thinking jackpots from one armed bandits happened every day! They were eagerly anticipating a repeat performance at the Green Dragon in Hereford. Sadly for them, the car over-heated and we had to stop as we approached Hereford. The A.A. came but we were unable to get the problem fixed on a Saturday morning so a dilemma presented itself, as we were many miles from both our destination and home. Should we attempt to get to Wales or stay in Hereford until Monday and get the car fixed there?

After much deliberation, no doubt influenced by the accommodation costs for two nights we decided that as the problem centred on the loss of water from the radiator we would buy a five gallon canister and press ahead. The journey was taken very steadily. We would cover some 20/25 miles, before the temperature gauge told us to stop. Then followed a period whilst the engine cooled down and very circumspectly the radiator cap was released to ease any remaining pressure before refilling with water. It was a torturous journey but we eventually arrived in Happy Valley, disappointed, but unscathed. The car was quickly unpacked and hurriedly parked on the local garage forecourt in Towyn for fear of it not starting again.

Despite the unsatisfactory start, this was still a good holiday. Unexpectedly, we were joined by the Comerford family who had previously showed interest in our '76 exploits. Whilst we knew they were planning a trip to Happy Valley, we didn't know when. Terry and Dee had two foster children with them, Steven & Sharon, the latter being mentally handicapped but with different problems from Philips. She was a good talker!

It was easy with us both having similar problems to get to know their family and to enjoy, with them, the pleasures of the locality. Our sorties to the beach necessitated walking over part of the Aberdovey Golf Club. Philip seemed to spot an errant golf ball in an instant. He was also highly amused if we heard the shout 'fore' from the distance and had to scuttle, heavily laden, out of the way of a bouncing ball. After a safe arrival on the beach with our needs for the day, we would settle in amongst the dunes. Towyn in Welsh is Tywyn, very aptly meaning 'sand dune' - they were everywhere!

With more people, particularly children around, the games on the beach took on a more competitive edge. These encompassed everything from cricket, with the usual arguments over whose turn it was to bat or bowl, to flying kites, which Philip enjoyed once his was airborne and overbearing parents left him alone, after taking some time to accept that he would not release the kite into the wide blue yonder. The large but potentially dangerous lagoons left by the ebbing tide, particularly near the river mouth, were explored for live creatures. We usually caught enough shrimps to boil up for Sharon's tea.

With no television in the chalets and no amusement arcades to blight the landscape everyone enjoyed and took part in the simple pleasures of life. They were happy days with a train excursion included in the late afternoon schedule followed by a game of cards or bingo in the evening. If it was the latter, Philip enjoyed being the caller; he knew his numbers!

The Comerford family had a collie named Bessie who was a quiet friendly dog. In an attempt to get Philip over his loathing of dogs we managed to persuade him to take her on a lead for walks. This was done along the sandy beach very much at arms length. Bessie, however, must have sensed the reluctance of Philip to do this as she was not an enthusiastic participant in his sole company. Philip would address other passing dog-walkers with 'dogs should be kept on a lead', much to people's amazement. This never led to any adverse or embarrassing comments - not that we heard anyway!

The gated roads as we approached our hill-top walks became great fun, with each child taking it in turns to open and close the gates to let the cars pass through, with the expectation of a tip, of nominal value, for their service. The walks were so relaxing, with sheep everywhere and the children free to roam, with the nattering parents coming along at their own pace behind.

Philip was in his element, never huffing and puffing as he ran vigorously up and down the hillocks at will. Having effortlessly conquered Cader Idris the next goal was Snowdon, some 600' higher. Mum was in favour of taking the train from Llanberis to the summit but as she was out-voted 3 – 1, the physical climb it would be.

On a bright sunny morning an expectant family rose early and set off for our conquest. At Dolgellau, I was bursting to spend a penny and in a wooded area with some urgency jumped out of the car only to find a silent Philip, obviously with the same problem, mirroring his father in trying to create a new waterfall attraction for the area!!!

Sadly, by the time we got to Snowdonia and in particular Capel Curig, often the wettest place in Wales, the cloud had descended and it was pouring with rain - our adventure was abandoned.

The children took the disappointment well and Mum was relieved. Instead the Ffestiniog and Bala miniature railways were given a visit.

Whilst not achieving our goal, we still had an exhilarating day with plenty to report in the evening to the Comerfords.

The children loved a visit to the pier at Aberdovey for a session of 'crabbing' before tea. On one such evening it was competition time with dozens of children lining the jetty in competitive mode to see who, over thirty minutes, could catch the most crabs. Neither Sharon nor Philip showed any interest in the competitive element of their endeavours but Alice and Steven were arch rivals.

Alice, with a fish-head as bait, much to the dismay of Steven, who fished next to her, was crowned champion, with many more crabs than anyone else. She was delighted with her success. Many more happy hours were spent by all four children catching, logging and releasing their ever-ravenous quarries. Simple but satisfying fun for them all; not forgetting the over-enthusiastic, supposedly supervising, but interfering parents. Do parents ever grow up? In my case I hope not!

By the time of our third annual visit to Wales, the party had grown to sixteen, split equally between adults and children with the youngsters all being around Philip's and Alice's age. They all gelled well and our largely happy times continued but amongst the children it was obvious Sharon and Philip were struggling to keep up, and were largely following what everyone else was doing.

Disappointingly for us, we could not attend the usual final night hotel meal as Philip was far from well. We had taken him to the local doctor who could not diagnose anything obvious but nevertheless routinely, I suppose, prescribed a course of antibiotics.

Although Philip manfully tried to put a brave face on his discomfort, we hurriedly packed and left Happy Valley on the Friday evening so that if necessary we could take him to Dr. Hill on the Saturday morning. We arrived home after midnight with Philip just pleased to snuggle down into his own bed. He slept well but the next morning he was covered in spots: he had measles.

Chapter 12 - Adolescence Strikes

Our years living at Old Stocks and my work at the bank produced many endearing friends and special occasions, particularly where the family became involved. Jack, a customer, invited me as a member's guest to a Test Match at Lords. It was a great day out and as Philip was already twelve, Jack asked whether, if he could get tickets for a game, Philip would enjoy watching cricket at Lords the next year. Remembering his interest in cricket at Bradenham I said I was sure he would love the build up and atmosphere of such a day out. My thoughts had already advanced to the abundance of open spaces and areas to explore within the ground if the day became too much for him and he became restless. There was no need to have worried.

Jack was as good as his word, and, produced tickets for the 1979 Gillette Cup Final, Somerset v Northamptonshire. There was a full house of some 25,000 people, many of whom came from Somerset. They were very vociferous, especially when the copious quantities of earlier- consumed scrumpy started to talk! This amused Philip greatly as he saw it as people misbehaving. It all made for an incredible atmosphere.

Our seats were in the front row of the intimate Allen Stand next to the pavilion - ideal for viewing, with plenty of freedom for movement during the day if it became necessary.

What a baptism for Philip. It was certainly a day to remember, with Viv Richards, Ian Botham and Joel Garner playing for Somerset, and Alan Lamb, Wayne Larkins and Peter Willey playing for Northants. The excitement and antics of the Somerset supporters crescendoed as the match progressed and they could sense their county was about to win its first trophy since formation 104 years ago. Philip was transfixed in his seat, logging the scores in the book bought for the occasion. Why did I worry that he would become restless? Getting him to leave his seat for the toilet was a major intrusion on his day.

Whilst the finer points of the game were lost on him, Philip enjoyed the action and the signals from the umpires, particularly when 4's and 6's were scored. Jack was thoughtful in asking Philip if he would like to stay to watch the presentation ceremony. The answer was, "A good idea," which in Philip's language is an option for "Yes."

With what already seemed like thousands of people running, jumping and cavorting all over the playing area and with Philip so obviously soaking up the occasion we stayed on - his face said it all. It was certainly a very special day to remember for all the right reasons and the first of many such days to come.

The success of the day and seeing it as another interest to cultivate for Philip, encouraged me to apply for MCC membership. How lucky can you be? Initially I thought it would be up to 20 years before membership would be offered but fortunately, in 1983 the membership numbers were increased by three thousand and I was elected a member of MCC on 1st January 1983. Even twenty seven years on I still see it as a privilege to be able to guarantee, for Philip's sake, to get at least one additional ticket, for even the biggest matches played at Lords. This one benefit alone makes the ever-increasing annual subscription worthwhile, particularly when one sees the pleasure emanating from him when he is ringing his Lords attendance dates on his new calendar each January. He is always asked if he wishes to go before booking the tickets and the answer is always unequivocally, "Yes."

Philip's fourteenth birthday was marked by the gift of a new bike, this time a silver 'racer' with drop handlebars. He was thrilled, especially as it had a milometer so that he could log how far we had ridden. Another statistic for him! Cycling was now a serious pastime which Philip and Dad could increasingly enjoy together.

Whilst Philip was growing up and developing physically, just as we would have wished, his ability to communicate through speech was still limited. Despite this he was easy enough to manage, and our lives, whilst blighted by his shortcomings, were still progressing quite serenely. There were inevitably plenty of heartaches but these were outweighed by a lot of happy memorable occasions.

We were content in that we had done all we could, for the time being, to look after Philip's future. What nothing or nobody could have prepared us for was the change that was to hit us so dramatically and unexpectedly. Seemingly in a matter of seconds, our world was turned upside down. From this change we have never fully recovered and now know we never will.

On a Friday evening in early summer we were later than usual travelling from Wooburn Green to East Anglia. We decided we would stop at Braintree for a Berni Inn meal. It was getting dusk by the time we arrived, with the journey, as far as we could recall, being perfectly normal with no traffic hold ups, arguments, unpleasantness or tensions along the way.

We duly parked the car and all alighted, except for Philip. He refused to budge and was obviously suddenly very agitated and cross about something. He exhibited a pent-up fury which we had never seen before. Much as we tried we could not establish what was annoying him so, if he even knew himself. Bewildered as we were, we coaxed him from the car with the overriding thought, "He'll soon get over it."

The meal was a very tense affair with Philip not wanting to eat anything that was on the menu. For the first time he was being 'bloody minded' and very obviously bristling and seeking confrontation over something, but over what we knew not.

Whilst the weekend with Nana and Grandpa passed off without incident it was very apparent something had gone sadly amiss within Philip's world during the journey from Wooburn Green to Braintree. He was suddenly tense, uncooperative and gone was the largely happy disposition we had previously enjoyed. Was it something we had said or something he had overheard, as he seemed perfectly O.K. when we left home? Wrack our brains we may, but all we could come up with were 'ifs' and 'buts' with not the slightest inkling of what had sparked off this rapid change. In a matter of a few bewildering minutes everyone's world, including his, was upside down.

"Oh dear, how do we cope with this and where do we go from here?" This was the nightmare we now faced as the confrontation continued. Our previously fairly calm world was suddenly shattered and we knew not what to do, or think, and nor for that matter did anyone else, except to say "It's the hormones." If it was adolescence it had certainly arrived with a vengeance.

Here we were with Philip, aged fourteen, whose previous social behaviour had been entirely acceptable, now erupting in frustration. No longer could we go out to eat, as embarrassing situations and tantrums would start without warning. We were reluctant to go out together and leave him in the care of a baby-sitter. As there were few people who understood and could cope with any problems, our options were fairly limited.

As we were unable to establish, or begin to understand, the underlying reasons for the sudden mood changes, life was all too suddenly like walking on broken glass. Tensions at home mounted, as, in frustration, Philip banged on windows which broke under the force of his flailing fists, walls in his bedroom were defaced and doors were kicked. Life became hell!

Whilst there may have been lulls for a couple of weeks between major outbursts, tension was always simmering below the surface. Philip had become quite unpredictable in his behaviour. Where had the easy going, amiable Philip gone? We were once more on our own and desperate, in that we now had a strong, intransigent and belligerent young man on our hands. The teenage syndrome had struck, and how.

Blood tests were taken, X-rays and more visits to psychologists revealed nothing, with the over-riding comment, "He will grow out of it." All we could do was pray that they would be right, but how long would it take, or whether it was likely to get worse, nobody knew or could even guess. We may at times previously have felt desperate but it was nothing compared to our feeling of desperation now.

With the ever-changing moods, life at home became very stressful as Philip strove to exert himself in an unpleasant and, at times, aggressive way. Household wares would be thrown if we sought to chastise him or to keep him to some sort of standard. Only with great fortitude could we even try to cope with this environment and at the same time give Alice the quality of life she deserved. Gone for ever were the invitations to Alice's friends to come for tea. There was no guarantee Philip would behave himself.

Living in Bucks, where Grammar Schools still existed and with the eleven plus examinations looming, we were petrified that the constant tensions at home would reflect in Alice's results and, in turn, penalise her for the rest of her life. Thankfully, Roy Harris, who was still the headmaster at St. Paul's, understood what was going on and reassured us that her school work was well up to standard and he had no doubt she would pass her examinations when the time came. At least there was some comfort there, but we had to do whatever we could to protect her from the constant traumas which she was enduring.

With Alice in mind, we made a specific visit to Dr. Hill who, in turn, made a strong case for Philip to receive Respite Care at the local council run hostel for one weekend in four. This was a bewildering change from where we were only months earlier.

Initially, we were desperately unhappy and felt guilty about having to put Philip into care, made even worse as his mournful face said it all - but it had to be. We ultimately looked forward to those few days of guaranteed peace, without Philip. This provided us with a chance to give Alice a 'normal' environment for a few hours. She was, however, very sensible and tolerant, although her life was now dominated by our need to try to keep a reasonably stable home. This invariably meant that her needs when Philip was around, whilst kept in mind, were seldom to the fore.

Whilst Alice never commented about it to us it was very apparent from Philip's looks that his attitude towards her had changed. From the earlier friendly, co-operative relationship it was now appearing to be one of utter contempt. Would this turn into a situation where Philip's irrational behaviour would one day be physically taken out on her? This was a scary and petrifying thought, but such were some of the outbursts that we were sure Philip was not in control of his actions. Poor chap, he had done nothing to deserve his state of mind.

Whilst we had become desperate for some respite to recharge our batteries, it was nevertheless distressing for us to hand over a bewildered, mournful-looking Philip to Sylvia, a cheery and very welcoming hostel manager. Such was the emotion, the handover was always rapid.

What a relief it was to us when, during term time, with the hostel in the same complex as Vinio House, Mrs. Quartermain arranged for him to be passed over straight from school on Friday afternoons. He returned to us via the coach on Monday evenings. This certainly made life easier for our consciences as, despite the troubles, we still held a deep love and affection for Philip - how could it be any different when we had such happy memories from only a few months earlier?

Relating to happier times, knowing that Philip had previously enjoyed his holidays in the Welsh chalet, we decided to continue with our plans to revisit Happy Valley in the hope that, despite his problems, this would help him to relax and find himself again. As usual, in the car Philip's world seemed perfectly O.K. We settled happily into the chalet after a warm welcome from the Comerford's, who were once again visiting for their holiday.

All appeared peaceful and calm within and we were outside talking to Terry and Dee on the Sunday morning when suddenly there was a loud bang from within the chalet. We all raced in to find that Philip, without any warning or provocation, had unceremoniously kicked a hole in the white painted hollow lounge door. He just stood there motionless, staring at his handiwork.

For the first time this was someone else's property now being defaced which really had us in a spin. What do you do in such bewildering circumstances? The suddenness of the eruption shocked us beyond all belief. Thankfully, we were in company, which tempered any immediate retribution we may have taken. It also helped to have good, understanding friends with whom to share our misery and shock at first hand.

A new door was the immediate thought so that the owner, who was a friend, didn't know what had occurred. Terry, a good DIY expert, thought otherwise and throughout the holiday we repeatedly filled and sanded the gaping hole until it was ready for painting. With the whole door repainted three times, by the time we left the damage had been miraculously repaired. A painful lesson had been learned and from that time on wherever we were, home or away, Philip always took his shoes off so that if he felt like kicking something he came off second best!

With Terry and Dee as buffers for us and their children as playmates for Alice, we set about trying to keep Philip occupied. Sadly, it seemed just being in Alice's presence may have been the provocation for his unhappiness. However, with the intensity of his moods, even in her absence he would soon have latched on to something else about which to create a scene. Where does one turn to for an inspirational remedy in an explosive situation like this?

Once more cycling came to the rescue. For two days we hired bikes at nearby Machynlleth for trips to Aberystwyth and a long circular trip involving Dolgellau. This certainly calmed the atmosphere down to a containable level but he was very reluctant to do the things he, and we, had previously enjoyed. Even the 'little trains' were taboo, with Philip not wanting to go on an evening excursion from Towyn to Abergynolwyn. He preferred to be with

Dad, riding to the destination in the car and having a walk in the village and a soft drink in the pub. Within this context he was quite happy to wave Helen and Alice off on their journey and to do the same at Abergynolwyn for their return. Was this further evidence of him avoiding the company of Alice? We thought so, but could not think why - she had never done anything but support him. His world most certainly prevented him from seeing life that way. We could only deduce jealousy was now rearing its ugly head!

Sitting on beaches was not on Philip's itinerary, unless it was for food. He was, however, intrigued by Terry cooking sausages using an old biscuit tin as his barbecue, amongst the well-sheltered sand dunes. He certainly tucked in to any morsels that were on offer, well done or simply burnt!

Walking and touring in the car were safe bets for defusing the gremlins so that whilst tensions arose, they were defused and we only had the one incident with the door during the two weeks. That was more than enough to keep our nerves jangling! It was at least a break for everyone in a different environment, but sadly without too much relaxation.

Chapter 13 - Autistic Traits & Personal Decisions

Schooling for Philip was not easy as his mood swings started to disrupt other students. His lack of ability to communicate and 'prickly' disposition made life uncertain for the staff. Not every day was a crisis by any means but a crisis was never far away, and life for everyone at Vinio House became more difficult. This can be no better relayed than through the following words of Margot Pottage, who knew Philip during the whole of his twelve years at Vinio House School:

My recollections of Philip by Margot Pottage

Philip, who was a pupil in my class for two years, is a person I will never forget. He was at that time 14-16 years old and a very complex and challenging character. He integrated well with his fellow pupils but did not have a specific friend, sometimes appearing quite aloof yet at the same time being aware of what was happening in the classroom around him.

He liked being helpful and was usually eager to please. Although very strong willed he could be persuaded to accept discipline when the consequences of irrational behaviour were quietly explained.

Like most of our pupils he liked constancy and routine which of course was interrupted or changed at times. This he did not like, becoming disturbed and/or disruptive if not calmed down with quiet reassurance. It was one of his traits we were keen to modify so he would learn to cope with changes.

Philip was a willing pupil and was eager to learn. He amazed everyone with his phenomenal memory, particularly dates and people's birthdays, or events that had happened long ago and which most of us had forgotten about. His recall was always accurate.

He was an endearing lad to the staff with his powers of observation which was unique amongst his peers. He would always notice a new hairdo or outfit. He would comment on it and compliment whoever it was by telling them how nice they looked. This is very unusual for any school boy to do and was very much appreciated by all. When this was reported to his mother she said "He never does it to me, and he most certainly wasn't copying his father!"

Philip enjoyed his school holidays, which consisted of Youth Hostelling, where everyone was expected to carry out chores. This was quite a challenge for someone of Philip's temperament as it involved strangers telling him what to do. In fact he could be quite over-enthusiastic, like taking plates of food away from people before they had finished eating because he was told to bring dirty crockery to the kitchen to be washed - well, he did as he was told. Usually these occasions could be resolved by explanation to the affected parties and often ended up with smiles all round.

Being out of doors suited Philip, he loved walking and visiting various venues, or taking part in activities like swimming, orienteering or abseiling, being quite proud of what he could achieve. He also enjoyed being 'put in charge' of a small group but this could lead to him being rather bossy and he needed to have his enthusiasm curbed a little, all part of his social education!

It was always a pleasure to take Philip out and about and I think he can be very proud of all he has achieved so far in his life, especially his sponsored bike rides which he has so enjoyed, thanks to his Dad. **MP**

Within the home, traits suddenly appeared along with his aggression. During Philip's life there had always been repetitive routine but one of the first serious and most disruptive foibles to rear its ugly head was Philip suddenly becoming obsessive at bedtime about the sheets on his bed not being creased. Helen would do her best in the morning, but come night time, when Philip and everyone else should be fast asleep, often after midnight, he would set out to remake his bed. With lots of banging and crashing about he would find he could not get things as perfect as he wished. As he would not tolerate our help, which he saw as interference, we just had to steel ourselves and nervously wait for the final commotion to occur. It always ended with a loud clatter as he unceremoniously upended his bed. When this had happened, up we got to remake the bed, and seemingly having got himself into an uncontrollable lather, the upending of the bed seemed to get the problem out of his system but only for the night in question. The next night would, in all probability see a repeat performance!

Bed remade he would then settle down for the night. Having gone through the build up to the finale there was no way we could then simply ignore what had gone on and drop off to sleep ourselves. Talk was all we could do but we had no answers, only a shattered sleep pattern.

Incidents such as the bed-making would often follow late night television, as being able to read the forthcoming television programmes in the newspaper he would insist on watching the zany antics of Laurel and Hardy! Their brand of mayhem seemed to inspire him to start banging and crashing about and to come in and out of our bedroom with a culmination of the bed saga bringing the evening's entertainment to a conclusion!

In an effort to combat the problem we tried late night viewing with him and hiding the newspapers so that he couldn't read what was on TV, and yet somehow he always knew! We had no idea there were so many of those damned films - they seemed to plague our lives for months!

Whatever was going on, we could not rest until Philip appeared settled and we could finally check the bathroom taps had been fully turned off and there was no plug left in the basin. Looking back I don't know how we coped with the tension, placation and compromise - an inner strength must have been inherited from somewhere to pull us through disturbed nights, constant unexplained mayhem and provocation. Giving him a good hiding often came to mind but we refrained from doing this as we did not wish to introduce violence into his troubled life. Where would it all end?

These inner strengths, if that is what they were, certainly made us realise just how on our own we are with our traumas. Whilst family and friends sympathised with our problems, some had little comprehension of what was going on and what we in turn were going through. Others simply had no understanding whatsoever, asking the same puerile questions time and time again. How can it be otherwise, unless within the rich tapestry of life they have experienced, at first hand, similar problems, or are carers themselves?

In these circumstances, as the problems roll on and intensify, we don't shout from the rooftops the stresses we are facing. Sadly this is a situation faced by most similarly placed families - whilst at the time we feel unique in our suffering there are many thousands of similar sufferers battling in the same way with not too much third party understanding.

With our charged and changed circumstances there was no way we could live a normal life and risk more family. It was agreed I should have 'a little op'. Serious as this decision was at the time, it produced its lighter side.

I was duly admitted to hospital for my 'routine' op. and who should walk into the room but Staff Nurse Heather Purves, whom I knew. She had a wicked grin on her face, and was gleefully waving a razor around in her hand. Being too embarrassed I never asked, but on seeing the admissions list I would wager she did this for devilment. She said with a wicked glint in her eyes, "I suppose you would prefer to do this yourself." Rather relieved and bashfully I replied in the affirmative. What a fist I made of it! I lived to tell the tale and left hospital with everything still intact, but in the process I had used the plaster I was given at the outset, in case of accidents, to patch up my finger which had got nicked in the nervous, trembling, self-inflicted shaving operation. The whole scene would have done justice to a Carry On movie.

This little episode had a further amusing family only side to it. Shortly after the operation we were walking along a rain sodden street in Bristol trying to keep dry. I had my hands in my pockets, quietly protecting my offended business so to speak when I was very firmly rebuked by Helen for what obviously appeared to be a very slovenly way of walking along. My reply of "It's bloody uncomfortable down there, my hair is starting to grow," brought tears of amusement to Helen's eyes. I was then permitted, without further ado, and an impish grin from Helen, to continue my slovenly posture!

Why were we in Bristol? We had an appointment with Mr. Les Fry the Social Work Director of HFT as Philip was now fifteen. In view of his, and our stressed circumstances over the past eighteen months, we had made further contact with the Head Office of the charity.

Although Philip had been confirmed as on their waiting list, this interview was by way of our first specific follow-up to the earlier submitted admission application form.

Mr. Fry was an avuncular gentleman and we were relieved to hear that he had assessed Philip as suitable to join 'their family', hopefully within a large property, with extensive grounds known as Downley Grange, which they were hoping to purchase within a few weeks. It was planned by HFT that this would be the core house of another 'Home', for some thirty mentally handicapped residents. The relief was enormous as we travelled back to Wooburn Green in the knowledge that although help was, we thought, at least four years away, there was light at the end of a very long dark tunnel.

We had by this time been working hard for some years raising money for HFT, very much with the future in mind, just as other like minded parents were doing. Eric Gibson was still the local High Wycombe Group of Friend's Chairman, and through his leadership we raised thousands of pounds for the prospective new 'home' in our midst. We all had a vested interest, and most certainly a worthwhile and tangible goal to aim at. When the first goal was achieved we all carried on working to help others in similar circumstances.

A further boon to our spirits was Alice passing her exams for entry to the High Wycombe High School for Girls. With no let-up in the home aggravation and despite Roy Harris's reassuring words we had serious doubts in our minds that she would make it.

We were thrilled for Alice and thought this was the time to do something positive for her. She had worked hard despite the upsets, never complaining about her lot. She had had riding lessons which she enjoyed and something we never thought we would own, a pony, was bought for her. What a wonderful distraction from her tensions this animal became! It was a sympathetic shoulder to cry on if she chose to do so. There was never a moment when she was late in attending to her new friend or shirked what needed to be done for him. Monty was a true investment in therapy for her!

Life at the bank, with the continuing problems, was difficult. Usually I managed to 'switch off' to concentrate on my work. Philip was never shielded from the staff and what was going on but he never misbehaved in their presence. If necessary, they were always quick to support or cover for me. This was in itself a great comfort and strength and helped in not letting my performance or commitment to work be undermined by Philip's antics. I considered myself lucky to have Helen's steadfast support to achieve this.

A breakthrough with the bed problem came at last. We realised Philip would be using a sleeping bag whilst on a school holiday.

Helen decided to strip his bed leaving just an under blanket and on his return from holiday his sleeping bag would be placed on it. With no fuss whatsoever, except that the pillow had to be just so, the new arrangement was adopted. It was not until some months later when asked if he would like to sleep in his sheeted bed again and he said an enthusiastic "Yes please" – that with great relief we realised the earlier pattern had been broken.

Although life was difficult, it was not all gloom. Philip thirsted for his cycle rides. This was certainly a way of harnessing his aggression and making him feel independent. We were often out at very unsociable hours, particularly in the summer, but it kept me fit. Philip was a very competent cyclist, usually following my lead as we travelled around the countryside. I therefore had to be very correct in my use of the Highway Code and take care not to be seen to take risks or jump traffic lights etc.

With the events at Happy Valley now twelve months in the past but still very graphic in our minds, we vowed to continue family holidays if we could. We all needed a change of scenery to recharge our batteries, even if the underlying tensions were still around.

Woodbridge in Suffolk was the choice, using a flat in the main street. We hired this from friends who knew of Philip and his outbursts. The venue gave us scope to involve the family living locally and to let Philip wander, if he chose to, without worries, into the little town or to walk by the river. As he was socially insecure we didn't expect him to take up these options but they were offered on the first day and it seemed to relax him. He was also aware the bikes were on the first floor landing ready for excursions touring the Suffolk countryside.

Cycling enabled days out to be arranged with both Alice and Philip in mind. During the holiday, whilst rumblings were usually just below the surface, they never erupted and his behaviour was a relief from what had gone on in the past and was totally acceptable. He seemed to reserve his outbursts for Wooburn Green and never in the presence of other family members. We were thankful for this on one hand but, on the other, they had no appreciation of what we were coping with as an almost daily routine.

Philip's interest in cricket from that first visit to Lords was developing nicely, principally through the statistics involved in the game as he poured over the newspapers, monitoring scores. He was, by this time, also interested in the horse racing results, and he happily trolled through the 'hatched', 'matched' and 'despatched' columns - no doubt through his continuing fascination with ages, birth-dates and days - a date committed to his memory was never to be forgotten.

Cricket became our first attempt at a meaningful way of disciplining Philip for his indiscretions. We felt on the one hand he knew what he was doing but, on the other, he sadly appeared to have little control over his actions and the circumstances which caused his wrath. Mood swings just happened, with conflict never far away - what a disturbed world he lived in!

On one such occasion we decided enough was enough, having had a serious upset on the Friday evening before a scheduled trip to Lords on the Saturday. When all had calmed down and we could think rationally, we decided, despite the consequences, there would be no visit to Lords the next day, but I would go, if possible, when Jack called.

The mood was calmer the next morning, probably as in his mind he was looking forward to 'going out' for the day to his favourite venue. The news that he would not be going, and why, did not bring the expected explosion, just the opposite - a very remorseful, silent young man. It would at that point have been so easy to weaken, but hard as it was, we had to stand firm. A nearly missed outing would have had no impact whatsoever.

Jack came to collect us and was visibly shocked that we had taken this stand and said, "Are you doing the right thing?"

We replied as one that we had to make a stand somewhere, and that we thought this was a real and understood form of punishment. Helen continued "As part of the punishment and to emphasise its implications we have agreed Andy should continue with his day out."

With heavy hearts and not without a lot of soul searching on my part, Jack and I left for Lords with Philip's tears streaming down his face as he mournfully looked out of the bedroom window. My heart was close to breaking as I looked back to give a feeble wave. Had I left Helen in the hands of a time bomb?

I could not relax and immediately upon arrival at Lords my first task was to find a kiosk to telephone Helen to ensure there had been no serious repercussions.   As it happened Philip had just sobbed his heart out after we had departed.

Having left the scene and the tensions behind me there was time to reflect.   Poor devil I thought, he can't help it, and I was sure he couldn't.

The punishment restored sanity for a short while ahead of normal service being resumed!!!

Chapter 14 - A Tormented Hero

Where do we go from here? Sadly there was plenty more of the same with no relief in sight through HFT for at least a further two years.

Life for everyone became increasingly tedious and exhausting. Crockery and glassware, including milk bottles, were still vulnerable to assault as were walls and windows, plus anything else that was nearby if a mood suddenly erupted. The breaking of a large bedroom window created sufficient shock to create a lull in the demolition activities. Derek came to our immediate rescue by getting it quickly repaired as the shards of glass hung precariously from the earlier impact – what a disaster!

We always seemed to be paying out for repairs or paint to redecorate. Time to do all that was necessary to keep the peace and other demands within the home became an issue, none more so than the priority to ensure Alice received the attention she never outwardly craved for but deserved nonetheless. She always, by necessity, came second, although never by choice - thank goodness she had her pony to confide in.

On numerous occasions we wondered whether Philip knew what he was doing - did he do it to seek attention - or had his mind become downright destructive and out of control? We always came to the conclusion that the first two options were the most likely as, despite the mayhem surrounding us we still did not see wanton destruction as being part of his normal make up.

The pressures, constant uncertainties and traumas we were suffering could not go on and be coped with without medical help. It seemed the authorities were happier for us to take the tranquillisers than Philip! They seemed afraid that if Philip took medication there could be other nasty side effects which could inflame our lives still further - was this possible we asked ourselves? All we were asking for was for something to suppress the unpredictable behaviour; he was taking no drugs and we were being stuffed with tranquillisers.

Philip enjoyed his music by this time, particularly Top of the Pops on Sunday evening. For him it was a must to listen to. Thankfully, with his acute hearing and aversion to noise, we were saved the further aggravation of music blaring throughout the chalet from his tape recorder! Habitual, copious writing, mainly copying statistics or pop charts would keep him occupied for hours on end in his bedroom. He would use reams of perforated computer paper. Despite the social problems we were enduring, we made no suggestion of a radio or television in his bedroom to keep him out of our way. We still tried, as much as possible, to keep him part of the family. We had to balance this with the likelihood of these facilities being used day and night if they were in the bedroom. As it was, despite actually going to bed often being a problem, once there and settled he slept peacefully without further disturbance - we had to be thankful for small mercies!

Philip's Attendance Allowance was due for review. The fact that he slept, when we finally got him to bed meant we did not qualify for the night time allowance, even though it was often one o'clock in the morning before he settled. What went on due to his behavioural problems before that occurred, and the disruption to our sleep, didn't seem to have any bearing on the decision-making process.

During the spring and summer months, the longer daylight hours gave us more scope to get Philip out of the confines of the house through planned walks and cycling. During the shorter, darker days it was a case of trying to keep the peace as the available time to express his frustrations and to use his energies was so much less.

In winter tensions often built in the evening when Philip undoubtedly felt constrained and hemmed in by drawn curtains and closed doors. During the day, a cycle ride would work off the frustrations and, in the evening, a ride in the car would usually defuse or reduce the agitation. Trying to head off trouble was all very time-consuming and often inconvenient, but it was a sacrifice we had to make to keep life on an even keel.

Out on his bike, where mood swings would have been disastrous, he was a model of concentration and good behaviour. The erratic and unpredictable youth disappeared as if by magic as soon as his 'bum hit the saddle' and his feet the pedals! It must have been his ability to express himself with only light supervision that made all the difference. On his bike he was the master of his own destiny.

At home there were unpleasant personal incidents which seemed to happen in a flash. Hard as we tried, we could seldom fathom the igniting spark. Only once, but it was enough, Philip went to hit Helen with a rolled up bundle of newspapers. This made us realise that anyone or anything that happened to be in the way when he lashed out was in peril. Actions of this nature were completely out of character with his previously good humoured disposition.

It was as if demons had invaded his soul. Difficult as it was we tried to sympathise because we were sure he couldn't control his mood swings as there were still short periods when his world was stable and charming. At such times we tried to make the most of it and to put the past where it belonged, as we knew the bonhomie wouldn't last.

Whilst neither Helen nor I are against a smack, if deserved, it is not with any pride to relate that we both just once lost control of our emotions. We always felt aggression from us was likely to be repaid by Philip thinking this was the way of life and would, himself, resort to physical retribution to relieve his frustrations.

Helen's indiscretion, created through absolute frustration, was to resort to a single hard smack. The shock of this really made him take notice and behave himself for a short time. Whilst Philip, at times, drove us to distraction, Alice was the one more likely to be on the receiving end of a corrective tap. My lapse was on a Saturday morning when Helen and Alice were out shopping. Philip and I were out in the garden when I saw him deliberately, as I interpreted it, drop a milk bottle. Being near at hand my spontaneous wrath was such that I grabbed him by his coat and threw him into the nearby laurel hedge. I do not know which of us was most upset by this exasperated action - it happened in an instant. Otherwise we somehow managed to keep our aggrieved emotions towards Philip under control.

Community work pressures were eased by a promotion to become an Inspector of the bank, heading a team based in London but with most of the work taking place within the South Midlands region, the area in which we lived.

Whilst our social life was curtailed by Philip's antics, we did still entertain our closest and more understanding friends. Though usually well behaved on these occasions Derek and Shirley do recall one evening when Philip appeared in the midst of dinner, sat rigidly on the floor and refused to budge. They were amused by this, but felt for us in realising what we were trying to contend with day after day - very few people witnessed at first hand our problems as it was unusual for anything to happen in company. On other more pleasant occasions both Alice and Philip would often appear at sweet time for a share of the spoils!

Alice was certainly enjoying the company and friendship of her pony. It took her away from the charged atmosphere of the chalet and into another little world. Philip had had a few riding lessons but it was Alice who so thoroughly enjoyed the activity. It was a pleasure to see her and her friends with a common purpose. Most importantly it was a pastime she could pursue without the influences of Philip getting in the way.

My membership of the MCC was now bearing welcome and additional fruit. Philip and I could leave Wooburn Green at 1 o'clock on Sundays and be parked, and in our seats at Lords, by the time play started for the John Player Forty Over matches involving Middlesex. Philip so obviously felt very important when he flashed my bright red membership pass at the entrance to the ground and the gateman doffed his cap and waved us through into the car park which was in those days situated in the confines of the ground.

With Philip grabbing the picnic, we would rush round to the pavilion where I would sign him in as my guest. We would then make our way to the most elevated area so that he could look down on the play. There were never any problems on those days!

In view of Philip's unpredictability, our family hotel breaks became things of the past. He could well have behaved himself but we did not feel able to take the risk.

When he was in the hostel for respite care at weekends we would, on occasions, ask in school holidays if an extra day was possible so that we could give Alice, and for that matter ourselves, a short break. At first it felt as though we were cheating on Philip but it was something we had to do. After a while, he was not unduly unhappy about his time at the hostel.

Philip was not completely left out of our time away as we continued to use the facilities of friends for weekends in East Anglia. These went well as the sun always seemed to shine and with the children we could explore, on our rickety old bikes, the pretty surrounding villages and countryside. This would be done without any aggravation whatsoever. Once again, what would we all have done without the safety valve provided by cycling? It gave Philip an element of self- expression and independence which, in his day-to-day life, he was yearning for but couldn't cope with. He continued to reserve his most troubled times for Wooburn Green.

In a period of calm we decided to look for pastures new for a holiday but, through a lack of confidence in Philip, it would just be for a week. We settled on Rothesay on the Isle of Bute. It would involve an early start followed by a long car journey to the west of Glasgow followed by a lengthy ferry crossing from Wemyss Bay. All in all it would be a completely different environment. It was a disaster – although not through any fault of Philip.

After a peaceful journey we arrived at the hotel. The ground floor was decked in gaudy Scottish tartan, nothing wrong in that, but the bedrooms were spartanly furnished with nothing particularly clean and no ceiling lampshade in one room. Altogether a rather shabby set-up - a complaint made little difference. Had it not been high season and the weather superb we would have left before the allotted time.

With wall-to-wall sunshine we kept busy walking and watching the boats in the busy Rothesay harbour. We toured the island and travelled to Oban by car to take a boat to Mull. We all hired bikes, Helen and Alice taking the more leisurely routes while Philip and I explored virtually every road on the island until they ran into the sea.

On our way home from Scotland we made a brief stop in the beautiful Lake District, taking in a boat trip on Lake Windermere which gave us a relaxing interlude. From a family point of view, the time went as well as could be expected. We were, however, always conscious we had to keep Philip on the go as sitting about would be asking for trouble.

On our return from holiday, Alice was due to start her education at High Wycombe High School. Having passed her exams to get there our worry was that, with the continuing upsets at home, she would not be able to cope, as the academic pressures would be so much greater than at St. Pauls.

Our problem was how to deal with this concern? Thankfully there was an Open Evening for the parents of First Year Students. This was the ideal opportunity, without making it an issue, to let Alice's form teacher know of the stresses she had to contend with at home. We felt we had to tell Alice we had mentioned this. She was far from impressed with the news - she felt she could cope. Whilst trying to calm her down with reasoning we became conscious that even without her brother as a distraction, she was going to be fully stretched in this environment.   We felt she would comfortably get an A level with honours in Common Sense, but would struggle with the academic subjects.   Ultimately we were correct in our assessment.

Vinio House schooling for Philip has been described earlier by Margot.   At sixteen he became part of the Further Education Group who stayed on at the school until eighteen, after which they moved to a sheltered workshop environment.   What an undertaking for the staff as the school catered for children aged from five to eighteen.

The one consistent area of enjoyment for Philip was his involvement with the local Venture Scouts.   They invited him to join their ranks, collecting him on a Wednesday evening and returning him at the conclusion of the evening's activities.   The leaders really looked after him and made him feel one of them.   He joined in all of their pursuits as best he could.

The leaders took the view that in addition to helping Philip it was good for the other lads in the troupe to work with someone less able than themselves. It worked well for everyone. Philip relished putting on his scout shirt and was always ready at the front door awaiting collection. There was no way he would allow us to take or collect him - it was very much something he did on his own away from the family. There was just the one permitted exception.

Still being seen as the local bank manager I was asked to give the troupe a talk on banking.   Philip was eagerly awaiting my arrival at the scout hut.   He sat transfixed that his Dad was talking to his friends.   As I concluded the talk a voice piped up - "Thank-you dad." What better vote of thanks could I have had?

We passed into 1983 little knowing what a traumatic year it would turn out to be.   Life was no easier and Philip was ever more agitated. We were coping, but with increasing difficulty, which was obvious to all around us.   We had to have help but what could it be without it being too drastic, such as a stay in a psychiatric hospital?   Hard pressed as we were we could not entertain this idea.   To us it was the next thing to a madhouse.   Surely Philip had not come to this?

Within a few weeks we finally succumbed to the pressures he was creating. We had to admit we were at the absolute end of our tethers. There was no alternative: we either had to carry on and as a result get more and more exhausted or let him be admitted to Manor House

Hospital in Aylesbury, the psychiatric unit, for observation and tests. We were, by this time, in such a state of turmoil and anguish that it had to be the latter.

Once again we thought we had seen it all as far as emotions were concerned but we had never for one moment thought Philip would come to this. It was upsetting in the extreme - had we failed him? We thought not but it felt as if we had.

The twenty-five mile journey to Aylesbury was purgatory. A pathetic, helpless, bewildered lad, our cherished son, was sitting in the rear of the car with Helen. Neither we nor he knew whether the proposed two-week admission was going to lead to something longer, particularly if he caused more chaos whilst there.

The admission procedure seemed to take an age. We were looking to escape as soon as possible but not without first trying to settle Philip into his new surroundings. His bed space was small and he looked pathetic as he watched Helen neatly place his few belongings into his battered wooden bedside chest.

It was with heavy hearts and some difficulty that we held back our emotions. We said our good-byes, with the promise we would be back to visit him in a few days, once he had settled in. We would also telephone each day to make sure he was alright.

Our journey back to Wooburn Green was one of near silence. At the end of our tethers we may have been but the necessity for this sort of remedial action brought guilt beyond belief to us both. Our emotions were completely addled, but there was no turning back.

We looked forward with some trepidation to the first hospital visit. It was a welcome relief to find Philip, whilst still looking like a 'lost soul', both calm and pleased to see us - he thought he would be coming home. He was behaving himself and being helpful and co-operative. Parting was again difficult but he was scheduled to come home again at the end of the next week, which we could talk to him about. In any event we would be visiting again in a few days.

During this upheaval Alice had been a tower of strength and maturity. She was quiet and obviously upset by losing 'her Philip', and insisted she came with us on the next visit. We did not prolong the occasion but we got strength from her support and the fact that Philip was pleased to see her.

He was a model patient during his two weeks at Manor House but the staff reported they thought they had observed a small fit. It was considered this was probably brought on by the incredible tensions he was suffering just from being where he was. We were amazed that still no medication was prescribed.

Despite the past we were pleased, and relieved, to have him home for us all to face the future together once again, whatever may be thrown at us. The two weeks had given us time to recharge our batteries and take stock, as well as the strength to look forward once again. We had all learned to adapt through this dramatic time and for a while life took on a more tranquil pattern, but we had decided Alice must have a holiday where she could relax away from Philip. How could we achieve this?

As The Home Farm Trust, who we hoped one day were destined to take him into care, had said they would need to make an assessment of Philip's needs before doing so, we updated them on our circumstances. This also had to include, more worryingly, details of his admission to Manor House Hospital. The news did not perturb them as they had probably seen it all before.

As far as we were concerned they were incredibly understanding and positive in their reply, advising us that they could allocate two weeks for a residential assessment at a local home in August. So soon after his two weeks at Manor House this was not news we could break to Philip for some time, and in no way could it be portrayed as punishment.

Alice agreed to go along with our thoughts regarding a holiday in August on the basis she could decide what she would like to do and could include her best friend Caroline in the plans. As they both loved horses, they decided they would like to spend a week at a riding school deep in the country in mid-Wales, followed by a week at Happy Valley. This they set up, with Helen and me to do the fetching and carrying and spending two weeks, once again, in Wales. It was no hardship to go along with their plans.

A few weeks after Philip's 17th birthday we were all watching the Sunday evening Nine O'clock News. In those less serious days the news usually concluded with a lighter topic. In this instance, a moment of inspiration shone through. It was reported that thirty thousand cyclists had taken part in the British Heart Foundation

(B.H.F.) London to Brighton Cycle Ride, a distance of some fifty-six miles. The screen showed an upended bike having a puncture repaired. This news item, as it involved cycling, commanded Philip's immediate attention. Spontaneously, and with Helen's face a picture of disbelief, I said to him, "Shall we do that next year?"

"In 1984 when I am eighteen" was the immediate response. It was bewildering: in a flash, when it suited him, he had connected and projected what it was all about. It was as if, given a jolly good shake, the workings of his brain would fall into place – oh, if only it were so simple!

How does one start to understand how the brain works, and in particular the one running Philip's life? We now had a goal in life but there would be plenty of water and some of it dirty to flow under the bridge before June 1984.

During the summer of 1983 we all had a break with Philip. Off we went to East Anglia for a few days. Grandpa had oiled and cleaned Philip's wreck of a bike and I borrowed his vintage 'sit up and beg' steed which had equally seen better days. With a cycle pump, puncture kit and two plastic bags containing a change of clothes (we didn't possess pannier bags) strapped to the rear of the saddles we set off. The plan was to stay overnight with friends Martin and Vivien, whom Philip liked and respected, near Bury St. Edmunds (26 miles) followed by cycling on to further respected friends Frank and June (30 miles) near Haverhill, before returning back to base (35 miles) on the third day. It is not difficult to envisage that our preparations before and during this excursion were minimal, to say the least.

The first stage, to stay with Martin and Vivien, was accomplished in bright sunshine on roads we had not cycled along before. In view of this, Philip kept close by. The weather closed in on the second day but we continued as planned and were soaked through on arrival at Frank and June's home. Philip didn't protest and looked forward to the third day, when we made detours before getting back to base unscathed and feeling pleased with ourselves. It was very obvious Philip had enjoyed his three days.

This was turning out to be a fraught year for us all. Nana, who had been in failing health for some time, became worse and died. This was the first such loss the children had experienced and both agreed to go to the funeral. The experience turned out to be a much more emotional day for the children than we ever imagined. As they had become older they had become closer to and had seen more of their grandparents than in earlier years.

The next dreaded phase of life was upon us; leaving Philip behind when going on holiday. He was not told the full story, but it was again traumatic breaking the news to him. He was told that in two weeks time he was to spend fourteen days nearby with a residential charity to see if, when he left school, he would be able to join other young people who were looked after by them.

During his stilted verbal outbursts he was always looking for pastures new, but didn't know what or where. We hoped and prayed this would appeal to him. We tried to enthuse about this as a new adventure where he would meet other people and be looked after by Barry the manager.

No hint was given that this was necessary as a rest for us or that we would be going on holiday without him. Such an approach would have been seen as another punishment, which we were trying to avoid at all cost. We were singularly unsuccessful in selling the benefits to him. It was very obvious despite the upsets that he loved his family and being at home.

The next two weeks until the placement seemed to drag, with Philip again being very quiet, although we had tried to convince him it would not be like Manor House. He was frightened, for all to see.

We duly took him on the Friday and Barry, a flamboyant, exuberant gentleman with a strong Irish accent, welcomed us. He quickly swept Philip off to see his bedroom before he had a chance to think. Barry suggested we said speedy farewells and as we did so we reminded Philip, probably as much for our benefit as his, that there was a family wedding to go to the day after we collected him. That it didn't register was clear from his sad and forlorn demeanour as we left.

Alice and Caroline enjoyed their break with the horses. On collection they looked as though their flannels had not been too over-worked. They then spent a further week with us at Happy Valley.

Our two weeks were a good rest but at the back of our minds we could not help wondering how Philip was faring in his strange new surroundings. Barry reported that he had behaved himself but had found it difficult to relate to other residents. Overall, he had done fine but the strain he had been under for the two weeks was very obvious in his eyes when we collected him. Whilst he was pleased to see us it was in a muted sort of way, just as, when we collected the cats from the kennels, it took a short while for them to forgive us for abandoning them!

We duly travelled to Whitstable the next day to the wedding. Whilst Philip obviously enjoyed seeing the family he was far from relaxed. This showed even more on photographs of the day. His whole body appeared rigid and full of tension.

The following weeks passed without major incidents, although awkwardness was still the order of the day. We could cope with this after what had gone before. As we hoped it would help Philip to accept more easily the next stage in his life we visited the house which, we had been told, HFT had earmarked for Philip, along with seventeen others, when the time came. It had now been purchased but it would be a further year before occupation. At this stage of his life Philip liked everything big and the bigger the better. This house certainly fitted that requirement.

It was a house which in the past had been rather grand. There was a coach house, dilapidated greenhouses and plenty of outbuildings, with areas of woods and gardens to set it off.

We could only view the house from the outside but we could appreciate, by peering through the windows, the large rooms with grand fireplaces and high ceilings. It was a building which cried out to be lived in and brought back to life. Philip wandered around the gardens looking very thoughtful. Did he fully understand, or appreciate what we were seeing and saying about the future? Probably not but at least it gave us comfort to see at first hand where his future might lie. As far as Philip was concerned there was a far more important date looming on his calendar; it was soon to be his 18th birthday, an event he was looking forward to.

A family lunch at home which included his Godparents was organised. Everyone made a big effort to attend and Philip responded by being quite the perfect host. Why couldn't he always behave like this, even without company? It was his big day and he made the most of it.

It suddenly seemed June was racing towards us. Whilst Philip and I had continued our cycling it now took on a new focus. In a matter of weeks we would be embarking on our biggest adventure to date - the B.H.F. London to Brighton Cycle Ride. As it was to be a journey of some fifty-six miles with plenty of byways and hills along the way we started to extend our outings, which took us much further from Wooburn Green. Philip thoroughly enjoyed these longer trips and was looking forward to June.

As Philip would be sponsored to achieve his goal we felt that his endeavours could not go solely towards the B.H.F., but, with Nana's death from heart failure, we had plenty of natural empathy with their cause. I disclosed on the entry forms that Philip was mentally handicapped but was an experienced cyclist and I would be his escort. Where it asked how much money we thought we could contribute from our sponsorship I put a few hundred pounds, which we would like to split with a charity for the mentally handicapped.

Within days, Miriam Collett, the Area Fundraiser for B.H.F., was on the telephone wanting to see me. Oh dear I thought, trouble, either because of Philip's status or because of our not wishing to donate everything raised to B.H.F., her charity. It was after all B.H.F.'s event and they were providing all the facilities on the day.

There was no need to have worried. Miriam was thrilled to have Philip taking part and, having discussed our plans for fundraising, was delighted, through their event, to also be contributing to another worthwhile charity. She was also grateful we had been honest and open with B.H.F. from the outset regarding the apportioning of any money raised.

As the day approached we all spent an enjoyable and fruitful day driving over the route and noting, as we saw them, any particular hazards to avoid. Why Philip was highly amused by Ditchling Beacon we had no idea - did he think he would cycle up it? Having seen it for the first time it was certainly not on my agenda to do so!

Our training was going well, with Philip enjoying the attention our efforts were creating - no problems in getting him into photographs, as the local newspapers became interested in what this mentally handicapped lad was doing. It was a good story for them to follow.

To help with money-raising my three assistants on the Inspection Team busily mailed the branches we had previously inspected, inviting sponsorship for Philip. Our incoming post bag grew by the day. With family and friends also providing generous and enthusiastic support it soon became apparent my few hundred pounds estimate would be comfortably exceeded.

With great excitement and expectation for Philip and no little apprehension for me, the long-awaited day arrived. On the previous evening the newly acquired roof rack was fitted onto the car, followed by the two cycles, ready for the next morning. Our pannier bags were filled with everything we could conceivably need. How many weeks were we going for??? Philip couldn't have been more helpful.

The alarm went off at 6 o'clock. It was a glorious sunny morning and the forecast was for a warm day. Alice was staying behind to have a day with Caroline and her pony. Leaving her behind, we were soon off to make our 8 o'clock start time at Clapham Common. The melee which greeted us was totally unexpected as thousands of people, along with us, tried to park cars and, having done so, get to the starting area. A quick recheck; were Philip's details still attached to his saddle as I feared losing him, and then what? As we struggled to the start I reminded him to keep close to me, which he did, chuntering at all and sundry in his limited way that he must keep close to his Dad. The message had got through!

After some jostling and trying to ensure that the frantic pedals of others were not taking lumps out of our ankles, we were funnelled through crash barriers into pens at the start.

There were no fond farewells or looking back to Mum as we were swept along in a tide of bikes. I purposely hung back so that we were at the rear of the pen holding our batch of starters. This, I thought, would give us a quieter send off, and in turn enable us to take a few minutes to acclimatise ourselves out on the road. All very well in theory, but what one didn't know was that dozens of non-registered riders would be imposing themselves onto the pack as soon as it left the gates. The first mile was bedlam, but Philip coped with the melee.

The outer streets of London were a seething mass of cyclists all jockeying for position at crossings and lights. Having thought I would get Philip to lead so that I could keep him in view, I soon realised he was easily put off by the masses and some stupidly aggressive riders who were treating the event as a time trial. He was worried by their antics and was pleased to move along behind me as if I was ploughing a furrow for him to follow.

Nevertheless, with some difficulty, as there were always streams of other cyclists just in front, who might without warning suddenly stop, it was necessary to frequently turn round to ensure Philip was with me. He always was. There were nasty crashes, attended by ambulances with sirens blaring; sights which provoked sobering thoughts. Despite this the day went well, with Philip obviously relishing the challenge, and the satisfaction of doing what everyone else was doing. In the searing heat, by the time we reached Ditchling Beacon we were tired. No heroics here - just a long walking slog up the hill where those not so fit and others carrying excess weight were sitting, lying down or simply standing gasping for air. Not so with our fit gazelle - he coped easily and was soon enjoying the long run down into Brighton. His concentration and application throughout the six hours had been unwavering. Not once did he cause me the slightest anxiety. What a hero!

When we checked in on the Brighton esplanade, to get our sponsor form stamped at the end of our fifty-six miles, there was a message from Miriam. Would we wait around, as she had gone to get Helen Worth so that she could say a 'well done' and 'hello' to Philip. It was a long wait but when she appeared he was completely taken aback by the attention being showered upon him - a Coronation Street Personality giving him a hug and talking just to him with crowds of other people looking on. He was a Star!!!

We found Mum, who had collected the car after our departure, and driven to Brighton. She was amongst a throng of people with Ann, Caroline's Mum, who had also travelled down independently to see us arrive. Alice had laid up the special tea at home which awaited our return. Philip retired for the night a very happy and contented young man - what a pleasant change! It had been a very rewarding weekend.

Chapter 15 - Overtaken by Events

Life was moving on much faster than we'd ever anticipated. A call from Bill Welsh, the newly appointed manager of HFT's new home Downley Grange, soon focused our minds. He wished to come and see us and Philip as he was putting together a list of potential initial residents to form the core of the 'new family' ready for the anticipated November opening. Was Philip really to be part of those plans and were we ready to also be part of them?

We immediately took to Bill. He was kindly yet, at the same time, obviously a no-nonsense committed carer - just right for Philip we thought. He was positive in his thoughts regarding his plans for the new home. Suddenly, we felt overwhelmed, because if this interview led to an offer of a placement for Philip it would be much sooner than we had ever envisaged. We hadn't even been thinking a placement might be near, or about anticipating such an event by making an approach to Bucks County Council (B.C.C.) for funding. Suddenly, we found it could be only some eighteen weeks before the first arrivals took up their places at Downley Grange. Bill left the problem with us.

Liz Arkell, our County Councillor and, luckily, Chairman and co-governor at Vinio House School, arranged for an application for county sponsorship to be received. The support we would be requesting would not be for a few weeks, it would be a life-long commitment of perhaps fifty or sixty years. It was most certainly not an undertaking to be taken lightly.

It was an emotional and daunting application to tackle but it had to be done, and quickly. Within forty-eight hours it was handed in at County Hall in Aylesbury.

In the meantime, the upshot of the London-to-Brighton endeavours created considerable local interest via the newspapers and brought Philip two further consecutive days of unexpected celebrity status. Miriam had telephoned asking if we would take him to Gt. Ormond Street Hospital for Sick Children. Despite only donating 50% of his sponsorship to B.H.F., Philip was the third highest sponsored rider and had won a bicycle. He was to be presented with the new bike by the Disc Jockey Steve Jones. He didn't need telling twice to get the gist of that message. He was beside himself with excitement!

What a message and a boost for us all. Despite his problems, Philip had achieved a major award and the resultant prize couldn't have been more apt. Would he now let me have his old bike?

The local Rotary Club, of which I had been an active member, had been monitoring Philip's success. Colin, The President, asked if the club could put on a cheque presentation ceremony as part of an evening meeting which would be held the day after the visit to London. We were all invited to join the club for dinner along with Miriam and Margaret Rundall, a regional fund raiser from HFT to whom Philip would present cheques totalling £4,290, directly as a result of his June endeavours - some increase on the initial £100's we had estimated we might raise!

Despite all the attention Philip was receiving, which he so obviously enjoyed, life at home was not all honey and roses. Moods still grabbed him and unpleasantness occurred. There was nothing we could do about it but to 'hang on' in the hope that Bill would offer a place, finance permitting, sooner rather than later. At least there was now light at the end of the tunnel but were we emotionally ready to grab it?

No doubt with confidence oozing through his veins (misplaced or not), came our biggest potential disaster to date. Alice was out with her pony and Philip was making a pest of himself in the garden - nothing new in that! Helen said to him, "Why don't you go and have a ride up and down on the road outside?" Without further ado, and with some relish, as this would be his first time on the road without fatherly supervision, he cycled in and out of the drive and up and down our quiet leafy lane. He was certainly pleased with himself when he came in for his lunch.

Lunch came and went and Philip agitated to get cycling again. As we were both still busy outside we suggested the success of the morning should be repeated, at least it would keep him quiet and occupied whilst we completed our chores.

Working around the bungalow and not taking too much notice of Philip's comings and goings we both suddenly realised neither of us had seen him for some time. "Ah well he'll be back, he's probably gone a little further this time," was my casual response. We were not unduly concerned, but an hour later we were. "He'll be back," had turned to "Where the devil is he?" or words to that effect!

Off I went for a tour round the immediate area, quite expecting to find him sitting by the roadside watching the traffic. All in vain, I returned home. "Where the hell has he gone?" I pondered.

We were helpless to know where to start searching. The police at this point showed little interest, their retort being along the lines that he had only been gone for two hours and it was too soon to mobilise forces.

Four o'clock turned to five, six and seven with no sight of him. He was ill-equipped to be out this length of time and with the previously hot sun setting in the sky. He only had the minimum of clothes on and was carrying nothing spare, no water or food nor the ability to mend or sort out any problems with his bike. In a distressed situation he most certainly would not be able to tell anyone who he was, or where he lived.

My mind went into panic mode. Was the label still on the seat of his bike? In such situations you are never sure, but you hope for the best. Although unlikely, had he cycled into an unfamiliar area and got lost? Had he fallen, or been knocked off his bike, and taken to hospital somewhere? Not for the first time in our lives there were no immediate answers.

Alice, by this time, although worried, offered a plausible suggestion. "He wants to come home with his lights on." Oh, how we wished she might be right and that would happen.

Completely bewildered and thinking the worst, at seven o'clock I made further contact with the police. Helpful as ever the duty constable drawled, "Well, you think your son is missing - what makes you think that?"

"We haven't seen him for over five hours, he's mentally handicapped and he is out unsupervised on his bike for the first time, without food or water" I replied.

Still with no great enthusiasm he then retorted, "Well you had better come over to Marlow and I will take some details." In the meantime, with some relief, we had drawn blanks on telephoning the Accident Departments of the surrounding hospitals.

By this time the light was starting to fade. We had marshalled every friend we could muster to drive the lanes and byways in the hope someone would spot Philip. Alice was left at home manning the telephone waiting for any sightings to be reported in - there were none.

We were powerless to co-ordinate particular areas to search as we simply had no idea whether he had gone north, east, south or west from Wooburn Green. We were completely helpless to know where to start looking - he could have gone anywhere.

Arriving at the police station, I had an agonising wait whilst some other seemingly petty issue was dealt with. There was nothing more important to me at that time than locating Philip. At this stage every delay, however small just heightened the frustration and tension.

Constable 'Dynamic' greeted me with "So your lad's missing." I assumed a description of him would immediately be circulated to all Panda Cars. Wrong - "Now let's fill up this form which will tell us all about him" - at last we were getting somewhere. Wrong - "Well before we post him as missing I shall have to send a colleague to have a look round your house to make sure he isn't hiding," was the next gem. "I should have a car free in about thirty minutes," he continued. "Now where do you live?"

"Wooburn Green," I blurted out in exasperation.

"Oh, that may come under High Wycombe," was the next pearl of wisdom. By this time, with the apparent lack of urgency I was trying, without too much success, to contain my increasing level of agitation. It was now getting dark and chilly and still no alert had been issued, not even an informal one.

Formalities over - where now? A call to Alice - relief at last! Helen had spotted him, in the dark, lights on, cycling between High Wycombe and Wooburn Green, seemingly none the worse for wear.

Helen, whilst mightily relieved, did not make contact, sensibly leaving him to make his own way home, arriving just before the police drew into the drive to search the chalet. To the relief of everyone they quickly turned tail and left. Was Alice's earlier theory right or had time just caught up with him? We shall never know. Frighteningly there was no identity label on his saddle.

Panic over, Philip tucked into a rather over-done and over-due roast tea as if nothing had happened, and seemingly not unduly tired. Where the devil had he been for the past six hours? Under pressure he couldn't tell us. He was not aware of the seriousness of his actions, the outcome of which could have been very different.

With still no idea where Philip had been the previous weekend we were travelling to Flitwick to visit Jack & Ellen, who had recently moved. The journey entailed passing along Cambourne Avenue in Aylesbury where Philip remarked in his clipped manner "John," who we knew as he was Alice's Godfather, "was in the garden last Sunday." Fortunately we understood exactly what he said as he never repeated himself if the odd utterance was missed the first time. What could he mean?

Suddenly it dawned, was this part of his escapade the previous week? We travelled along the A41 as far as the Tring roundabout to further gather from Philip that he had, we thought, turned round there. Our thoughts were reinforced when John confirmed he was in his front garden at around 3.30 that bewildering afternoon. The puzzle was complete: Philip had cycled anything up to fifty-five miles, on his own, thankfully without mishap.

In the heat of the afternoon, with no drink or food, he could have become dehydrated, faint with hunger or had a puncture. Someone looked after him and he survived! One may ask how he found his way, but he did. What else could this young man possibly have in store for us?

After this escapade, a leather label was permanently fixed to the rear of his saddle giving his personal details. It was an oversight not to have ensured continuance of the practice after his London-to-Brighton run. It was important for his safety and also as back-up information if, when I was cycling with him, I had a serious problem, as he would not be able to communicate with a stranger and even less so in a stressful type of situation.

A few weeks later we had a variation on a theme. Philip and I were cycling home approaching the Bicester side of Aylesbury. As I often did, I turned round to make sure he was O.K. and following, even if at a distance. To my horror, on a long straight road he was not in sight. In some desperation against the prevailing wind I quickly retraced my journey for the two miles to where we had earlier had a drinks break. He was nowhere to be seen: he had again disappeared. Which by-road had he taken? There were plenty to take. Where had he gone, and why? I hadn't a clue. He was again on his own and exposed to potential danger, but this time with, I hoped, a label on his saddle.

Despite anticipating that the label was intact, without further ado I charged to Aylesbury Police Station to report him missing. The duty officer was much more alert to the potential problems than his Marlow colleague. As Philip was wearing distinctive clothing he quickly alerted the cars in the area.

Some feverish three hours after discovering Philip had 'lost me' and making detours on the way, I arrived home. I was greeted with an agitated, "Where the hell have you been?" Before I could answer Helen went on "Philip has been home for over an hour and said you were coming; where the hell have you been?" or words to that effect! After calming the atmosphere down a trifle I related the happenings of the latest little escapade. Again he had traversed at least thirty miles under his own steam with me having no idea of the route he had taken to get back to Wooburn Green - who needs Sat. Nav. when Philip's around?

This second incident could not be treated with kid gloves. Philip had to be read the riot act whatever the reaction. He was told in no uncertain terms that there would be no more cycle rides if I could not trust him to keep with me. The reason was explained and how stupid and dangerous it was to do this and probably the most poignant fact which hit home was that it made Mum and Dad feel quite ill with worry. The message got through and there were no more problems, although it took a few weeks before my confidence in him was restored.

Alice was continuing to grow up, having now reached the age when Philip first started to have his problems. Thankfully, she was very much involved with her pony, and adolescence had not reared its ugly head. She never 'kicked over the traces'. We were certainly grateful for that.

It had to come sometime that she would outgrow Monty, her pony. When the time finally came it was the cause of a double dose of grief. Alice cried herself to sleep because she was losing her loyal and trusted friend and the little girl who took the pony was so excited she had a series of migraines. Ryan, a much larger animal, soon replaced Monty and all was well in Alice's world again.

On a more serious note, the feedback from school was that Alice was likely to struggle with her O levels in two years time. Her mocks would probably confirm this the next year. We were not surprised.

We knew she was no academic and would be unlikely to become a vet, her early wish. To her, a Veterinary Nurse was not an acceptable substitute option. As far as we were concerned she did all we could have asked. She unstintingly supported us with Philip's problems and was working hard at her studies. Sadly she simply 'freaked out' when it came to exam time.

However, to her credit, there was never any suggestion of making excuses which she could with some justification have done. We were already anticipating that she could leave the High School at sixteen, as even at this early stage we could see that a two year 'A' level course would be an unfair burden to her. We had seen too many young people's parents pushing their children to the limit and some over it. We already had one problem. We didn't want two!

We returned to the comfort of Woodbridge for what could have been one of our last family holidays. By the next summer Philip might be in care and taking holidays with his fellow residents. What a sobering thought!

It turned out to be a super holiday with the usual cycling, picking blackberries and, most exciting of all, with cousin Diane in attendance, netting the tidal creeks at high water at Waldringfield to trap Grey Mullet. Philip would often be the first to spot a trapped fish and eagerly await the falling tide.

On return from holiday, Liz called to ask how our application for Philip's funding was going with B.C.C. We simply reported that we had not had an acknowledgement, or any contact with our Social Worker. She was furious. "That's simply not good enough," she rather haughtily replied. "I am going into Aylesbury tomorrow and will find out what is going on." Good, we thought, as we don't have any clout; but after such a good holiday, once again, were we really ready for Philip to go away just yet? Suddenly, events were moving on and potentially becoming much too close for comfort.

Liz telephoned after visiting Aylesbury. "I have been to see the Director of Social Services. He will acknowledge your application for funding and be in touch again fairly shortly." She continued, "Please let me know in two weeks what is going on." What did she really mean? What had she stirred up? We didn't know. We soon found out.

Within ten days, not only had we had an acknowledgement of our application but also the commitment of funding for Philip. We were overwhelmed, Philip's life was moving on too quickly for us to comprehend. What do we do now? In rather a shocked stupor we telephoned Bill to tell him Philip had funding. "Excellent," he said. "We are having an Open Day for prospective parents in two weeks, can you come?"

We duly attended the Open Day along with other aspiring parents, some of whom were expecting to have their offspring transferred from other more distant homes to the new facility.

In a quieter moment Bill told us Philip was earmarked to be one of the early in-take of new residents to the charity. He was likely to be placed in a dormitory of four in one of the large upper front rooms of the building. We wished to view the room but as the house was in a state of chaos there was little we could see; it would have to wait until another day.

The defining moment arrived. A letter was received from HFT confirming Philip's six months probationary period of residency. If that was satisfactorily completed, a commitment would be made for his lifelong future care. The letter also confirmed an estimated occupation date a few weeks hence during November. What a bombshell. Were we really ready for this?

Whilst we knew we should have been delighted and grateful, as there were plenty of other parents who would have given anything to get such privileged news, the answer was still a resounding NO. We were not ready. However, the clock was now remorselessly ticking towards November and his anticipated new life.

As Philip, at eighteen, would not be returning to Vinio House we asked for an appointment with Mrs. Quartermain. We really had no one else to talk to about our feelings. With her experience and knowledge of us, Mrs. Quartermain was the one person who we felt would understand what we were going through in sending our son away in such circumstances. She let us pour out our misgivings and unease about this stage of Philip's life. As ever, she fixed a gaze on us both and quietly and purposefully said, "I can understand most of your feelings but what you must realise is that Philip is entitled to a life of his own and this is the first step. Others go off to university and leave home for a variety of reasons, so what is so different? Just think for a moment, what is the alternative? He is finished here, dislikes the Work Centre and one day you will not be able to care for him." She had to be right and it was all put so succinctly.

Although Mrs. Quartermain's thoughts made it easier to come to terms with the change which was upon us, the feeling of guilt about how Philip's life had stumbled along was no less painful. We had no reason to feel this way as we had done all we could for him and the scenario we now faced had been our chosen way forward for many years. We knew we were fortunate to have his future settled so quickly but we could still not see it as a time for elation. We were now about to enter what would be for us a torturous period, embracing the next stage of his life.

Whilst we had talked to Philip about the likely changes to his life it had been pitched very much into the future. Although he thought he thirsted for a new environment away from Wooburn Green he had no idea what he wanted, or where it should be. If it came to leaving home he would have no idea what it would entail and how he would be affected!

To ease the likely transition we made an effort to call at Downley Grange, the new site, so that we could all walk around it and get used to the open spaces and enthuse about the many plus points. At no stage did we sense any feelings of enthusiasm from Philip for his potential new home. This was certainly making our existence more difficult.

We tried to keep life as normal as possible as the clock ticked away towards November. It seemed to be an eternity coming. In the meantime, there was an eerie calm centred around Philip. He was a lost soul, once more bewildered by what was happening in his life. The strain was no less severe on Helen who had unstintingly always been at the forefront in both the good and the bad times, particularly during the past few years of his life.

Bill telephoned and a November date was fixed for the opening of Downley Grange. Philip, with his B.C.C. sponsorship in place was to be one of the first five residents - four boys and a girl. We now had to change our attitude and be positive with Philip. The build up to the final days before admission seemed unreal. Philip was apprehensive in the extreme and we were relieved that the waiting was over. We just hoped he would settle down in his new environment. Bill had suggested that in order to help with the transition Philip should bring his bicycle with him as he had active young staff who would enjoy taking him out for rides. This was the first news to please Philip who decreed he would reclaim his old bike from me and take this with him and leave his coveted possession, the B.H.F. prize, at Wooburn Green.

For Philip, it was a sad time saying his good-byes to the Wooburn Green Venture Scout troupe who had, over the previous months, looked after him in such a dedicated way.

Packing the bulk of Philip's belongings was extremely difficult and emotional for Helen. It was the culmination of eighteen years of love and devotion, the last four of which had been particularly harrowing. Whereas I went to work, she was always around and fully involved in both the good and more recently, the disagreeable times.

Regarding Philip, whilst we felt an element of relief, the apprehension was already enormous. He was going away, or was it being 'put away,' for a probationary six month period? What then, if it didn't work out? Mrs. Quartermain's earlier words of wisdom were very much in our thoughts as we still struggled with our emotions.

Alice had said her farewell and wished good luck to Philip before she left for school on the day of admission - we were scheduled to arrive at Downley Grange after lunch. It was an empty feeling as we packed the car without too much help from Philip. He was very much wrapped up in his own thoughts. Enthuse though we may about the future – the freedom he would enjoy with his new friends, holidays at Old Stocks where his bedroom would always be ready for him, and how lucky he would be to have two homes, nothing we said lifted his spirits, even momentarily.

It was a strange and strained atmosphere in the car during the hour-long journey. We arrived in the central courtyard of the large core house to be welcomed by Bill and his staff. Everyone was bright and enthusiastic about this new beginning. We tried to put on a brave face but Philip certainly wasn't in a euphoric frame of mind; he was just very quiet and nervous.

Bill escorted us to Philip's room, or better described as bed space as the large front upper room with its high ceilings had been partitioned off at head height into four units. Our first thoughts on seeing this arrangement were not favourable but we could not talk about it until we were on our way home. Philip had never previously shared a bedroom, except with Alice on holiday. He was now faced with three other lads, whom he had not previously met or seen, being his partners. How would he take to this arrangement and cope with the lack of privacy? There would undoubtedly be disturbances, noise, and conflict as he and others tried to come to terms with their new surroundings. Based on our knowledge of him our fear was that this arrangement was likely to be a recipe for problems, if not disaster. We could only hope our fears would be unfounded!

With his belongings crammed into cupboards he was finally unpacked. We then gravitated to the dining room to rejoin Bill and his staff along with the other parents and incoming offspring. We were all strangers but for the Open Day when we didn't know who would be part of the first intake of residents. One resident was being transferred from another home in the North. The remainder were new to this environment.

Bill formally welcomed us all with the suggestion that, although there was free access to residents, a period of some six weeks should elapse before a return home, which would coincide with Christmas. This certainly made sense but we reassured Philip we would telephone him in the meantime.

Whilst we were pleased to be part of the initial plans we were still in a sense of profound shock, coupled with an overriding sense of guilt that we were placing him into care. We found we were not alone in our thoughts as the other parents who had been waiting and planning for some time for a placement were in a similar mental turmoil. Now that the awaited change was taking place, a big mental adjustment on our part was needed.

To save prolonging the agony for Philip we departed the scene as graciously as possible, leaving him with his new colleagues and surroundings. A new chapter was about to unfold in his life. Please please we prayed, may it be a happy and successful one.

Chapter 16 - On Probation

Without the daily ups and downs and the inherent tensions, life seemed quietly strange without Philip around although he was constantly in our thoughts. How was he getting on? Was he behaving himself? The Sunday evening telephone calls were very stilted and one sided in content. They told us nothing except that he was pleased to hear from us. Bill had reported how he was being slow to settle, which was not totally unexpected.

Hardly had Philip left us for his new life than disaster struck. We had recently become the unofficial guardians of Caroline, Alice's best friend, as her parents were in the Middle East where David was working for Cable and Wireless. She boarded at Dean Court School in Cheltenham.

After the autumn half-term we took her back to Cheltenham, stopping at picturesque Bibury on the way for tea. It was dark when we arrived home, to be faced with the previously locked garage door wide open. OH NO! Philip's prized bike of only a few weeks was missing. It had been stolen!

The earlier newspaper coverage of Philip's award included our address and had obviously alerted a heartless and ever-opportunist thief. The bike was the only thing missing and, with Christmas approaching, it was probably the acquisition of an early present for someone living locally. The offender must have been a tall adult as the bike had been lifted over the car, slightly scratching the roof. How could we break the news to Philip? He would be mortified. We couldn't just replace it, he would know.

The Bucks Free Press carried a prominent article reporting the theft the following week. From that article, another Guardian Angel appeared. Whilst not recovering the bike, Cycle Care in Desborough Road, High Wycombe, most generously offered to replace the one that had been stolen. Super, a solution was at hand.

We would tell Philip the truth when he returned for Christmas, along with telling him he was being presented with a gleaming replacement later on in the holiday. He took the news remarkably well, in his way having nothing but contempt for the 'bad man' who had pinched his bike. The new bike was kept firmly secured.

The eagerly awaited break for Christmas arrived. We were relieved to see him looking so well. Bill reported that his first six weeks had been a struggle but had basically gone O.K. His slowness in settling had not been helped by the shared sleeping arrangements! He was also finding it difficult to relate to the other residents, but these were early days.

We were introduced to Debbie, who was to be Philip's Key Worker. In addition to being the person most closely associated with him during his time at Downley Grange, she was our designated contact within the home.

Armed with the presents he had bought with the help of Debbie, Philip said his quick good-byes and leapt into the car and off we went to Wooburn Green. We were hardly inside the door before he was bounding upstairs to see that his bedroom was still intact. It was, and nothing had been changed except for a spruce up by way of redecoration. This done, he soon settled down and was so very obviously pleased to be back. When they met, Alice received a cursory sort of greeting.

We had an enjoyable and trouble-free Christmas but with a big underlying worry. How would Philip react when it was time to take him back? Would it lead to a major confrontation? We need not have worried as, on the appointed day he was quiet, but his bags were packed and he returned without fuss. It was, again, a strange feeling as we left him with Tony the Assistant Manager who was on duty, and returned home. So far so good!

A few weeks after Christmas we began getting telephone calls from Bill telling us that Philip's behaviour was becoming erratic and he was starting to misbehave. At times anything to hand in his frustration would act as a missile. Whilst this sort of unacceptable behaviour sounded horrendous to us, Bill didn't seem to consider it too serious although he thought we should know. Oh dear, we thought, he is finding his feet - what now?

Bill's calls continued, reporting a worsening pattern of misdemeanours to the extent that we came to dread the telephone ringing. Our dread of hearing his voice soon became apparent to Bill. If his call related to the forthcoming Summer Fete I was organising for the home on the front lawn of the main house, or any other matter unrelated to Philip's behaviour, he would start his conversation with

"Everything's O.K." This at least took the immediate panic out of some of the calls, although he would always mention whether or not Philip was behaving himself.

We continued to bring Philip 'home' every six weeks, for a long weekend. He was always ready to greet us and apparently looked forward to his forthcoming days at Wooburn Green. We kept him busy whilst he was with us and with this came a lessening apprehension of an adverse reaction when the time came to return. On each occasion when we collected him we would get the same theme in reply to our enquiry of "How is he getting on?"

"He is taking a while to settle in," would be the reply. Was this just Philip?

As a consequence of opening the home in the previous November, and being staffed ready for a full compliment of residents, as each new phase arrived the staff ratios per head automatically lessened. The upshot of this was staff had less individual time available to give to Philip. The direct result was that his behaviour continued to deteriorate. Without doubt, in his distorted way of seeing the world, he was seeking attention and looking for one-to-one type relationships.

Time was certainly passing quickly and suddenly it was Panic Stations! Philip was shortly due for his six months probationary review. With no yardstick by which to gauge his progress, our thoughts were full of frightened foreboding.

Surely we thought, with the trouble he was creating they would never keep him. What then, we wondered, as we'd already realised returning home would not be a welcome option. Could we now even cope if it came to that? With those thoughts the build-up to the date of the review was worrying in the extreme.

'Reading between the lines,' we had not heard too many positive comments about our son from Bill or his staff. They always appeared guarded in what they said. In fairness could they be otherwise, bearing in mind Philip's reported conduct?

Within months of Downley Grange opening we were being asked if we would take part in two five-minute television programmes which were being filmed by Thames T.V, for their programme, 'Help'.

With Helen and Philip in attendance, my contribution featured our fundraising activities through cycling and how the money raised had been apportioned. Other parents, in addition to extolling the standards set by HFT, also expressed their appreciation of being able to arrange for their offspring to be placed in a settled environment during their life time. The programme certainly showed the workings of HFT in good light.

With the build up to Alice's GCSE examinations which were, we knew, going to be difficult for her, and with everything else which was going on, our lives were in mayhem. The six monthly review of Philip's progress was suddenly upon us. What an ordeal this was likely to be! This would be the first time we had been faced with the catalogued facts of Philip's misdemeanours - not a pleasant prospect.

The appointed day duly came. There were five others present, including the local GP and the Social Worker from B.C.C. who was responsible for Philip's welfare in care.

Bill and Debbie, Philip's appointed Key Worker, supported HFT's Social Work Manager in setting out how the first six months had gone. Bill detailed the developing behavioural problems and how he and his staff were trying to counter these. Philip was far from settled and this was disturbing for other residents and beginning to affect the confidence of the staff dealing with him. Summarising the review at it's conclusion, the Social Work Manager said, "Having to take a long term view of Philip's problems, and in particular his, at times, aggressive behaviour, it has been decided his probationary period will have to be extended by three months." It was agreed in the meantime Bill would seek an in-house assessment from Dr. Jack. The meeting concluded with us being told, regretfully, that it would therefore be necessary for a further review to take place in August.

This was completely shattering news to hear at first hand. To be fair, and having taken heed of the earlier comments, we were to a certain extent relieved that he was to be further reviewed and not immediately jettisoned. It was also of some comfort that Philip's problems were to be looked at in some depth. Perhaps after the forthcoming assessment he would receive some much needed help.

We were also consoled to learn, without being specific, that other new residents also had their own set of problems. This helped to ease our worried minds but, not for the first time, nor probably the last, we were powerless to assist in settling him down. All we could do was to work closely with Bill and his staff and to support any initiatives they were taking.   Debbie now kept us routinely up to date, and considering all of the traumas faced by the staff, we only had the utmost admiration for everyone's fortitude and endeavours on our son's behalf - they were most certainly long-suffering.

Whilst Philip's emotional problems were on-going, he was, through the energies of the staff at Downley Grange, continuing with his cycling.   It was undoubtedly his emotional safety valve.

To give him a new focus for a few weeks we were again entered for the June B.H.F. London-to-Brighton Cycle Ride.   Miriam was delighted; at least someone was pleased with him!

On a fine sunny morning a more positive party than that of the previous year set out for London.

On reaching Clapham Common we found exactly the same format as twelve months earlier, seemingly hundreds of fellow-cyclists pushing and shoving to get to the starting pens followed by a hazardous start.   The starting times allocated bore little resemblance to reality.

Philip had obviously gained in confidence from his experience of the previous year.   Riding along, he was tending to get himself attached to the numerous groups of other riders rather than closely following my lead.   With some difficulty I managed to keep track of him, but over the first ten miles, with so many other bunched cyclists, it was a nightmare.   He would do as he was told for a short while and then drift off again.   I had to be ever alert for him passing me without warning tucked onto the rear of another group.   Had I not seen him I would not have had a clue where he was and more importantly, whether he was O.K.   Thankfully he was wearing a very distinctive top, and despite the odd scare we both arrived in Brighton safely to be met by our ever-faithful chauffeur - Mum.

The financial support flowed in.   My assistants at the bank again worked hard and with generous support from friends a further £3,623 was raised to add to the previous year's £4,290.   Philip wasn't bothered about the financial aspect of his success; to him it was a great day out.

To bring some variety to our exploits we also cycled in another charity event, from Crystal Palace to Cambridge.   We just made a donation on this occasion to the organising charity.   It was an easier event as there were considerably fewer cyclists around, added to which Philip was in largely unfamiliar territory which meant he again needed my leadership to get him safely to Cambridge.

Philip took these fifty/sixty-mile jaunts in his stride with no apparent physical distress. There was always an air of disappointment when the journey had been completed such was his enjoyment of these events.

Philip was certainly enjoying the afterglow his success created. However his general behaviour, coupled with his lack of fellowship with the other residents, was still a cause for serious concern.

To further help the staff bonding process at Downley Grange I would order and pass on cricket tickets for special one-day matches at Lords. It is a ground which has a special feeling, and just being there creates a feeling of well being. The announcements over the public address system, the informal jazz band comprised of 'old codgers' playing at the entrance to the Harris Gardens and the buzz from the good natured crowd makes for an air of excited anticipation. The red and yellow striped jackets worn by some of the M.C.C. members also add colour and splendour to the day. These factors all contributed to an air of expectation which would build-up to the result as play progressed. Helen would prepare the picnic and I would depart early to reserve seats with a good view in the Member's Stand. Philip, and a carer, would meet me later on in the morning inside the ground.

Philip would score, in his way, all day without a murmur and though this did not disguise the apparent prickly tensions invading his body he always behaved himself and would be pleased if we bought a small cricket year-book so that he could devour the details of the featured players. To cap the day he would always want to watch the presentation ceremony. It was as if he was sad the outing was coming to an end.

The staff accompanying him were always amazed how quickly Philip knew the travel routines. Knowing the routines when they work is one thing but getting on the right train if something goes awry would be a different kettle of fish altogether!

Philip was also now an avid 'reader' of The Daily Telegraph, copying the lead of his cousin of the same name. It was nice to see the two of them were forming a strong bond of mutual respect. My nephew always made an effort to get onto our Philip's wavelength and discussed current cricket happenings and statistics with him. Philip could, in his way, respond to this leadership. A sympathetic dialogue certainly achieved results and his cousin Philip had that knack.

On getting his daily newspaper Philip would immediately devour the 'hatched, matched and despatched' columns and then spend hours logging cricket scores and looking at the racing pages. His main interest was scouring the pages and taking on board dates of birth and statistics.

His newspaper had become synonymous with a feeling of well being, as he would regularly be seen marching around the residential site with it neatly rolled and tucked firmly under his arm.

If we visited cousin Philip, who then lived in London, his collection of Wisden Annuals, spanning some forty years, was like a magnet to our Philip. As soon as the pleasantries of welcome were over he would quickly lope up the stairs to the bookshelf, where they were displayed. All would be peace and quiet as he poured over these books taking even more statistics into his troubled little brain.

Along with the 'Cricketer's Whose Who,' our Philip now has his own collection of statistical and event books. Each new one is always of immediate interest.

After leaving the May Review, little had been said on our way home. There was nothing positive we could offer each other; once more we felt helpless. Bill was aware how distraught we had been with the decision to extend Philip's probationary period but we accepted that, as the manager, he had to report on Philip's antics accurately, as he saw them, as part of his endeavours to weld a largely compatible 'family' unit together. True to his word, however, he had quickly enlisted the help of Dr. Jack, the 'in-house' Consultant Psychiatrist, who'd said he would ensure that his report would be available before the next review, which had been scheduled for August.

In the meantime, with a heavy heart I had committed myself to seeing the September fete through come what may. It was, however, difficult to think positively whilst Philip's future was still so uncertain. A good level of momentum had already been built up which I was determined would not fall away because of our personal problems. Whilst we were both disappointed and continually worried about the future, it was through no fault of HFT. They were doing all they could to get help for Philip and we couldn't ask for more.

With the approach of the August Review looming and Philip's behaviour, as far as we were aware, little different, we felt our lives were in limbo. We could not see how we would be offered a permanent placement. We were irritable with each other, as in our minds loomed a huge dilemma – what could we do thereafter, if a halt was called to Philip's care with HFT? We had no idea what alternatives there were – if any.

At the August review, unbeknown to us, it was revealed that at the outset of the psychiatrist's investigation, in addition to the behavioural problems to be addressed there were also concerns that Philip's detached disposition, at times, may be symptomatic of a psychotic condition. We were already worried in the extreme on the one hand regarding what may be revealed by a third party using his expertise to assess him, yet on the other hand we were both thankful and grateful that Bill had enlisted the help of a colleague for his opinion Had we been aware of the full story our worries, which were already at breaking point, would have been greatly compounded.

The three months to August passed agonisingly by with, as far as we could deduce, little change in Philip's behaviour. Debbie, in her written reports, was always loyal to him, trying to find plus points to comment upon, but she could not ignore how he was misbehaving. Because of this Bill was, by necessity, the interim mouthpiece.

We were late arriving for the review as the motorway had been like a vast traffic jam on the move. We felt we were walking into a court which was about to pass sentence, particularly as everyone was already seated in the room awaiting our arrival. They all stopped their discussion and, as one, looked up as we entered the room.

The format was similar to the May Review. It was again being chaired by Robert, the head of the Social Work Department. It was agonising listening to him recalling the circumstances under which Philip's placement had been deferred. This was followed by the list of the many misdemeanours which had occurred during the intervening three months.

Milk bottles used as missiles, broken windows, flooded rooms, hiding on site and missing for hours at a time by losing his escort on cycle rides or simply taking off from the site on his own. It certainly didn't make for pleasant listening. In fact it was down right depressing.

Attention then turned to the findings from Dr. Jack's report. From his relatively short time with Philip what a factual and positive revelation he produced. In short, he said, Philip was not psychotic, but he had without any doubt an Autism Spectrum Disorder - he was Autistic. What did this mean? Here were words we had never previously heard. Philip had always been referred to as mentally handicapped and now he was having a label attached to his condition. To us it was a startling and bewildering revelation. What now?

The findings upon which the prognosis was based were explained to us. We could quite easily identify with virtually every one.

For the record they are worthy of recall:-

a) *Tics - Involuntary or habitual movement of face and or hands.*

b) *Mechanical Voice - Sing Song in sound.*

c) *Echolalia - Repeating questions before answering.*

d) *Obsessional Traits - Steers conversation into cycling and carries 'The Daily Telegraph' around under arm.*

e) *Visual Avoidance - In a tight spot closes eyes or drops gaze.*

f) *Rocking motions - Seated on a chair.*

g) *Behaviour - Impression of tense, stilted, stereotypical conversation.*

h) *Rote Memory - Obsession with dates and birthdays.*

i) *Barks at 'print' - Some words clearly enunciated whilst others are rubbish with little or no comprehension of what is being read i.e. from the newspaper. Wales and Abergynolwyn and Dolgellau quickly sprang to mind.*

With these facts placed before us we could not but agree that Dr. Jack's prognosis must be correct. It was not that we were seeking to dispute the findings but quite simply that we could only lament the fact that this succinct series of facts had not been revealed by others over many previous years. If they had been, where would Philip be today - in our view with no better placement than he now had, but would it last?

What is an Autism Spectrum Disorder which is the label Philip has now been given? Bill did his best to explain.

It is a life long brain disorder which is normally diagnosed in early childhood - not so in our case. Within the U.K. there are estimated to be over 500,000 people with the disorder. It appears males are four times more likely to be affected than females.

The condition is no respecter of creed or social standing. It is a severe mental illness in which sufferers are absorbed in their own minds and imaginations, coupled with limited ability to communicate with others or create relationships. Sufferers find it hard to make sense of their surroundings.

Those with autism can have challenging behaviour caused by their frustrations and if this is the case, they will need specialist care and support. Anyone with a Spectrum Disorder can have a multitude of traits, extremes and impacts. Speech ability can be very varied, with limited ability to learn by observation and reasoning.

Those with high IQ's can have intensely focused interests and capabilities. This sort of ability has recently been highlighted by the film The Rain Man and TV coverage of a young man who could memorise and, from visual impact, create a most detailed and intricate drawing.

Taking the above as a whole it all adds up to an Autistic person's brain being an extremely complex, and perplexing, piece of equipment. Philip seemed to fit perfectly a number of those complexities. What a mish-mash of problems!

Having, to a certain extent, been relieved that at last someone had put a label, however unpleasant, on the problems Philip faced, it did not take away the immediate stress we were under regarding his future. Rather, it immediately added to those concerns. I glanced towards Helen; she was clenching her hands so tightly, they were ashen. She was very close to tears such was the strain of the discussion taking place. I felt no less secure with my emotions. It was as if a noose was slowly being tightened around our necks. The report then came to Dr. Jack's summary of opinion:-

Some of Philip's behaviour, if not all, can be modified beneficially if he receives a consistent programme which would entail adequate staff training. He should then gradually become less tense with less frequent mood changes and the violence at present experienced diminish or be extinguished – the first positive guidance and thoughts we or anyone else had received.

The summary concluded - *he should therefore benefit from his existing environment and it should be possible to accept him into long term care.* I RECOMMEND ACCEPTANCE.

Did we hear correctly? I RECOMMEND ACCEPTANCE. Whilst he did not have the final say, to hear those words from Dr. Jack's report was like music to our ears - it was an unbelievable relief.

From that defining moment we knew we had an awful lot to be grateful for and nobody had contributed to this more than Bill. From our first impressions of him we knew he was a professional carer of the first order. This had now been borne out by his patience, dedication and caring attitude towards Philip. Without him would we have ever heard the final three words of Dr. Jack's report? We doubted it. Also coupled with his care for Philip, during some very harrowing reports and telephone calls, had come many reassuring words of tolerance and comfort for us. This was the mark of a true and highly respected professional.

Without those final three oh so important words where would we have been with Philip's life and for that matter our own? It just did not bear thinking about but it was not a thought we could easily jettison from our minds.

We were quickly reassured that Dr. Jack's recommendations would be accepted and from that time the tenor of the review took on a more positive perspective. We were informed of the care recommendations which came with the report and were again reassured to hear that, whilst looking after Philip was, as we already knew, far from easy, with those recommendations of action a plan of campaign would be put into place. How long it would take, or if it would work, nobody at this point dared to prophesy. To our surprise there was still no recommendation in the report for prescribed medication.

Our journey back to Wooburn Green was one of thankful relief that Philip's future was well on the way to becoming assured. How different from some ten months previously when we had been so uncertain and ungrateful when the letter setting out the details for Philip's probationary admission had been received. It had been, as we recalled, with an element of reticence that we had left him in the care of Bill and his staff. In hindsight, we now realised that in our isolation we had become too immersed in our own emotions to be thinking straight for Philip's sake.

Within a few days of the review a letter franked from Bristol arrived. We trembled as we opened the envelope - it contained the letter we had thought we would probably never see. It was the confirmatory letter from HFT of Philip's acceptance into lifelong care. (By the necessity of changing circumstances with all residents the words 'lifelong care' have now been removed, as it is impossible to know what the future holds regarding mobility and other ailments which may occur in later life).

In a reserved yet emotional state we went out that evening together with Alice to celebrate Philip's acceptance into the care of HFT. On toasting Bill and his staff along with Philip's good fortune we soon felt a whole lot better. Typically, Alice put it all in perspective when she said, "Mum you could not have coped for much longer; what then?" What a tower of strength she has been to us in some very difficult times.

Despite the problems we had faced both Helen and I were still able to be thankful for the gift of our children and how in our different ways over the years we had all enjoyed many happy occasions together - there was no reason why that could not continue. We were thankfully still a close family unit.

The prime responsibility for Philip's care was now, for the first time, removed from us. We would not, however, be divorcing ourselves from the responsibilities of helping with his care where we could. We loved him too much, despite everything we had endured, to do otherwise.

With the prime responsibility removed we were not naive enough to think there would not be many more heartbreaks and upsets to face along the way, and so it proved to be.

By this time Alice had received her mock GCSE results. For her, the results were disappointing, but to us not totally unexpected. She hated exams, and the ongoing problems with Philip would not have helped. She was, as ever, practical about the future. Although the decision time was still twelve months away, she had already decided she wished to work with horses. We suggested she search for a college with an equine facility and, when the time came to apply, we would fund her excess fees. Our taking this attitude regarding her future certainly helped her to relax and to look forward with a degree of confidence.

With Philip's future settled we ventured to Portugal for a holiday. It was our first time abroad. As a bank manager I had extolled to my customers the necessity of making a will, but Helen and I had always funked the issue. We could not get our heads round what to do about making provision for Philip, as he would never be able to manage his own affairs. Taking advice, we created Discretionary Trusts with the dual purpose of appointing third parties to look after his financial affairs and to also save later complications with his B.C.C. sponsorship which could easily be put in jeopardy if he inherited capital.

Setting off for a two week holiday in Portugal was a break we were looking forward to, but it was with heavy hearts we left Gatwick Airport. It was our first holiday without either of the children and rather meanly we dared not divulge to Philip what we planned to do. We kept in touch by telephoning, as usual, on the Sunday evenings we were away.

Arrangements for the fete at Downley Grange were going well. Bill suggested that to bring his cycling achievements to the fore, Philip should hold centre stage for a few minutes during the afternoon by presenting him with a cheque for £4,413 from the two London to Brighton runs. He said it would be a pertinent time to do it as the money had been earmarked specifically for use to renovate the dilapidated greenhouses at Downley Grange. The supporters present could see, at first hand, and immediately appreciate, how the money raised was to be used.

Miriam, to add to the presentation build up, agreed to attend and to receive, on behalf of B.H.F. a cheque for £3,500. Whilst this was regurgitating the first year's money everyone agreed that by combining the two years into one presentation it would serve to emphasise the magnitude of Philip's achievements in raising a total of £7,913 through his cycling expertise.

On a warm sunny afternoon in early September the stage was set. With Bill having set the scene with a few well-chosen words, and the large gathering of supporters all around the central ring, bang on schedule at 4 o'clock, to a loud triumphal blast of 'The March of the Gladiators,' Philip cycled across the large front lawn, through a gap in the crowd and into the ring. He very carefully stood his bike up on its stand. Looking sheepish but very pleased with himself he extracted the two large presentation cheques from his pannier bag. With great aplomb he unrolled them and handed them over to Bill and Miriam.

Now that the scene was so firmly set, Bill repeated to the audience what his cheque would be used for and Miriam, after praising Philip, concluded her thanks with a completely unexpected presentation to him of a B.H.F. Honours Award.   Unashamedly, tears filled Helen's eyes, and mine too, as Philip, momentarily completely overwhelmed, stood, eyes glistening, transfixed to the spot.   Suddenly, holding the B.H.F. award in both hands, he triumphantly threw it up over his head, just like the F.A. Cup winners do!   He soaked up the atmosphere he had created as complete strangers pushed forward to shake his hand. He loved it, the smile on his face said it all – once again I'm a hero!

Personal Recollections

Having asked the following for their comments some twenty years after they happened these are unabridged recollections from Bill (Manager), Barbara, David, Derrick, Jill and Joyce, all of whom worked with Philip in his early days in care.

When Helen read these recollections she just said - "He was more of a sod than we ever imagined!"   This one comment made the writer change the format of this story to one with the true facts retained but the names of the key characters changed.   To do otherwise would have watered down the benefit that others in similar situations may have gained in knowing they are not the only ones to be bewildered by the actions of an autistic soul.

Changing the book's format has taken away the planned use of photographs which would have helped to provide a balance by showing the growing up process.

Fond Memories of Philip's Early Days in Care

The Sunday morning when he thought he would water the seedlings in the long greenhouse - from the doorway - with the hose full on.   RESULT - a heap of compost at one end of the greenhouse, and a lot of empty trays

THEN, staff drawing lots as to 'Who would tell Trish on Monday morning?????

It's only now that we have an allotment that we can fully appreciate all the time and effort that went into planting the seeds in the first place, especially as it was other residents who had painstakingly planted many of them.

Philip helping Derrick to do some maintenance. When instructed to 'foot the ladder' he twisted the ladder and was later seen being chased across the lawn by an irate Derrick.

Philip was duly brought back to 'foot the ladder' as initially instructed. He then did as requested but refused to get off the ladder when Derrick had finished the job.

Cycling - A very considerable worry to us - A safety valve for Philip. He would make his own marmalade sandwiches if he was going cycling. They would leak all over his cycling bag – Ugh.

Name and address stickers were placed on his bike. Philip accepted these were so the police would know where to return the bike to if it were stolen The truth was he would be unable to tell anyone where he came from if he had an accident or something caused him to be upset.

The police knew Philip, calling one evening to reprimand him for being out in the dark without lights - a very salutary lesson to him. He was always back before night-fall after that.

Being an early riser, when Philip first arrived he cycled into the local village to pick-up his morning newspaper. He then realised that he didn't have to return straight away.

He usually went for his newspaper during the time when all the other residents were getting up and breakfasting etc., so the staff were pretty occupied and he found he could cycle off into the wide blue yonder and be gone for hours, perhaps not cycling very far. To combat this we took to locking the bicycle up to 'keep it safe' and so he would then walk the mile or so to get his newspaper. Philip enjoyed being accompanied on cycle rides by staff. That is until he was nearing base and would, if not watched, dash off down a side road and not be seen again for some hours. The one exception to this was if he were out cycling with Will, the manager's son, who was then Fifteen years old. Perhaps he felt the need to "look after Will!"

Philip would attack his bicycle if something was wrong with it as he was unable to sort anything out for himself. Putting a chain back on was messy and modern valves too complicated. On one such Saturday morning he was making one heck of a racket at 9 a.m. outside Will's bedroom. Seeing that Philip was attempting to put his bike into the industrial bin Will opened his window and shouted down "Philip if you will be quiet for half an hour so that I can get to sleep I will help you sort out your bike. Without further ado the bike was removed from the bin.

Staff were amazed by this act of compliance. As Will was not staff and was younger than Philip did he need to be looked after and helped? - Who knows?

Philip especially enjoyed watching the evening traffic from the motorway bridges. Much to our concern one wild and windy night he had been gone for hours. On his return, expecting to be told off he was greeted by Jill who opened her arms wide and said "Come here Philip you must be frozen," and then foolishly continued, "Put your hands under my arms Philip, I will warm them up for you just like my Dad did for me," quite forgetting he had man-sized hands, not those of a child. His hands covered most of her bust - Philip was quite oblivious to Jill's predicament!

Not so the other male members of staff who witnessed this, and claimed they also had cold hands. Jill enjoyed the experience!

One afternoon Bill came across Philip some fifteen miles from base in a conurbation sitting at traffic lights. A big decision; was he lost, do I interfere? He decided to leave well alone. Philip was back at base within an hour of Bill's return. His ability to find his way around was amazing. He only had to go along a road once to know where he was on a re-visit.

Philip would go on cycling holidays with Alan and never once shirked, on his old bike, even the toughest terrain. To give Philip a change of scenery Alan, who cycled the ten miles to work, would take Philip home for tea if he was on duty on a Sunday. Philip would return under his own steam with Alan worrying like a father until he got a call letting him know Philip was back - he always arrived safely and within the timescale set for his return.

The Lighter Side of Life -

Joyce and Bill both recalled taking Philip on the train and underground to meet Dad at Lord's. Both were impressed how very aware he was of how to get there and seemed pleased to know more than they about the journey. His concentration lasted all day sitting, watching and marking every ball. He was also pleased to act as Will's escort on another occasion, not realising the plan was really the other way round.

Being at a W.I. event in the local Village Hall with Philip exclaiming in a loud voice that the room was full of Old Ladies. On being shushed he said, "But they are OLD, Miss Tennant is 93, Mrs Birley is 95 and Josie Gilbey is 87 - he was of course correct and had he been asked could probably have reeled off their birthdays. We tried explaining that the ladies probably wouldn't like to be reminded of exactly how old they were. This was totally beyond his understanding.

Bill is a bandsman and Philip loved to 'BLOW' Bill's Tuba. When loading or unloading the Tuba into or out of the car, Philip would instinctively be there. To BLOW a very large Tuba, very loudly indeed, would not be every-ones' idea of "soothing music." However after a five minute BLOW, Philip would hand the instrument back to Bill, perfectly calm and very happy and contented. On these occasions 'patience had to be a virtue.'

Philip adored the Levi 501 advert where Nick Kamen stripped off in the launderette and put all his clothes in the washer. This began a phase of everyone's washing being done for them regardless of colour or fabric BUT on seeing the same advert at the cinema on the huge screen, Philip had (on the small screen) obviously missed the fact that the chap also put his trainers in the wash. After this, no-one's trainers were safe either!

Philip loved Tony Hancock and would mimic his voice and had some of his sketches off pat.   Jill well remembers sitting typing away in her office off the Pool room, when Philip entered.

"Get your clothes off" said Philip.
"Certainly not" said Jill not looking up.
"Get your clothes off" repeated Philip.
"Certainly not" said Jill.
"Get your clothes off" said Philip again.
for a final time Jill said "Certainly not, I'm not that sort of girl."
She then looked up from typing and saw that Philip was not alone but had with him two visitors from the Local Council who were obviously quite concerned about this bizarre conversation.
She tried to explain this was a dialogue from 'The Blood Donor' but she was not sure if they were convinced.

Philip enjoyed his holidays but usually on a 1 to 1 basis.   David took him to a YMCA.   They cheated by driving to just around the corner and then walking up to the front door.   On arrival Philip had got a splinter in his foot.   He would not let anyone near the offending appendage, not even David, but he did nevertheless want him to remove it.   He made such a song and dance about it, he quite cleared the dorm until the foreign body was removed and his foot bathed.

Philip was fondly remembered helping in the garden by raking up the leaves and driving the ride-on tractor mower.   It would all start in very orderly fashion with neat straight lines, then in zig zags followed by going round and round.   This all made interesting crop circle type patterns on the large front lawn.

On wild, windy, moonlit nights, he would often run into the house woods.   Staff in their endeavours to find him would come and ask us to walk Kelly (our Labrador) so we could ask Philip to help find her and to then take her lead and to bring her back.   Much as he loathed dogs he was happy to do this.

In his early days Philip didn't work in the kitchen very much but Barbara well remembered him tying the cord on his apron so tight she thought they would have to sever it to release him because he was in danger of cutting himself in two. Prior to the kitchens being phased out he used to enjoy his time carrying out the chores.

Tormented Behaviour

We had to ask for the milk to be delivered in plastic bottles because if Philip was upset he could rival 'Barnes Wallace with his Bouncing Bomb'. He would stand behind the kitchen servery and bounce one bottle after another - many made it through to the carpeted end of the dining room. Some were full, others awaiting collection in crates. He didn't mind. All were good as missiles, it was just unfortunate if someone was still eating at one of the tables.

Likewise at weekend lunch times - possibly due to his routines being broken from the normal weekday patterns Philip could flip over four tables if he placed himself in the middle of all four. Food and crockery would fly, some residents would be off like startled rabbits, others would hang on to their plates for grim death.

Staff would expect him to return to clear everything up immediately, feeling he had 'got away with his behaviour,' but on some occasions he would respond to "Come here Philip and let me give you a cuddle and you can tell me what is bothering you." He would be so tense, rigid to hold, with sweat pouring out of him. So embarrassed were his parents after one crockery-breaking session they completely replaced our crockery on what they called a 'Royal Worcester Run'.

He had a habit of flooding bathrooms, probably on purpose. After one such incident Derrick stormed through the house and pulled every plug from its mooring. No one could have a bath, or shave, without having to resort to having their own personal plug in their pocket. Not to be thwarted - Philip unravelled the hose pipe all the way from the outside tap into the Pool Room, as if to say to Derrick - so you think you've won!

In Conclusion

We must say we all learned a lot from Philip. Staff often approached him with some trepidation. But, as with the incidents with the milk bottles, when he did let you near him it was obvious he was very distressed. His whole body was quivering. We were able to say to staff that however upsetting they, and the other residents found it they would most certainly have hated to be Philip at that moment. This was something they had previously not taken account of. Likewise, we are led to believe that in any upsetting situation (for any of us) the adrenaline is still pumping through our body for over an hour after the initial incident. That is why things often 'flare up again' if people insist on addressing issues immediately, rather than to allow an amount of 'time out'. We certainly found that if we did this with Philip he would come back and help clear up. Not 'in his own time' but when he had indeed calmed down.

One of our original staff, Rachel, went from us to a boarding school in Bristol. We met her 12 months after she left us and she commented how invaluable her time with us had been and how her work with Philip, and others, had guided her when working with school age boys and girls. She felt able to pass on her knowledge and experiences in advising staff at the school that if they didn't challenge behavioural problems now, they would be doing their clients a disservice, because it would be much more of a problem when the youngsters became adults.

Chapter 17 - Reality or Simply Madness?

With Philip's future now, in our minds, more settled, the same could not be said for his state of mind. There were stable, helpful periods and then, for apparently no discernible reason, more outbursts. He was far from balanced. Because of this the telephone calls from Bill or David, who was now Deputy Manager, continued to report to us if there had been a particularly unpleasant outburst or misdemeanour. Those calls were no less devastating to our morale than when they first started. We may not now be at the 'sharp end', and in direct receipt of the traumas, but they were still just as upsetting.

Until it was locked up, Philip would take off at will on his bike, without warning, into the wide open surrounding countryside. On one such occasion, after he had been missing for a much longer period than usual, and as nightfall approached, David telephoned as he thought he should alert us to the looming problem.

Helen was the recipient of the call, being greeted by an agitated and no doubt very worried David, who opened the conversation with the words, "Hello Helen, there is no other way to say this than he has buggered off." Whilst obviously powerless, at sixty miles away, to do anything about Philip's lengthy absence, Helen related the two instances when he had 'buggered off', so to speak, with ourselves, before he became a resident under their care. David felt mightily reassured on hearing this information and thirty minutes later telephoned again, with a much calmer voice and obviously relieved to report Philip's safe return. Where he had been or what he had been doing David couldn't ascertain. Another budding drama was over!

Whilst obviously not knowing where Philip passed his time when he 'took off', we assumed he would have been somewhere fairly local. Our guess was he would have been sitting on a bridge over a main road watching the speeding traffic below. He seemed fascinated by this movement, particularly the large container lorries and buses. They were always picked out for a mention when in the car with us.

To emphasise our assumption of only very local movement we were once returning from the North and thought we would call, unannounced to see Philip. As we were about to leave the motorway we spied him, minding his own business, sitting on his bike looking over the railings of the bridge. We drove slowly round the junction island, wound down the car window and quietly said, "Hello Philip." He was so startled he dropped his marmalade sandwiches all over the path! Having got over the initial shock he was delighted to see us. We suggested if he would return to Bill we would meet him there and then go to the airport to watch the aeroplanes and have some tea. This outing always found favour and off we went, leaving him to follow in his own time.

David was the first person we saw when we arrived. He greeted us with the words, "Philip's not here he's been gone for almost two hours: where he is at present goodness knows." We related our story and Philip arrived back within a matter of minutes.

With Alice coming to the end of her days at Wycombe High School and my hours of work for the bank, as an inspector, much more predictable than as a branch manager, we had become much more involved with Eric's High Wycombe Group of Friends of HFT. We were an active practical group of a dozen people who were prepared to support whatever venture we arranged to undertake. Other than Eric we all had a mentally-handicapped child so the consensus to work together was easily achieved. I had become the Treasurer with a philosophy that whilst we appreciated everyone in the group giving freely of their time they were not expected to do this at an additional financial cost to themselves. All out of pocket expenses should be, and were, reimbursed. This worked well to the ultimate benefit of our endeavours as nobody, in volunteering their services for any events we were running, was likely to be out of pocket. This still remains my strategy.

Our annual fundraising events were largely repetitive but soon became finely honed. We raised thousands of pounds from Barn Dances, High Wycombe Flag Days and Sponsored Darts Evenings involving the local area pubs. We also received generous ongoing support through donations from the local Ladies Auxiliary of the Licensed Victualler's Association. They also willingly applied for licences for our bar facilities at evening events. At those events we worked hard and through this, gained a reputation for giving value for money, together with a happy, informal evening. This was none more so than at our summer barbecues, held at Hugh and Muriel

Wilson's period cottage, where a fast-flowing tributary to the River Thames ran through their garden.

The setting was idyllic, and so British, with the local High Wycombe Youth Orchestra all resplendently dressed in their black trousers and white shirts. They always relished being asked to give a live performance from the garden patio overlooking the stream. Joining in our barbecue no doubt also had its attractions! What could be nicer on a summer's evening? We may have feared the worst on wet afternoons ahead of the event but somehow the sun always shone on us in the evening!

Despite having to transport everything we needed to the venue for 120 guests, including an awful lot of sausages and burgers it was, with our large group of willing volunteers, always set up and cleared up with a minimum of fuss. Hugh and Muriel appreciated this. It was hard work but enjoyable and rewarding, especially when the takings were added up!

Peter, who worked for Guinness, always managed to provide gratis a Harp Lager keg and a few cans of Guinness from the 'Toocan' for our social events. These along with other drinks were cooled naturally in baskets in the river - there was no going to the fridge to get a chilled drink. These were successful events with a touch of chaos thrown in especially on the first occasion when the wine bottle labels came off and had floated down the river between placement in the afternoon, and our return in the evening - not deterred everything was consumed. It all added to the mirth!

We had a loyal following of supporters for our functions and always sold every available ticket. Our biggest dilemma on our social occasions was how much dare we charge without being seen as taking our supporters for granted.

The upshot of these efforts was truly emphasised when Bill on one occasion telephoned, and from his voice he very obviously had a serious question to pose. He quickly reassured us that, on this occasion, Philip did not come into the equation, saying, "We have very serious problems with the Craft Area electric's and it will take £6,000 to sort it out. In the meantime it will have to be closed. Is there any way your Friend's Group can do anything towards helping us?"

I replied, "We have a meeting on Thursday, I'll see what we can do." At the meeting the problem was posed. Without quibble the Friend's Group agreed that as we had more than £6,000 in the bank we would be more than happy to help. Specifically allocating money was not a popular pastime with HFT's Head Office but the cheque for £6,000 was immediately drawn with the proviso that it was earmarked for the repair of Bill's electrical problems in the Craft Shop.

Bill, who had hoped for some modest help from us towards the overall cost, could hardly believe the news. Only three days after he had made his plea his problem was on the way to being solved!

Being able to be positive in helping Bill in this way was related by Eric to over a hundred of our supporters at the next social function, a Barn Dance. It was a great fillip to the group's endeavours. Success, and being able to communicate that success, which Eric always did very well, bred even more success. Communication and saying thank-you for successful fundraising is so important, but in my experience is all too frequently neglected or not done very well.

Although Philip had now been accepted into care it did not mean the end of regular reviews of his progress, including his behaviour. The intervening period through to March 1986 encompassed the winter season of shorter days. The dark evenings created more tensions, as the relief obtained through cycling and thereby releasing the ongoing agitation was not so readily available. He was cooped up and not able to cycle to goodness knows where! No doubt to compensate for this Philip would wander off by himself into the gardens in the pitch black of night, always, in his own time, returning but in the meantime creating staff concern. In the acres of uneven grounds he could so easily have fallen and broken a leg. He never, as far as was known had any problems but it created additional concerns and worries within the 'home' environment. How the staff continued to cope one doesn't know, but they did.

The build up to the March Review, whilst there would not be the earlier uncertainties and tensions, was nevertheless still going to be a nerve-wracking affair, and so it proved. We were well aware that Philip had during the intervening period been no angel; far from it.

Philip's behaviour had been helped by moving him to a single occupation room. This enabled him to sit, uninterrupted, to copy and assimilate copious amounts of printed matter, usually of a statistical nature. It was useless ongoing information but it served a purpose in that it kept him quiet and occupied.

His behaviour was still the major subject at the Review, particularly as there were still very serious concerns relating to his continued periods of agitation and aggression. Despite charting moon phases and any other likely warning sequences, nothing in particular had emerged. There would be, on average, at least one such outburst per week. These would be aimed either at the duty staff, usually female, or towards the fabric or the contents of the building. Agitation with the staff was a real worry as he was now a well-proportioned six foot tall strapping young man. It was, however, noted for the first time that, after an outburst, if another person had been caught up in it, when it was all over he would show an element of remorse.

The catalogue of outbursts went on and on:-

September 21st Broke milk bottle and upturned table.

        23rd Flooded bathroom.

        28th Throwing jars etc.

October 5th Flooded bathroom.

        11th Broke window and record player in pool room.

        18th Flooded bathroom.

        23rd Jostled night staff.

To see and hear for ourselves what had been going on was like having a knife thrust into us and turned between the shoulder blades. It was harrowing. As if it was of any comfort we were told the violent frustrations appeared to be reserved for the 'home' environment and not outside it. He always walked the two miles to get his daily newspaper as a model citizen. This was not unlike the pattern of his moods and behaviour when he lived with us at Wooburn Green.

Because of the additional demands made by Philip's behaviour it was reported that a case was being made to B.C.C. for additional funding to increase the staff one-to-one time available to him. This certainly made sense to us.

The request, which was to be made through the B.C.C. Social Worker present at the review, raised another unwelcome issue. He suggested Philip should have a further in-county assessment to see if the environment in which he was now placed was really suitable for his needs. We were flabbergasted and dumbfounded to even hear this being suggested so soon after Philip's acceptance into permanent care.

Whilst his management was extremely fraught the charity, through its 'no bolts and gates' policy, did provide, as far as possible, an ideal environment in which he could develop and hopefully, as predicted, stabilise. It was already known and accepted that this would not happen overnight, it may take ten years, of which six had already passed. To move Philip would no doubt have completely removed any freedom he had and he would be institutionalised. Difficult he may have been but we didn't see the need for this draconian action.

Thankfully, the staff at the review, which was led by Bill, were very obviously indignant at this suggestion and made a strong case for not creating further changes to Philip's routines. In any event Dr. Jack's assessment only a few months earlier had been searching and thorough. It had now been established what the problems were but how to deal with them effectively was the ongoing issue. Hearing these strong, supportive words made us extremely grateful and also thankful that we had chosen HFT for Philip's care. Neither we nor Philip could have asked for greater support or commitment.

Dr. Hazard, the GP who looked after the resident's medical needs at the home volunteered to make contact on behalf of Philip with a Dr. Hughes, a highly respected Consultant Psychiatrist in Oxford. This he did and, along with Bill, we took Philip to see her. It was soon obvious she was very well briefed but what would she tell us that we didn't already know?

Philip was well aware this appointment was all to do with his welfare and moods. He was pensive during the journey as a result. We were all shown to her room. She was a mature, quietly spoken lady with a kindly face and, on first impression, created an air of professional authority very reminiscent of that which Mrs. Quartermain brought to her work. Dr. Hughes was somewhat taken aback when Philip stepped forward without uttering a word to shake her hand. She immediately responded most graciously and welcomed him to Oxford. The scene was set to yet again go through Philip's historical past.

At the conclusion of the up-date we expressed thanks for her honest plain-speaking approach but added our bewilderment at the current state of affairs with Philip and his mind set. Without ceremony she quickly turned to us and said sharply, "Your son is autistic and, as such, you would not wish to cope with what his mind has to put up with for five minutes. His world is something you would find it impossible to comprehend." We could only humbly nod our acquiescence, and meekly left the room.

Those were very salutary words spoken in such an authoritative manner they have remained with us ever since. They helped to put things in perspective - poor Philip.

At the conclusion of the meeting we felt, for the first time, that we had a better understanding of the ongoing mental torments Philip faced. Or did we? Sadly we could do little about them other than to continue to support Bill and his staff.

At Bill's request, Dr. Hughes agreed to visit the home to talk the staff through the traits and problems faced by those unfortunate enough to be afflicted with autism. He was sure this would enhance, at first hand, the staff's understanding of dealing with Philip and other autistic residents at Downley Grange as each one had differing problems. It was a steep learning curve for everyone.

Whilst Philip's behaviour and how to cope with it occupied large portions of the review, other aspects of his welfare were also given an airing. Everyone seemed to comment on his erratic behaviour in that at work in the garden, kitchen, woodwork shop or craft room, on some days he was diligent and co-operative and on others he was the complete opposite. He was a real Jeckyl and Hyde character, one minute full of bonhomie and the next all agitation and fury with no apparent reason for the sudden change. The staff never knew which version of Philip would turn up, or if he would even appear! It was soon realised that on a one-to-one basis he was more likely to be at his best than if he was in a group. Wherever he was it was always necessary to keep a close watch on him. He could not be trusted without constant supervision.

Keeping an eye on him was not always easy in that, on the leisure front, he enjoyed his cycling, television, writing and twice-weekly swimming. Whilst he was very fit his personal hygiene regarding changing clothes and shaving left a lot to be desired. He just didn't seem able or willing to transfer his Wooburn Green living skills to his care environment. Dr. Hughes told us the inability to transfer skills or experiences from one situation to another, was not unusual with an autistic person. This is a syndrome still applicable some twenty years on. Mum's constant nagging over the years to do these things could also have had a bearing on her success!

Socially, on his own terms within the home, small improvements were being seen, initially with members of staff and then with other residents. Basically, Philip was a loner and didn't thirst for company. This was a further trait of his autism.

Whilst cycling was his safety valve, it now had to be controlled by keeping his bike under lock and key in order to know where he was, on or off site. Where he was when he was off site was another, largely uncontrollable matter, with the consolation that, left alone, he was a capable, safety-conscious cyclist. However, in a confrontational external situation, which never, to anyone's knowledge, occurred, goodness knows what might have happened.

One dark evening Philip had a run in with the local police as he was returning from a solo jaunt with no visible lights on his bike. They were obviously sensitive to the situation and, using common sense, reprimanded him and escorted him back to base. After this he was organised into ensuring the first thing he did after being out in the dark was to put his batteries on charge ready for the next outing. This reprimand by the police proved to be a very salutary lesson to him. To this day he still looks for and chastises, from the safety of the car, erring cyclists with no lights as dusk falls. Otherwise if anything went amiss with the bike it was likely to get a good kicking which necessitated a repair!

Visits to see Philip or, as he preferred, to visit us, were as regular as possible without in any way undermining the ongoing residential aspect of his care. We wished for him to see where he was now living as 'home', with Wooburn Green being a place to visit for a break. This seemed to work well as we always pencilled in the diary the next visit at the conclusion of the current one, usually four weeks hence. Our attitude in this respect was often favourably commented upon at reviews. HFT were very relaxed about the frequency of home visits but as Philip was now always well behaved in our company and willingly co-operative it had become a pleasure to have him with us. At least it gave the staff at the home some respite but they never complained. They were always quick to point out that worried as we were by Philip's behaviour there were plenty of upsets with the other seventeen residents.   We were grateful for this - we were not alone!!!

The summer months of '86 were busily spent keeping Philip occupied as far as we could. This included the usual three trips to Lords for the One Day Internationals or Domestic Finals. These were still days he looked forward to, especially as on occasions his cousin Philip, along with Uncle Robert, would join us.   It didn't seem to matter what frame of mind he was in when the day started because by the end of it he was always in fine form.   At Lords he always remained calm and diligent throughout the day with his scoring. Having once, in his younger days, been denied the pleasure of his day at the cricket he was not going to jeopardise it again!

The B.H.F. London to Brighton cycle ride was safely undertaken for the third year, with a repeat of the London-to-Cambridge ride. The latter was still a much more relaxed affair, once out of London. However this excursion was not without its lessons.

As I approached Clavering on a quiet stretch of road, I turned round for one of my periodic checks on Philip's progress to find, to my horror that he was nowhere to be seen. I had been wrapped up in my own thoughts and not fully concentrating, and as a result I thought I had been cycling too quickly for him.   Philip would not be hurried and always cycled very much within himself.   Sitting on the bank by the roadside I waited and waited, still thinking he'd be along shortly, but he didn't appear.

I retraced the route for over two miles to find him remounting his bike with an elderly, immaculately togged-out gentleman cyclist just leaving his side and bidding him a friendly farewell.   Philip returned the pleasantries, thanking him in his stilted way for his help. Philip had had a puncture and this kindly gentleman had thoughtfully and without fuss stopped to help – a real knight of the road who could so easily have ignored Philip's plight, but thankfully didn't.   I was extremely grateful and relieved, but the gent in question was out of sight before I could establish how Philip's misfortune had shown itself – was he riding on a flat tyre, shouting by the roadside, abusing his bike or simply looking forlorn and helpless when his rescuer came upon him?

Whatever had happened Philip was very pleased to see me appearing as, by the time I had returned, it had probably been at least thirty minutes since we had last been together.

For all his years of cycling Philip has no ability to fend for himself in times of adversity, involving his bike. In fact adversity, and with it pressure, would most likely see him at his most belligerent. He is not a natural mechanic; nor for that matter, is his father! If there is a right and wrong way to do something I will always choose the latter. An unexpected spring will pop out from somewhere which I cannot get back to whence it came or even establish where it popped out from in the first place. Alternatively I finish with a bit over. I am sure I am dyslexic when it comes to interpreting diagrams which describe the assembly of even the simplest of objects. In fact I am an acknowledged mechanical disaster!!!

Philip's relationship with Alice was showing distinct signs of improvement, particularly when he learnt she would also be going away very soon. She had done moderately well with her exams and had secured a place at Newark College, where there was an established Equestrian Course. As a fall back option Helen had sensibly suggested that Alice should take a Secretarial Course alongside her chosen subject, and this she was prepared to do. In her absence Ryan, her beloved horse, would be loaned to and stabled with Caroline.

Whilst to outsiders, unless directly involved with them, Philip was still a loner, his wider family was however important to him He was always pleased to see them, particularly if they were attending and running stalls at the fetes I organised at Downley Grange in 1985 and 1986. These were large, well publicised affairs which enabled the local area to support and see at first hand what HFT was doing within their community. In a single afternoon each of these fetes raised over £4,000 for the charity's funds in a single afternoon.

As if in charge, Philip would happily flit, without commitment, between family members as the afternoon progressed and, at the conclusion, thank them in his way for coming and helping. In such circumstances he is always the perfect gentleman!

I had earlier asked Philip whether he would like to go on a long, long cycle ride with me, staying at a different place and with different people each night, spanning fourteen days and covering 874 miles. I showed him a map and pointed out where we would go, visiting Land's End, Bristol, Kidderminster, Manchester, Hawick, Edinburgh, The Forth Bridge, Perth, Inverness and finally stop before we went into the sea at John O'Groats. We would be cycling from Land's End to John O'Groats, the longest journey we could make. It would be like cycling from London to Brighton every day for fourteen days. His eyes lit up, he was unusually positive and decreed it was a "good idea" - a resounding 'Yes' in Philip's world. Did he understand the implications of what I was suggesting? You bet he did!

"Bloody hell, oh no, you can't be serious!" This was Helen's very measured response to the thought. Very quickly realising that it was more than a pipe dream it was not long before the inquisition started.
"When?"
"In May of next year."
"How long will it take?"
"Fourteen days."
"How many miles will you cycle a day?"
"Fifty to seventy miles depending on available areas to stop."
"When will you start training?"
"Probably February."
"How will you train?"
"Just cycling."
"I know that but how far?"
"On two consecutive days we will cycle twenty-five miles for two weeks and increase this by five miles every two weeks."
"Will you have rest days?"
"Probably not."
"Will there be just two of you?"
"I was thinking we need an escort vehicle."
"Where will you stay?"
"Once the day-to-day route is worked out I will approach Round Tables and Rotary Clubs along the way for overnight help."
"What if Philip plays up?"
"I think there needs to be another cyclist to act as a foil for me."
"Where is that foil to come from?"
"I don't know."
"Where is the escort vehicle to come from?"
"I don't know."

"How will you get to Lands End?"

"Train."

"How will you get back from John O'Groats?"

"Train or aeroplane from Wick."

"Philip won't fly, will he?"

"We'll worry about that later."

"Will you do it for money?"

"Most certainly."

"How do you reckon you will raise money?"

"Sponsorship and buying some coins."

"What coins?"

"I had thought of getting £100 of five different commemorative crowns (25p each) from the bank."

"Can they get 2000 coins?"

"Yes, they are lying in the bank's Cash Centre vaults in London."

"How will you use the coins?"

"Send them out to local voluntary service clubs and ask them to multiply the face value of £1.25 by say twenty times on our behalf."

"How long has this been going on in your mind?"

"About two months."

"Two months? and the rest! Is it settled then?"

"No, but I think it is a real possibility. I would like to do it and it would be a wonderful experience for Philip. There is still plenty of water to flow under the bridge before it becomes finalised, if it ever does!"

Alice was equally aghast when she learnt what was proposed but knowing how her father's mind worked accepted that it may happen and that it was not just 'pie in the sky'. From my point of view at least the subject had been broached and not been immediately kicked into the long grass.

Shortly after this searching conversation, Princess Anne was scheduled to visit Downley Grange. Helen and I were to be presented to her along with Philip in the greenhouse complex which had now been repaired with the aid of his London-to-Brighton fundraising money. He was scheduled to present the Princess with a shrub grown in the garden.

It was a cold wet day and, though dry, we got perished waiting in the unheated greenhouse for her to arrive. Under a large protective umbrella The Princess duly strode through the outer door of the greenhouse. She was taller than I expected, or was it the hair do? What a charming bright figure she cut even in those dark and dank conditions.

She was well briefed, knowing what Philip had achieved through his cycling. Before she was presented with the shrub the Princess was completely taken aback by Philip telling her when her birthday was. He had obviously been doing his own research! The Princess agreed he was correct and, with a warm smile, she responded to his gift of the shrub and continued by congratulating him on raising so much money. This was followed by her asking him if he had any other long cycle rides planned. He instantly replied, all in one quick breath, in his clipped way, "Lands End John O'Groats 874 miles." She asked him to repeat what he said, not fully appreciating, or believing what she thought she had heard. Royalty she may be but he declined! This brought us into the conversation and it was confirmed that she had indeed accurately heard and understood exactly what he had said.

As The Princess moved on she turned to Philip and said, "Keep me informed and let me know how you get on." Philip said nothing and with a new mannerism, simply raised his thumb as if to say O.K. ma'am. There's no need to talk if you don't have to! As they left, Bill, who was escorting The Princess, dabbed a tear of amusement from his eye. Had the project been borne with royal approval? Were we under way?

With Helen's reluctance removed, the proposed adventure passed quickly from a distant dream towards reality.

At the next High Wycombe Friends Group meeting I mentioned my thoughts for eight months hence. I advised I would be looking to recruit an escorting van and a third cyclist but how, and who I was going to involve, had not as yet entered the equation. Amazement was expressed that, knowing how Philip was behaving, I was even contemplating such an adventure. At the time it didn't seem to be too pertinent as it was the following year we were talking about.

Eric, undeterred by the doubters, had put this news on a back burner. It was not there for long as, at the end of the meeting, he came over to me and said, "I have a camper van, would that do?"

I replied "It would be just the job but it will need a driver."

"I will have a word with Muriel (his wife) as its something I would like to do. We could make it into a holiday," he said. Could this really be true - the first major hurdle cleared at a stroke?

My Inspection Assistants were well aware of their 'mad cap' boss's plans. It was a source, at my expense, of some good-hearted wee-wee taking. To update them, despite their mirth I mentioned that Eric had confirmed his wish to be involved by providing, and driving, his camper van as our escorting vehicle. John, who had only been part of our team for a few weeks suddenly piped up, "I've got an old bike and what you are planning is something I would like to do one day. It sounds a great idea: I think I would like to come along if it's O.K. I could help you with Philip, he knows me a little and we seem to get on fine." It was a great offer. He was young and the sort of chap with whom Philip would easily associate and who would be a perfect foil for me if difficulties occurred.

The plans just kept rolling along, with Brian, a first-class printer whom I knew well from my time in Round Table, wishing to get involved. On hearing about our plans he immediately said without being asked, "You do it and I'll get my artist at work to do the graphics for an A3 poster and an A4 leaflet. I'll produce the first 6,000 for you." With the ever-increasing momentum it would have been both difficult and embarrassing to stop the band-waggon rolling!

Ill advised, or naïve, I remained confident we could complete the journey. I was really too busy for it to enter my little head that we mightn't. Misplaced or not I had complete faith in Philip's ability. Failure was not something I readily accepted, but had I really thought through the mechanics of taking a mentally-handicapped lad on a two week 874 mile cycle ride? There was lots to do and only time would tell if my scheming would turn out to be a foolhardy and fruitless exercise. It was after all, completely unknown territory for us all!

Chapter 18 - Adventurous Times

Undeterred by the 'Doubting Thomases' regarding the sense, or largely otherwise, of taking Philip on such an outrageous adventure, by November 1986 the dates were set. We would travel to Cornwall on Friday 8th May and commence cycling at 9 o'clock the following morning. Our arrival at John O'Groats was scheduled for the afternoon of Friday 22nd May. Put so simply that's all there is to it. Easy ain't it?

Despite his now more interesting and, through the prospect of the mammoth cycle ride, more attentive world, there was no lessening of Philip's outbursts. Upsets, remorse, quiet periods, followed inevitably by the next explosion.

When life was quiet it was always a case of, 'I wonder for how long' and so it went on month after month. He could be so pleasant and helpful one day and the complete opposite on another. At least we were not seeing at first hand what was going on, but it was impossible to ignore how unpredictable Philip's behaviour continued to be.

Whilst one could not other than admire the continuing forbearance of the staff, their ongoing lack of confidence in dealing with Philip had now become very apparent. For our part, when we visited the home and saw a broken window, furniture damaged or something drying out, we would always initially suspect it was the aftermath of yet another of his incidents. What a relief when, as was often the case, it had nothing whatsoever to do with him. Oh ye of little faith!

It was not all doom and gloom surrounding Philip's welfare. He had developed quite a sense of humour, evil though it may from time to time have been. He loved to mimic TV programmes such as Hancock's Half Hour with some of his catch phrases becoming a regular feature of his vocabulary. Zany adverts also seemed to catch his imagination. At times he would see himself as an authoritative member of staff and would quite knowingly send other, more gullible residents off to incorrect locations for their work or craft within the home. He then enjoyed watching the fruits of his mischief. He always knew what everyone else should be doing but was not too industrious himself!

Meanwhile, Alice had quickly settled into the routines of her college life at Newark. At Christmas there was a genuine 'pleased to see you, how are you getting on?' type of greeting towards each other. In Philip's eyes they were probably now on a par with each other, both living elsewhere.

Over the following months and leading up to May, there would be lots to do and little time in which to do it. Eric and John continued their commitment, which enabled me to concentrate on the logistics of the event. The areas I identified as needing to be covered were as follows:-

Publicity - This would be an important part of our strategy if we were to have a chance of raising a serious amount of money.

Travel - The logistics of movement from the time of leaving Wooburn Green until our return. To this would be added the daily route, coupled with the nightly accommodation. This had to be a priority as there was no way, even with the camper-van in attendance we could set out with a mentally-handicapped young man not knowing exactly where we planned to go each day or whether there would be a guaranteed evening resting place.

Training - Working out a schedule which was linked to cycling, gradually building up our strength and stamina - included in this there would be no visits to a gym. It would be roadwork only. It would be madness to set off without adequate physical preparation. It is a fallacy to think that, as the days pass, one will get fit as one goes along. You most certainly don't, you just get tired, sore and finally exhausted to such an extent concentration wanes and you are very likely to have an accident. There was no way either of us was going to be exposed to that sort of outcome.

By way of a cause and purpose the event would be linked to HFT's 25th birthday, Philip's 21st and my 50th. John, my planned foil, was happy for our endeavours to be solely in aid of the next proposed HFT home in Bedfordshire, for which, through the readers of the Herald newspaper in Luton, a very substantial appeal had recently been launched. Our efforts would be a natural story for them to follow and publicise.

Having sorted out in my mind the strategy of the event it was then time to decide on the finer details of each aspect:-

1.   **Publicity** – A letter to Princess Anne recalling the earlier meeting with Philip in the greenhouses at Downley Grange and another to Brian Johnston, the radio cricket commentator who I was aware had a daughter in care with HFT.   These approaches produced their pertinent personal comments to insert into our 'Balloons' on our leaflets and posters.   Peter Edwards, the then President of the Bourne End and Cookham Rotary Club, added the good wishes of the club's members.   The fourth balloon would be a message scribed by Philip, "Please help me to help others."   This was an impressive and eye-catching array of support.   It also gave us much needed credibility which, in turn, grabbed the attention of other, as yet unsuspecting, third parties!   Brian's artist was delighted - she had some real ideas with which to work.

2.   **Route Accommodation and Transport** - Working on travelling distances of fifty to seventy miles per day, we would stay in or near towns along the way.   I thought that, other than in Scotland, it could be worked out quite easily.   In the event it was not as simple as I first thought, but it was an interesting exercise to undertake.   It occupied me for a whole evening.   With the route largely settled in my mind it was a case of poring through the club directories, which I should not have had access to, of Round Tables, 41 Clubs (Ex-Round Tablers) and Rotary Clubs looking for potential accommodation each evening from their club membership for four weary travellers.   It was incredible,   the   reaction   to   my   13   unsolicited   letters   for accommodation was positive and, above all, speedy.   The route and overnight stays were quickly firmed up.

At this point of detail Philip's interest became very apparent.   The potential daily mileage was a statistic for him to follow.   I drew red rings on the map of England and Scotland showing where we would rest our weary heads each night.   He simply named the days 1,2,3 and so on.   It was great to hear - he most certainly did understand what was going to happen.

The arrangements for transport soon fell into place.   British Rail donated tickets from Paddington to Penzance (see later what a furore that generosity caused).   We would be met by staff from Cable and Wireless at Penzance, staying at their centre at Porthcurno where we would meet Eric with his camper van, and stay overnight.   On the

Saturday, Cable and Wireless would take us to Land's End and see us on our way. Shell donated £200 to cover Eric's fuel costs and Loganair donated tickets from Wick to Edinburgh with British Airways completing the round trip by donating tickets from Edinburgh to Heathrow where our long suffering chauffer Helen would await our return. These were some very generous offers and again all very simple, if it worked!

3.   Training - The late 1986/87 winter was quite harsh, which curtailed the February training plans which should have started with twenty-five miles on two consecutive days, rising by five miles every two weeks. Not cycling on icy roads was the only concession I would permit to stop our ongoing preparation and that was just what we got for the first two weeks. As it was necessary to get my legs into trim earlier rather than later I borrowed our next-door neighbour's exercise bike. What a mindless occupation riding one of those is!

By early March, come rain, wind or shine we were out on our thirty-five mile outings. We could not now be fair-weather cyclists as we had no idea what weather May would throw at us. We had to be both fit, and prepared for nature's little surprises.

Everything appeared to be organised and set up but we had hardly settled into our training routine when the bank intervened in our progress. At short notice I was required to undertake a three week inspection of the International Branch in Guernsey, flying out on Sunday evening. That was it, with no room for negotiation.

'Oh what a nuisance' was not quite the tone of the words I used on hearing this inconvenient and most unexpected news! Initially there was an air of disbelief, followed by panic. As it was a fait accompli the turmoil soon turned into reflective and thoughtful calm. What could we do about the training schedule? It was such a vital part of our preparation!

Putting the upset to one side I decided that as the costs of travel to the bank would be the same, Helen should spend the middle weekend with me in Guernsey. I could make up my lost training miles when I returned home. By chance, no doubt currying favour with his inspector, the manager of the branch dusted down his old redundant bike and offered it to me for use whilst on the island. I enthusiastically took up his offer.

Before breakfast I would get up in the dark, often on cold mornings, tiptoe out of the hotel, collect the bike from an outside shed and cycle the eighteen miles round the island clockwise. In the evening, before dinner, I would reverse the journey. These were varied and undulating miles totalling, more than I was scheduling to do at this stage. It was fun: I got to waving acquaintance with fellow cyclists going to work in the morning and would see the dawn breaking whilst out on the road. Without a rest I would get round the island in ninety minutes. These were good work-outs which took the pressure off the weekends.

For a week during April, to further supplement my mileage and to build my stamina I cycled, as an inspector, from Wooburn Green to a branch of the bank in Reading and returned in the evening. The staff who worked at the branch were highly amused to see me arrive in this way and it gave my assistants a further cause for wee-wee taking. I had always arrived, washed and changed, before they put in an appearance each morning.

True to his word, Bill kept Philip's training going, and by the end of March we were back on the projected schedule. By mid-April, as planned, we were cycling our 50 miles on consecutive days. For good measure, at Easter, we added a third day - all very time consuming. During this time John, who was looking after his own fitness, rode out with us twice for Philip to get used to his company. They soon formed an easy relationship.

The weekend following Easter was the big and final effort. I drove to collect Philip from Downley Grange, taking our two bikes with me. Bill saw us off to cycle sixty miles to friends on the Saturday, returning on the Sunday.

Philip in particular coped easily with the Saturday journey, with a light tail wind and sunny skies. Sunday was a different story. The sun had 'shut up shop' and we were now cycling into a cold head-wind with intermittent snow and hail showers to wet our appetites for what may be in store in May. It was a most unpleasant day but we battled on for forty miles, before stopping at a pub for a cooked lunch rather than resting in a bus shelter to eat our prepared sandwiches. It was bliss to see a blazing fire as we walked into the warmth of the pub.

Philip hankered for a roast and his usual pint of shandy. To pass the time I was reading his Sunday Telegraph which, to keep him onside, was a must to buy along the way. Suddenly I heard a little snort. He was sitting, bolt upright, blissfully fast asleep. The struggle of the earlier hours had taken its toll.

We completed the one hundred and twenty mile round trip and our training was complete. I had cycled over a thousand miles, accompanied by Philip for six hundred of them. To his credit, Philip had battled on in some atrocious conditions. He had been the model of application and concentration. Whilst obviously not relishing some of the training stints he never protested - a good sign for the future?

4. Sponsorship and Fund Raising - Whilst it was easy to get too immersed in the fundraising of the event we had to remember cycling from Land's End to John O'Groats was primarily an experience of life for Philip. That was how it started and that was, despite everything else going on, how the event should be.

The Herald free newspaper in Luton as part of its appeal for the new home printed a short list of our needs. It produced yet another new bike for Philip and waterproof clothing. Isostar provided a consignment of their isotonic drinks, Avery Labels produced adhesive labels, Basildon Bond boxes of envelopes and the bank provided as many T- shirts as we needed. With another bike readily available we could now carry a spare on top of the camper van.

The volume of copying and letters needing to be sent was quite incredible. At all levels the necessary help was willingly offered and gratefully received. Everywhere our inspection team went our plans grabbed the attention of the staff. Time was our biggest enemy: suddenly there were simply not enough hours in the day.

Our neighbour's nephew was the chairman of Woolworth's. With that connection, and introduction I was confident this was a good source to tap for corporate sponsorship. What a positive start that would be. The reply to our letter was a bit like the curates egg. "I know this answer will come as a great disappointment," followed by, "In conclusion can I wish you well in your endeavours and I will pass your details on to a trust with which I am involved." Seven days later a cheque from the Trust for £1,000 arrived. Any expenses were now well and truly covered. In the event, as our hosts generously fed and watered us, the only expenses incurred for four people were, one nights dinner and the carriage costs of getting one bike to Penzance and, on completion, returning the bikes to High Wycombe. To minimise the costs and, in turn, to maximise the benefits to HFT, we all agreed we would pay for any incidental costs during the journey. Quite incredibly the total charge to the event covering the fourteen days came to the grand total of £110.50!

The initial welcome success of the fundraising prompted the need to keep any income and expenses at arms length from the participants. Joan, who was part of the Friends Group, acted as our 'Post Office'.

I bought £500 of Commemorative Crowns (£100 each of Churchill, Silver Wedding, Silver Jubilee, Queen Mum's 80th and Royal Wedding, Charles & Diana) which were lying in the bank's vaults in London. My assistants joined an evening work party at High Wycombe Cricket Club where 240 packages were prepared to be sent unsolicited to Round Tables, Rotary Clubs, 41 Clubs, Ladies Circles, Tangent Clubs, Inner Wheels, Lions Clubs and Rotaract Clubs, asking that they multiply the face value of £1.25 of the crowns by twenty by whatever means they chose. The clubs for mailing were centred around High Wycombe and Downley Grange where I and Philip respectively resided, hoping that the clubs would wish to be associated with our forthcoming adventure.

Overall the coins were well received and a very worthwhile exercise, with donations ranging from £100's in a single response to zilch, plus an aggrieved letter that we should ask for support in this way. Some of the crowns were never seen or heard of again - that's life!

Whilst the local newspapers gave us copious coverage it produced virtually nothing by way of financial support from their readers.

It is a fact that raising money for a charity such as HFT is five times more difficult than for locally based emotive charities connected with Cancer, Hospices, the Blind or Lifeboats unless there is local flavour to the appeal. We had no such benefit.

A silver lining appeared from my three weeks working in Guernsey. As my evenings were free after dinner, I would retire to my bedroom and with the aid of the Lloyds Bank Manager's Directory, personalised and collated a letter together with a sponsor form to over 2000 branches and departments of the bank.

John, who was by this time working in London, in Head Office, approached the messengers in the bank's Post Room. He asked if they would send out our massive mailing through the internal post. They immediately agreed which saved a vast postage bill and the necessity of fully addressing the envelopes.

Each weekend my excess baggage related to a weighty consignment of internal mailings to be passed on to John. The help received from those learning of the background to our activities was incredible. We were all working hard to succeed and appeared likely to do so, assuming of course we safely completed our assignment.

Having received help and co-operation from all walks of life, at last the long awaited day arrived. Eric had earlier taken our luggage, including lots and lots of clean clothes just waiting to become soiled clothes, ready for our return in two weeks. Phew, what a lovely hygienic thought!

Philip had been collected the previous day and was given a right royal send off. Every resident and on-duty staff member gathered in the courtyard to wish him well and a safe return. He was handed a large good luck card and we were on our way. Arriving at Wooburn Green, he was not too happy and not able to appreciate 100% what had been loaded into the camper van for his use. In his case, seeing was believing. Not travelling to Penzance with Eric in the van was probably the missing cog in his mind.

How we managed to get four bikes and four people into, and on top of, our fairly standard car for the eighteen mile journey to Reading still amazes me in retrospect. Somehow we managed it!

We arrived at Reading station full of nervous, bubbling apprehension. We unloaded and each took charge of a bike. Clutching our British Rail tickets and Helen her platform ticket we approached the ticket barrier. What a welcome greeted us - diplomacy at its best! "You can't take those bikes on a 125, the guard won't let you," said the collector on seeing our tickets.

"But we have tickets given to us by British Rail which includes the four bikes," I countered.

"Makes no odds mate, the guard is in charge of the train and what he says goes," sharply retorted the ticket collector. Having completed his spiel and no doubt to get us out of his way he let us through the barrier. A tense period then elapsed, not knowing what was going to happen when the train arrived from Paddington.

Despite the earlier rebuff, on the train's arrival we headed straight for the guard's van which, as it happened, was virtually empty. Upon seeing the bikes, the short rather rotund but so obviously very important guard was out of his van like a whippet out of a trap. "You can't bring those bikes on here," was his greeting.

Again I was the mouthpiece. "Why not, British Rail is one of our sponsors for a sponsored cycle ride starting at Land's End tomorrow morning! It includes the bikes. Here's the letter."

"I don't care," was the most indignant and helpful retort.

By this time, with John, at a distance, looking after an agitated Philip and with Helen equally disturbed, I had raised a good head of steam. Not to be beaten, I said, "If I have to lie in front of this train it will not leave this station until the bikes are on board." Pointing to my camera which was slung round my neck I continued, "I have a photograph of you looking out of the carriage as the train approached the station. The newspapers and ITV London who are to report our progress will love this story with you as the central character and villain - what will British Rail think of that?"

By this time a number of bystanders had gathered and were intrigued by, but not involved in, this impasse. I was also conscious that passengers on the train were starting to lean impatiently out of windows. Silence followed whilst my comments, which were a complete bluff, were digested. He was digging a hole for himself and didn't know how to back down without losing face.

In the meantime, the 125 driver, an avuncular sort of chap, had also arrived along the platform to see what was holding up the departure of his train. I repeated the story and told him the action I proposed to take and made to walk along the platform. He muttered something to the guard, who by this time was getting redder and redder in the face and looked as though at any minute he was likely to 'blow a gasket.' The driver shrugged his shoulders and wandered off.

Suddenly there was grudging progress amounting to almost a climb-down by the guard, but with a sting in the tail. With all the good grace of a snarling hyena he condescendingly said, "You can put three bikes in the van but not the fourth that will have to go on a slow train." In a far from calm state of mind we did as we were told and placed the three bikes to be used in the almost empty van and boarded the train.

Without time to say proper good-byes we left a bewildered looking Helen standing forlornly on the platform propping up the spare bike as the train pulled out of the station. We could only wave and hope she could sort out its onward transmission to Penzance. What an inglorious start to our adventure!

Whilst Philip was not 100% aware of what was going on he nevertheless fully appreciated that his Dad was annoyed. Having safely loaded the bikes ourselves we left the guards van and out of earshot he quietly said "silly man." He was of course right, what a Wally!

To make sure the bikes were not being damaged as the train headed west, after each stop I visited the guard's van, much to our new friend's irritation. Nothing appeared to change and after each visit I was able to reassure Philip everything was alright. Fascinated as he was watching the wires and pylons flash past as we sped along, he was still on edge and restless. Had the guard's attitude upset him more than we realised?

When the train crew changed and he saw the 'silly man' depart Philip seemed much better. Ironically, the new guard on the next inspection had a completely different attitude and told me not to worry. He would see the bikes were safe and sound. When told the story of the happenings at Reading he couldn't understand what the fuss had been about - he didn't run his train like that. We had been unlucky to meet a 'Little Hitler' and it spoilt the start of our journey and certainly increased Philip's unease.

After collecting her shattered thoughts, Helen went to the ticket office to put the remaining bike, as she thought, on the next slow train. The station staff had yet to finish their charm offensive. On asking for a ticket to transport the fourth bike to Penzance she was told "You can't send an unaccompanied bike on a train, it will have to go by Red Star."

"Where do I find that?" asked Helen.

"Down those stairs over there," was the next gem. Nobody offered to help her, so, with some difficulty, she descended the stairs with the bike, and for her trouble got a generous covering of oil from the chain as she went.   She paid for overnight carriage, BY TRAIN, to Penzance. Would it get there in time for collection the next morning?

We were duly met by an open-backed lorry at Penzance and transported to the Cable and Wireless College at Porthcurno, where a beaming Eric awaited our arrival.   Suddenly the previously pensive Philip was like a different person.   He was so pleased to see and address his friend Mr. Gibson.   It seemed he had not been able to fully comprehend what was going to happen and where the camper van, which he had not seen, would fit in?   Was the van the missing bit in his jig-saw puzzle, complete with our cases and more importantly his books?

There was a friendly welcome for us at the college and we soon settled in.   After dinner, the banner advertising our jaunt was fixed onto the camper van, which Philip read out aloud. After a quiet walk in the warm evening sunlight we retired for the night.   As a precaution for the next morning I suggested to Philip that he should not lock his bedroom door, just in case he was feeling awkward and I could not get into his room.

My night's sleep was virtually non-existent.   Suddenly, as I lay there my 'banking-bad-debt-type-syndrome' appeared and all that could go wrong during the following two weeks flashed through my mind.   Would the spare bike be at Penzance in the morning?   We would have to go on without it if it wasn't.   Would we have lots of bad weather? Would the bikes be O.K?   Would we somehow lose each other? Would one of us be ill?   Would we have an accident? Would our hosts be expecting us? I had organised everything and now was the time of reckoning. I would ring each of our hosts on the evening before our arrival to make sure they were expecting us. There was nothing I could do about the other worries but they just would not go away. The one justifiable worry, Philip, did not enter the equation!

Rising at 7 o'clock, I went to Philip's room.   No sign of worries with him - he was still fast asleep. I gently roused him and he was out of bed in a flash, all bright-eyed and bushy-tailed.   Quickly washed and shaved, he was soon ready for the day ahead. We all ate a hearty breakfast and were well set up for the long day in front of us. As we posed for photographs in the early morning sunlight prior to departure for Land's End, the chef very kindly passed a hamper to Eric - it was our provisions for the day.   Philip grabbed it and quickly loaded it onto the camper van.   He was in such a bubbly mood.   I thought, long may it last!

The small convoy departed for Land's End. We were ready for the start of Philip's adventure!

Chapter 19 - Land's End to John O'Groats - Our Daily Diary

Saturday 9th May - Lands End to Bodmin, 58miles - With our bikes unloaded from the lorry, Philip was still doing his impression of a rubber ball.   He was obviously very excited but sadly could not express his thoughts in words.

The staff from Cable & Wireless, who had looked after us well, remained to see us off along with a group of staff from Lloyds Bank, who had travelled from Penzance.   After a series of photographs to record the beginning of Philip's epic journey, and a final check to ensure the label identifying him was safely attached to the rear of his bicycle seat, we were ready for the off.   At 08.40 hours we started off on our momentous journey.

Philip charged off as if the 874 miles ahead of us would be completed before lunch!   John called for him to slow down and he did so, turning round with a big ear-to-ear grin on his face.

On such a beautiful spring morning this was a positive start but both John and I were aware we had fourteen long days ahead of us, with the sole mission of getting Philip safely to John O'Groats.   It seemed an awfully long way away at this particular juncture.   Would Philip get bored, tired or saddle-sore?   The possibilities were endless.

Eric, having seen us on our way, left for Penzance where we would join him to put the spare bike onto the roof of the camper van.   The first concern, would it be there?   By the time we arrived Eric had retrieved it from the parcel office and had bought a Daily Telegraph for Philip.   That pleased him, and the first likely tension had been catered for before it began!

The ride to Bodmin along the A38 was uneventful, except that Philip seemed displeased that we were later than anticipated in having lunch.   So well was the journey going we decided to cycle on an unscheduled twelve miles further to the Jamaica Inn on Bodmin Moor, where we left the bikes overnight and Eric ferried us back to the Tamblyn's home outside Bodmin.   John made a point of congratulating Philip on his cycling during the day, which pleased him.   Our only discomfort from our exertions, which we did not immediately realise, was the cumulative affect of the sun, which had shone onto our unprotected legs throughout the day.

The Tamblyn's had arranged a party with the local Group of Friends. It was very kind of them but it was hardly something we thirsted for after cycling some seventy miles! It was time for bed, and also, as it turned out, for our first problem. Philip, despite having a single bed, refused to have me sleeping in his bedroom. We were both very tired and whether he was trying to create an incident I didn't wait to see. I simply said, "O.K., so I'll go and sleep in the camper van," - which I did. It was a chilly uncomfortable night and I hoped this was not going to be the pattern of the next two weeks.

Sunday - Bodmin to Tiverton, 71 miles - All was well in the morning, with another sunny day in prospect. What a psychological boost it was to retrace our journey of the previous evening and be driven twelve miles over the moor to collect our bikes! Thankfully, we had reduced the day's potential journey as, whilst I had realised from the map contours there would be ups and downs passing through Devon, I had had no idea how severe and frequent those hills would be. Surely we went up more than down, it certainly seemed like it!

On stopping for lunch, Philip homed in on a sign in the lay-by that read, 'Take your litter home'. We were reminded of this for the remainder of the trip. It was with some relief, after a 1 in 7 descent into Bickleigh, that we saw ahead a relatively flat landscape. At Tiverton, our scheduled destination, we again decided to travel on for a few miles and left our machines at a garage. For some reason it was now quite acceptable for me to share Philip's bedroom. Had I called his bluff the previous evening?

Monday – Tiverton to Bristol, 70 miles – True to the weather forecast we awoke to a cold wet morning. As we prepared for the day ahead and started our journey there was not too much enthusiasm from Philip - he lagged behind. Eric then suffered an escort's nightmare. In writing up his log for the previous day as he was sitting in a lay-by he missed us passing him and, when he came to move on, realised he had no idea if we were behind or ahead of him. He had to retrace the last few miles before he could move forward to find us, twenty miles up the road, sitting on a garage wall having the much-needed cup of coffee he had been scheduled to provide.

Eric's daily routine was to leave us at a given point, with his first priority to buy Philip's Daily Telegraph, along with the ingredients for sandwiches for lunch. He would then return and announce he would stop ahead, having made the coffee ready for our arrival. It would only be a short rest, so it saved time.

As part of our day we had a nightmare of a cyclist's detour to make in Bristol to the H.Q. of HFT where a celebratory cake awaited Philip. He was very much the centre of attention. It was such a relief to get out of Bristol and back onto the open road. Although it entailed a later than anticipated finish, we kept our twelve miles in hand.

Tuesday - Bristol to Kidderminster, 70 miles - Another miserable day, with an unwelcome detour into Gloucester to receive a cheque from the staff of the branch where David, one of my ex-assistants now worked. It was not that we were ungrateful for their support but quite simply that, in cold wet weather, I now had only one thing on my mind - getting from A to B each day as simply and quickly as possible. Stopping and starting, coupled with detours, breaks up the cycling rhythm. With Philip having to be coerced by John to ride after lunch it was a seemingly long and uninteresting ride to Kidderminster. We arrived in pouring rain and were thankful for the earlier miles in hand. Our hosts quickly dealt with our wet clothes and we were ready for the next morning.

Wednesday - Kidderminster to Tarporley, 65 miles – It was still a northerly wind as we headed for Tarporley, using the busy A41 for a time. James was making good progress, with John and me now realising that he would come along in his own time and if he wanted to stop to watch traffic on a bridge, so be it. At least he was happy and looking forward to meeting new hosts each evening.

By late afternoon it was sunny again and, as the wind had veered in our favour, we recovered our miles in hand. It is amazing how one always feels a certain element of fatigue as the final miles towards the completion of a gruelling day's schedule slowly count down and then suddenly, it becomes much easier to cycle when the allotted miles for the day have been completed. The fatigue goes, the legs seem to get stronger and the additional miles peel away. We always asked Philip if we should continue. He never protested at our plans, he was simply enjoying the daily journey wherever it went and however long it took. Each night we would look at the map and talk about where we were going the next day. Philip would always conclude with the number of the cycling day just passed and how many more days there were to go.

During our quest for publicity we had interested ITV London who, that night, were going to include Philip's exploits in their six-o'clock show, 'Help'. Reading in the morning newspaper the headline, 'Reporting on the progress of Philip Childs, who is cycling from Lands End to John O'Groats' was exciting for Philip. Before departure they had photographed him riding along a country road with yellow oilseed rape as a background. In the studio they panned onto the photographs to create cycling movement within their report. Sadly we missed the programme as we were still cycling. Imagine a simple story like that getting reported in today's drama filled world. We would need, at the very least to have had a serious accident to get a mention!

Thursday – Tarporley to Lancaster, 70 miles - Oh no, what had we done to deserve those continuing northerly winds coupled with heavy squally showers as we negotiated the dangerous, polluted east to west trunk roads linking Manchester and Liverpool, and the appalling water-filled potholes and cobbled roads of Warrington and Wigan! It was slippery and treacherous riding.

With poor conditions this, of course, would be the day when we needed all our patience with Philip. Early on we found he was not behind us. We waited but he didn't appear. In a state of panic we retraced our route and found he had decided to take a longer than normal look at the traffic below and was still happily sitting on a bridge. Seeing us returning he decided to get under way again. It was only a few miles later, again hanging back, with John and I having passed an exit slip road on the A49 and passing under a junction bridge, that we realised Philip had shot up the exit slip road. "Oh s**t now what's the little s*d up to" was the lament. Hardly had we thought that we'd have to slip back and retrieve him than, with a big grin on his face, he merrily flashed down the entrance slip road on the other side of the bridge. He had overtaken us! It was left to John to issue a mild rebuke.

John's and to a lesser extent Mr. Gibson's presence in acting as foils for me in counter-acting Philip's wayward demeanour was working well. He had the utmost respect for both of them.

During lunch it rained heavily, causing us to shelter in the van for $1\frac{1}{2}$ hours. As we had twenty-six miles to go to reach Lancaster, we decided we must make a dash for it, if you can, over that distance on a bike into the gusting wind! Now was the time for enthusiastic encouragement from John, resulting in Philip, who at first had been reluctant even to pop his head out of the van into the elements, becoming a hero during that afternoon. He rode on gamely and quickly learnt to slip-stream the camper van, whenever he could. If, however, John or I joined him in getting a tow so to speak, he would quietly fall back and be exposed to the elements. We left him to it and, three hours later, we all arrived bedraggled at the 3* hotel where we had been billeted for the night by the Lancaster Rotary Club.

After a hard day what bliss it was to be shepherded to a comfortable warm room. As soon as our showers and dinner were over Philip soon settled down in front of the television and fell asleep, not for the first time, exhausted and still sitting in a chair!

By the next morning our clothes had been laundered and dried and awaited our collection at the reception desk, along with a donation of £20. The continuing kindness we were experiencing was amazing. It seemed that everywhere we went folk wanted to identify with us and what we were setting out to do.

Friday – Lancaster to Penrith, 55 miles - Philip was counting the days down as we progressed. We enjoyed a comfortable ride to Kendal, with a stop for mint cake, followed by the long haul up Shap amid blustery hailstorms. Philip made remarkably steady progress but protested about the cold as we descended from the summit into the bitter northerly wind. Our early evening arrival into Penrith saw the distant Lake District hills turn white with snow as we watched.

Saturday 16th May – Penrith to Hawick, 61 miles - It was good to be alive. We enjoyed a most pleasant day as we cycled through the beautiful Border Country. We had been on the road for a week and what a thrill to cross over into Scotland but seemingly not for Philip. Neither by this time was he too interested in the commemorative photographs we wished to take under the sign depicting the border. Did he see this as the start of the rundown of his adventure, as we were in our eighth day and only six to go? He probably didn't appreciate that Scotland was nearly as 'long' as England – it was just the number of outstanding days which were important to him. Later on in the morning he was far from impressed when Eric handed him a copy of the Scotsman, as we had now left Daily Telegraph country. He thumbed through the paper during the coffee break and, after finding the 'hatched, matched and despatched' columns seemed to be more at peace with his new newspaper.

We overshot Hawick, travelling on to Galashiels, leaving our bikes at the nearby fire station. We had regained our miles in hand once more.

Sunday - Hawick to Edinburgh, 45 miles - Not the best of days, with yes, a northerly wind and light rain all day. Even our miles in hand and a shorter journey scheduled, not everything went according to plan – far from it! Our first problem was soon upon us, and it was a major one.

As we were approaching the suburbs of Edinburgh with, most unusually, the camper van close behind, with some very obvious urgency Eric gave a loud and lengthy blast on his horn. The van had conked out with what was later diagnosed as a broken timing belt. With no chance of a repair on a Sunday and the Monday being a local holiday we were faced with cycling without escort for probably two days.

We felt naked as we filled our pannier bags with everything we could carry and set off for Edinburgh, leaving Eric to sort out the van as best he could. An added complication was that he was due to meet Muriel, his wife, (Mrs. Gibson to Philip) from a train as she was joining us for the remainder of the journey. As Muriel and Eric were scheduled to stay with friends on the other side of the city in the evening this added to Eric's problems. There was nothing we could do to help so we left a forlorn looking Eric at the roadside awaiting a recovery vehicle.

In our hour of need we made contact with our hosts for the night, and they were both positive and kind. With us having no idea where we were in relation to their house within the vastness of Edinburgh they simply said, "Ride to the Forth Bridge if you want, leave your bikes at the garage there and we will collect you when you are ready and return you tomorrow morning." How kind of them. The immediate problem was solved!

Our Perth hosts, when I made the evening call, were also ready to do whatever was necessary on the Monday to keep us on schedule. We began to feel much more secure.

Monday – Edinburgh to Perth, 54 miles – It was a still fine morning as we crossed the Forth Bridge. Philip was interested in the lorries and trains also crossing. With full pannier bags we were now cycling with much more weight than previously, and it felt like it. Philip, without Mr. Gibson, was in a different and unsure frame of mind, keeping very close to John and me on the road. There was no dawdling behind us today! We made good progress to Perth, with new road layouts reducing the planned mileage. We made the most of this as the next day would be a difficult journey through the Grampian Mountains.

Having overshot Perth by eighteen miles we were almost to Pitlochry, from where our hosts very kindly collected us. What a surprise and relief to find, on our way back to Perth, Eric and Muriel in their camper van approaching from the opposite direction, trying to find us. Philip was pleased, as we all were, to again have the company of Mr. and Mrs. Gibson. In 1987 mobile phones were not available as they are today.

Tuesday – Perth to Kingussie, 72 miles - What a day! Although Philip climbed steadily up the Drumochter Pass he complained about the biting winds, which became stronger as we reached the 1507 foot summit of the pass. With the bitter wind still in our faces we descended to Kingussie, but not before my lowest mental point on the trip. I stopped to take some photographs and by the time I remounted, the rest of the party were round the corner and out of sight. Tired and struggling to get any momentum into the wind, despite cycling downhill, I could have cried I felt so forlorn. It was with great relief I reached the camper van, parked up for lunch, a mile or so further on.

After lunch, with a strengthening wind, Eric, with the aid of slip-streaming, virtually pulled us down to Kingussie. Philip had by now become very adept at using this form of assistance. What a picturesque scene Kingussie made in the setting sun, with the snow-clad Grampians in the distance. Surprisingly Philip was not a problem with the sleeping arrangements, as he was to sleep in a bunk bed. With Muriel now with us and the camper van fully in use there was no margin for nonsense. Philip retained his thirst for meeting his new hosts each evening. He couldn't wait to be introduced. He was the celebrity and we were the bit-parts in his adventure. Without exception, every host soon got onto his wavelength and made him feel very special. They always made a point of wishing him well and waving us off on our way. We arrived as strangers and left as friends.

Wednesday – Kingussie to Munlochy (Black Isle), 58 miles - An early start today as, complete with hats, gloves and scarves we passed Aviemore and set off up the 987 foot Slochd Pass. At the summit we were looking forward to the long run down into Inverness. All was going too well and, at coffee, we were too confident and cock-a-hoop regarding our progress to date. Hardly had we restarted when John's front wheel suddenly collapsed and he was left writhing in agony in the middle of the busy A9. It seemed to happen in an instant but fortunately, at that moment, none of the heavy lorries were thundering past. Philip, at that point, had already started his descent. Cycling into the headwind, he couldn't hear my calls and I had to cycle as quickly as I could to catch up with him and bring him back. On seeing John, his friend, in some distress, and the buckled wheel of his bike, Philip was visibly upset. Being highly agitated he stomped up and down the grass verge, unable to express his feelings. He didn't calm down again until the wheel was changed and we were once more underway. Thank goodness we had the replacement bike available, for the use its spare wheel.

Rather deflated, with John in some discomfort, we descended the long gradient into Inverness in bright sunshine. There, for the first time, Philip saw John O'Groats marked on a signpost. He was clearly excited and read the distance of 125 miles out loud. We carried on, and during the afternoon crossed the Black Isle.

In the evening the care rolls were reversed. Philip became very attentive about his friend John's poorly swollen arm. Keeping his arm covered John reassured him that he was not too badly hurt and would be able to ride again in the morning. But would he?

The accident wasn't mentioned during the routine evening calls home to either Helen or Chris, John's wife. Our progress was reported, together with a map reference so that Bill, on receiving Helen's daily call, could mark the map hanging in the hall at Downley Grange, to show how close we were to our destination.

Thursday – Munlochy to Brora, 60 miles - John had a poor night's rest but was determined to continue. Philip was still showing real signs of concern for John's welfare and again John reassured him that he wasn't going to be beaten and give up at this late stage. Philip's concern dissipated as soon as we were back on the road.

Off we went, crossing the Cromarty Firth, where we had a choice between the easier coastal road or the harder, but shorter climb over Struie to Bonar Bridge. Despite being in some pain, from what was later diagnosed as two cracked bones in his elbow, John said we should go the shorter way. We made quite remarkable progress but the descent from the summit was obviously painful for him, particularly when he had, by necessity, to continually apply his brakes – Ouch!

We rode down to Bonar Bridge and stopped to watch the fishermen in coracles trying to net salmon. This was followed by a glorious ride, in bright sunshine, along the yellow-gorse-lined roads of the Dornoch Firth. Twenty years on it is still an unforgettable memory, such was the warmth, beauty, and stillness of those few miles.

During our break for lunch beside Loch Brora the northerly wind was again strengthening. Despite this we decided to cycle beyond Brora (our next scheduled stop), but not without a protest from Philip. We had asked him what he wanted to do but, just like the army sergeant major asking his recruits if everything is alright, we didn't listen to the answer and continued with our plans. "Why oh why did we ignore Philip?," we were soon to ask ourselves as, immediately after leaving Brora, we had no alternative but to abandon our efforts for the day. The now gale-force winds were swirling down off the surrounding mountains to such an extent that we had little control over our bikes. It was quite frightening, and dangerous in the extreme to continue.

The wind was not the only looming problem. To date, Philip was assuming we would have a long train journey back to Reading. He was not aware of our intention to fly home. Having not flown before this would most certainly have given him something to get wound up about. As a team effort we casually mentioned the bad weather in the south and the havoc it was causing and left it at that. Seeds were, however, being gently sown regarding alternative modes of transport.

I hardly slept that night - what would Philip's reaction be on learning about the flight and would the wind continue to rage and stop us completing the final leg of our journey the next day? If necessary could we complete, with a lot of hassle, on the Saturday and still be ready to catch our flight. It may have been only sixty-five miles to John O'Groats but it would have been madness to even entertain cycling in such conditions if the gales continued.

Friday – Brora to John O'Groats, 65 miles - My prayers were answered! Overnight the wind had moderated although it didn't sound like it in the exposed, very basic skiing chalets where we were billeted.

Despite the severity of the terrain, we enjoyed the rides over Helmsdale and Berriedale. Although John's arm was easier the descents still caused him great discomfort. With lunch taken at the 'dead centre' of Wick in a lay-by outside the cemetery, we were ready for the final seventeen miles of our adventure.

After a hurried lunch, Philip could not wait to get started and soon he was off, just like the rocket which left Land's End two weeks earlier, so much so we had to remind him that he could still have an accident. He didn't listen, here was a man with a mission, and sped down the slope into the John O'Groats clinker-covered car park to announce to our small but triumphant group, "**Philip** was first and Dad and John were dead heat second." It was amazing - where did that vocabulary suddenly spring from?

* * * * * * *

Set out below are the recollections of Eric, (Mr. Gibson) and John regarding their association with Philip. I am pleased to say they are both held in the highest regard by him and he is always pleased to renew his acquaintance with them.

Memories of Time Spent with Philip Childs by Eric Gibson

In my early acquaintance with Philip, he always seemed to be a very likeable lad, with a phenomenal memory for birthdays. His reaction to unforeseen events was sometimes unpredictable. To him, small things could loom very large, but there were times when he would accept unexpected events quite calmly. When trying to deal with such situations, he seemed to be locked up within himself, no doubt struggling to understand what was happening.

On the 1987 Cycle Ride, he was quite reliable on the road, happy to cycle ahead of the other members of the team. When leading he confidentially negotiated roundabouts and road junctions. The prospect of having to cycle day after day did not appear to worry him, though on one day he did not want to ride into a strong wind and cycled most of the day sheltering closely behind the escorting van - and who could blame him? Only on one day did he need a lot of persuading to restart after a lunch break - the weather was unpleasantly wet.

He liked to have the Daily Telegraph each day (mostly to find the cricket scores): this was not possible in Scotland, and he was not keen to accept the Scotsman as the next best thing.

A few memories from the ride illustrate his character.

One evening, I think at Kinguissie, he was not able to watch a particular television programme, and he was very awkward the whole evening - typical of a teenager but not perhaps a 21 year old.

At the overnight stop on the Black Isle, he was not in a particularly good mood as the cycling had not been very pleasant, but he suddenly decided that he would allocate the bedrooms to the various members of the party - all in a very pleasant and acceptable manner.

Once the ride had finished, the cyclists were booked to return to London by air. Philip did not think he wanted to fly, but wanted to go home by train. He was persuaded that the train service had closed down and the only way he could get back quickly to see his mum was to fly.

On the drive to the airport at Wick, he was not happy and sat holding his copies of the accumulated newspapers and locked up within himself. As soon as we reached the airport, he jumped out of the van calling to the others to join him getting to the plane. What a change, and a relief to us all.

* * * * * * *

My Friend Philip Childs by John Parker

I probably first met Philip in late 1985 but I only came to "know" him when I committed to joining him and his father, Andy, on the project to release the potential within Philip to cycle from Land's End to John O'Groats. It was during the two week 874 mile ride that Philip and I became friends and started a friendship that is still on-going, after twenty years. I think a shared goal in the first phase and then a shared achievement brought out a friendship that did not necessarily rely on communication. Philip just knew that we were doing something worthwhile together and added to this was that he was with his father as well which made the ride even more special for him. Philip and I seem to connect on a level that does not require either of us to be overly emotional towards each other, we have just settled on a mutual acceptance of unspoken friendship. So, given this almost contradictory position, how do I know we are friends?

A few examples come to mind that also demonstrate to me that Philip is more aware of what is around him than perhaps he consistently demonstrates. During the ride we awoke to a pretty foul weather day and Philip would have been very happy to stay watching the television rather than getting out on our bikes in the wet. I think Andy had given up on convincing Philip, so it was my turn. I decided not to appeal to Philip but rather lay out that we had no choice if we were to achieve our challenge and at one point just tossed a bag of kit to him as I moved to leave the room. Our world moved into slow motion as Philip weighed up his options, decided to catch the kit bag and, without any protest, followed me and we were off on another day's ride.

A year or so later, by which time I was living on the Island of Jersey, Andy asked Philip if he would like to visit us. One known problem though from the cycle ride journey home was Philip's fear of flying so there was every chance he would decline. Happily, if getting on a plane was the only way for him to visit his friend John Parker, then so be it and fly he did. Each time we now meet, not usually more than once a year, there is no doubt in my mind that when we shake hands we are both pleased to re-connect. I am naturally the more enthusiastic but I am never less than certain that Philip is equally happy for us to catch up, albeit for a two minute exchange of communication on a standard level. As evidence to support instinct, on one occasion we telephoned from the car to say we would arrive in ten minutes' time. Much to the amazement of Helen, his mum, on hearing this Philip proceeded to comb his hair so as to be presentable for our arrival.

Philip knows me, remembers our shared experiences and we both accept a friendship that is based on a handshake and brief hello, how are you etc. and then contented shared silence with gentle interruption from time to time. No need to push at doors - we know each other and long may that continue. (John has been a special friend of Philip for twenty years. This friendship was initially cemented during his time as the riding escort on the 1987 Land's End to John O'Groats Cycle Ride.)

Chapter 20 - Celebrity Status

On a cold, overcast afternoon in May, with the wind gusting from the north what a cheerless, godforsaken appearance John O'Groats portrayed. Across the Pentland Firth, the nearby Orkney Islands were shrouded in mist and on the mainland there was not a soul in sight to share in our triumph. The much photographed sign post pointing to Land's End 874 miles away, stood in splendid isolation, with the forlorn looking waterside John O'Groats hotel looking tired and drab - what an anti-climax. Although it was such a melancholy scene, the gloomy surroundings could not stop us, adorned in our hooded anoraks, from celebrating and basking in our success for a short while. Helen had put a bottle of champagne aboard the camper van which, after two weeks of being, 'shaken, but not stirred,' was very carefully uncorked, ready for Philip to spray anyone within range. He loved the experience, and he knew exactly what to do, he had seen it all on the telly many times, and now it was his turn. His face said it all.

After posing for photographs by the signpost, and with the excitement subsiding, Muriel took the initiative, as the best teller of 'white lies" we had on board to talk to Philip about getting home. She told him there had been, through the bad weather in England, land-slides which had blocked some of the railway lines. This would mean the only way to get home to see Mum on Saturday, would be to go to Wick and catch an aeroplane to London.

This news was obviously a 'bolt out of the blue' to Philip. He froze and incoherently muttered something, which he continued to repeat whilst he mulled over the issue. Were we now in for trouble?

With the bikes loaded into the camper van we returned to Wick. The adventure was over and, whilst feeling pleased, relieved and elated for Philip there was an underlying feeling of anti-climax as we left the four bikes in the care of the station master at Wick. Sending them by rail to High Wycombe, not just one bike but four unaccompanied was no problem whatsoever and it belied the nonsense endured at Reading two weeks earlier. Perhaps they were accompanying each other!

John, in praising Philip, said how much he had enjoyed his company and was looking forward to flying with him to London. Philip was not so sure but the previously terrified look had gone.

Our hosts in Wick were certainly charming, but I found it almost impossible to enthuse with them about our achievement. Was I physically or mentally exhausted through our endeavours over the past fourteen days? Had looking after Philip taken its toll or was it all now an anti-climax having completed his experience of a life time? A bit of each I suspect but all I wanted to do was to just sit quietly and let events pass me by.

Having briefed our hosts regarding our foreseen travel problems the next day they casually mentioned the rail delays during dinner. There was no visual reaction from Philip. Was it sinking in?

On rising on the Saturday morning, Philip enjoyed his breakfast and, to my great relief, seemed in good form. Having slept I also felt more sociable and apologised for my apparent lethargy the previous evening.

Upon us all meeting up later in the morning it was agreed we would treat flying home as a fait accompli. We bought Philip his copy of the Scotsman, which had now become an acceptable alternative to the Daily Telegraph. Whilst he was thoughtful, he appeared quite content collecting up his newspapers covering the past two weeks.

Purposely leaving little time to spare, Eric drove us all to the airport. What now, I thought, if Philip refuses to budge? I kept my distance as John and Muriel chatted to him about the events of the past two weeks and praised him for his cycling expertise. Flying was not mentioned. I wondered, was he listening to a word they were saying?

OH YES he was! Hardly had the van stopped than up leapt Philip. He was out of the door in a trice, carrying his heavy plastic bag full of newspapers. Without a shred of inhibition he loudly announced to us, "This is Wick Airport." All was well and he was obviously relishing the thought of this new experience. If only he could or would communicate his feelings!

Our plans to leave little time to reflect at the airport were soon in tatters. The Loganair flight to Orkney and Shetland had yet to pass through going north. There would be a ninety-minute delay. Just what we didn't need!

As Philip and I stood gazing into the clear atmosphere with high white cloud cover he excitedly pointed and said, "Here it is." A small white twin-engined plane with a red stripe around the body at passenger window level was coming in to land. Despite the strong cross-wind buffeting the plane on its approach to the runway the touch down was perfect. So far so good! It was an agonising wait for G-BMAR to reappear from the north and for it to become our turn to board. Philip, by this time, had taken on the air of an 'old campaigner'. "This way please," he said to John, me and the other six passengers. He was up the steps and on board with his safety belt fastened in a flash - another worry was over.

It was a glorious flight to Edinburgh over the snow-covered peaks of the Grampian Mountains and, further south, to see the patchwork quilt of fields below - they were dominated by the bright yellow oil seed rape flowers.

John explained to Philip we had another flight to catch. It would be a much larger aeroplane, the British Airways Super Shuttle to Heathrow, London. Philip was far from overawed as we waited in the departure lounge; he was taking it all in his stride. As the now-seasoned traveller he confidently alighted from his second flight at Heathrow, complete with his W.H. Smith plastic bag full of old newspapers, and his Saturday copy of the Scotsman tucked firmly under his arm.

Helen and Alice, along with John's wife Chris, were at the airport to meet us. We were whisked off to a Welcome Home party at Wooburn Green, but not before Chris asked John what was wrong with his arm. Our secret about the fall had never been a secret as both Helen and Chris, on receipt of the Wednesday evening telephone call, knew something was amiss - ugh, women's intuition!

Philip was quite overwhelmed with the excitement of the day and, for the first time, I was able to relax.

The bikes arrived safely back at High Wycombe and Philip returned to his life in care with HFT.

What a welcome back to Downley Grange he received! Bill had asked for us to telephone him when we were some fifteen minutes away so that he could gather the residents and staff together to await our arrival. Everyone was assembled in the central courtyard, which was decked with bunting. There was a large "Congratulations and Welcome Back" sign together with a table laden with food and pomagne.

Bill toasted Philip's achievement and his safe return. To our amazement Philip responded by popping his head out through the bars of the cycle rack covering the open sun roof of the car and, with a raised glass, called out, "Cheers everybody!"

Before Helen and I left for home Bill said a quiet well done and confided he had had serious doubts we would ever start the journey let alone complete it. It had never seriously crossed my mind that we mightn't be successful. I hadn't had the time to think otherwise. Philip had been superb in concentration and endeavour and once again confounded his doubters.

The two weeks had benefited Philip's confidence, misplaced as it often was. It was there for all to see, so much so that on the 1987 B.H.F. London to Brighton Cycle Ride, being as fit as fleas from our endeavours of only three weeks earlier, he simply did not want to cycle with me. As he tagged onto other groups it was such a worry keeping track of him that it became our last such ride.

At the July meeting of Downley Grange's Family Staff Association, Joe Ede, the Chairman, had asked Philip to come along to the start of the meeting. The room was full of staff and other resident's parents, which made for an intimate atmosphere. Joe, in congratulating Philip on his successful completion of the Lands End to John O'Groats cycle ride, presented him with his first ever silver trophy. He was quite overcome with emotion on being recognised in this way. His eyes glistened as he thrust the cup up over his head.

Despite the increased attention on his return to Downley Grange, the feel-good factor soon diminished and the frustrations resurfaced. Normal service was resumed with HFT!

By the time of the September '87 Review, Philip had moved into a newly located ground floor single room within the main house, which resulted in bed-times being easier to manage. There had been ten outbursts during July, when Bill was away, and five during August. Philip undoubtedly responded to Bill's style of management, as did we all. It had been observed he was often agitated around tea time. Helen mentioned that, at Wooburn Green he was always allowed to watch the 6 o'clock News. Could this have been a contributory factor?

HFT, through Bill, had been enquiring of The Burden Institute in Bristol whether they could make any recommendations for possible medical control of Philip's outbursts.   Their Consultant Neuro-psychiatrist suggested Carbomasapine as a likely drug.   Dr. Hughes concurred, as it was quite possible Philip was suffering from epileptic-form brain activity.   To monitor its success a base line observation of him would be essential, with stability of his life style also being imperative.

To us anything was now worth a try.   Having been in the care of the Trust for almost three years he could not go on as he was and something had to be done.   To hear about and understand the continuing outbursts and aggression towards others at this stage was no less upsetting now than it had been when it started.

On the home front, Alice was happy, and doing well at Newark. Out of the blue I received a surprise telephone call from the Regional General Manager of the bank offering me promotion to the post of District Manager responsible for Oxfordshire, based in Aylesbury.   I was delighted to accept his offer and another move of house was in the offing.

Sadly, this would upset Helen's first employment, as a Special Welfare Assistant looking after a young boy at a school in Beaconsfield with Oriel's Disease (brittle bones).   With her experience of life she was ideal for the job and loved the challenge.

With the sponsor money from Philip's Land's End to John O'Groats cycle ride now only trickling in, and as HFT were celebrating their 25th Anniversary with a Sunday evening 'Stars and Brass Charity Gala Night' at the Bristol Hippodrome, I suggested this would be an opportune time for Philip to formally make a cheque presentation to the Trust.   It was agreed that this would set the seal on his achievement.   We travelled to Bristol on the previous Friday for a photo call.   The local newspapers took photographs outside the theatre of Philip sitting astride his bike, holding the proposed presentation cheque aloft.

The lady organising the event was charming but infuriating.   She insisted on holding Philip's arm and shepherding him along as if he was fragile and would fall to bits if he wasn't closely monitored. Philip tried to pull away from her.   He didn't need a guiding or supporting arm, far from it.

On this occasion as there was a current production at the theatre we were only briefly permitted to see inside and behind the scenes.

Sunday came, and along with Helen we made our second 200 mile round trip taking two bikes with us to Bristol. I decided I would not be involved and that this should be Philip's evening. The presentation was scheduled to open the second half of the show. On our arrival at the theatre, as the North Skelton BSC Teeside Band, followed by the Band of the Royal Marines were rehearsing, we did not have an opportunity to mount the stage to work out a routine. How was Philip going to cope with this? He needed to know exactly what he would be expected to do.

Philip and I missed Richard Stilgoe's contribution, which concluded the first half. Whilst we waited in the wings, Philip was completely overawed to find both Leslie Crowther and Lonnie Donegan, whose rendering of 'My Old Man's a Dustman' always tickled his sense of humour, congratulating him on his cycling feats. Both were interested enough to want to know what the financial result was. To their amusement I helped Philip to tell them, as he was getting his hundreds, thousands, and pounds in a bit of a pickle.

With the curtain down and the stage deserted, Philip in his blue shorts and grey John O'Groats sweater practised cycling onto the centre of the stage, pulling his bike onto a borrowed stand, removing the large presentation cheque from his pannier and handing it over to a vacant Master of Ceremonies podium at the front edge of the stage. In real time the cheque was to be accepted on behalf of HFT by Richard Baker.

As the interval concluded, a concerned Richard Baker appeared holding a cardboard box, asking what was to happen when the film about the work of HFT, which was preceding the presentation, had concluded. Tensions rose as the curtain remained closed due to delays because of a malfunction of the projector. Philip continued rehearsing, watched by Richard, who appeared petrified that something completely unscheduled might occur during the presentation. I assured him Philip would not be erratic in his behaviour. He was in good form so there would be nothing to worry about.

After what seemed an eternity, the short film concluded with a brief reference to Philip's Land's End to John O'Groats journey on behalf of HFT. As Philip's face faded from the screen the curtains opened and the stage was illuminated. Richard referred to the film and announced, as it was not printed in the programme, the presence of Philip to make his unscheduled presentation.

Having held him back until the introduction was over, the spotlight suddenly swung from Richard to Philip and I gave him a gentle push from the wings of the stage. Off he went to the small stand centrally placed so that he had to walk a few paces to reach Richard. To polite applause, and with great aplomb, our earlier brief rehearsals were carried out to perfection. As the spotlight brightened Philip grabbed the presentation cheque from his pannier, which was large in more ways than one, and right on queue he unfurled it above his head. There were gasps from those in the front rows who could see the amount. Having been handed the cheque, Richard immediately announced to the 75% of the audience who could not see the amount that it was for £53,590.22. (Based on inflation of 104% since 1987 and with say 80% of the donations Gift Aided an equivalent amount in 2010 would be some £135.000)

The earlier reserved applause crescendoed and died again, ahead of Philip being presented by Richard with a pewter mug in recognition of his endeavours on behalf of the Trust.

The earlier acknowledgement was but a whimper compared to the thunderous acclamation received when the mug was triumphantly thrown up above his head. They loved the spontaneity of his action as he left the stage. By now tears were streaming down my face and there was a dabbing of eyes in the audience. Whilst he obviously enjoyed the ceremony and adulation, as he came off stage it was very much a case of 'job done' as we made our way back to our seats.

As part of our celebrations the following Christmas we were invited to Hampton to visit Ed., Mary and their three girls. It was arranged 'the children' should go to the races at Kempton Park.

We all viewed the horses as they paraded and Philip chose a scruffy looking little nag for the first race. It won easily and standing aloof, some fifteen yards from the rest of us, as it safely negotiated the last fence he turned to us with a big knowing smile on his face.

Whether it was expertise or just knowing the names of the horses from his copious reading of the Daily Telegraph we will never know but the only person to have a profitable afternoon was Philip. He picked three winners and very proudly placed his four £10 notes on the tea table. His expertise was the evening's talking point!

As a direct consequence of the May Cycle Ride in having travelled from one end of the country to the other, by whatever means, we were entitled to, and became, members of the Jogle Association. We sent the editor of their magazine a copy of our diary, which was received by members a few days before we attended their winter weekend at Newquay. The event incorporated their annual dinner on the Saturday evening. This would be another new experience for Philip as a direct result of his earlier endeavours. I had told him that he would, during the evening, be presented with a certificate in front of everyone to commemorate our big cycle ride last May. The thought of this pleased him.

On arrival in Newquay, we entered the foyer of the hotel to see on a side table a whole array of trophies on display. They belonged to the Jogle Association. Philip was quick to spot the name of one of his cricketing heroes, Ian Botham on the centrally placed large Eagle Trophy.

Looking very smart and so obviously very pleased with himself in his sports jacket, complete with his emblazoned Jogle tie, we joined the pre-dinner bar reception.

Most of the members present had read our Cycle Ride diary, with Tricia, the editor, having added at the end, in very bold type 'words fail me on such a tremendous achievement. Many, many congratulations Philip.' He virtually purred with pride when a number of them, on realising who he was, came over to congratulate him on his endeavours.

Unusually, he seemed to enjoy being part of the large gathering. Just to see him in such fine form made the long journey worthwhile.

At the table of ten for dinner there was a common conversation theme from members, relating to their travels in making the 'end to end' journey. One had walked, another had ridden a vintage motor cycle and two others had cycled. Whilst Philip was not able to contribute in other than single words by way of reply to questions put his way, he was very obviously aware of the implications of the tales and place names being mentioned. Via my recollections, some of the chatter involved Philip and how we had fared on our memorable journey some eight months earlier. He seemed to relish his first attendance at such an occasion, and the noise and numbers in the crowded room did not faze him.

With his pint of shandy in front of him he was totally relaxed. He obviously felt part of the scene and important. After it had been 'piped in', he tucked into his first ever portion of haggis, followed by a good helping of roast beef.

At the conclusion of the meal chairman Dennis rose to say a few words before the presentation ceremony. He welcomed everyone and advised, after the celebrity status of the previous year's winner that the 1987 Eagle Trophy winner was of no lesser status. Hearing those words and knowing the Eagle Trophy was awarded to the person who had raised the largest amount of money from their 'End to End' trip, for the first time I fleetingly wondered if Philip was being referred to.

After a short comfort break the presentation ceremony was set to commence. On being re-seated I noticed Jerry, the custodian of the certificates to be presented, briefing Dennis about something in the direction of our table. On seeing this, my mind was in a tailspin. Could it imply that Philip was involved? With just the thought that it may be I already had a lump in my throat.

"The winner of our principal Eagle Trophy this year in cycling from Land's End to John O'Groats over the period 9th to 22nd May," began the Chairman, and on hearing these words I instantly knew the winner! As the tears poured down my cheeks, Dennis continued, "raising the incredible sum of £53,590.22 for The Home Farm Trust, a charity which provides residential care for the mentally handicapped, the trophy this year is awarded to –," (with a pronounced and dramatic pause) "- PHILIP CHILDS."

Philip had heard his name but did not realise the significance. With tears still streaming down my face, I said, "Philip! You've won a cup so go and get it." Needing no second bidding he jumped up and strode purposely to the 'top table' to collect his trophy, happily posing for photographs. With the formalities over, before returning to the table, the large glinting trophy was thrust gleefully above his head to milk the acclaim of the assembled diners. By now there was hardly a dry eye in the room!

Neither I nor Philip really took in the remainder of the ceremony. He simply stared in some disbelief at the shining trophy before him and I in turn simply stared at him, enjoying the greatest moment of his young life. Both our cups were overflowing. His eyes were sparkling in a way I had never seen before.

As soon as the meal was over and we were able, with good grace, to get away from the enthusiastic back-slapping members, we made for the nearest phone box, as a call to Mum was paramount. With my own excitement running high and hands trembling, I dialled the number. On hearing Helen's voice I simply said "Philip's here and he's got something to tell you." He grabbed the receiver and, without any greeting blurted out "I've won the cup and had 'aggis for tea!" That was it, a man of few words! I then had to explain to a by now equally excited, tearful Helen, the totally unexpected happy events of the evening.

The cup stood by his bed all night. After posing for more photographs the following morning it was handed back to Gerry for safe keeping, never to be held again - but was it really to be the end of the story?

Chapter 21 - Welcome Changes?

With the excitement of the Jogle Association Dinner weekend at Newquay over with, we made the long journey back to Downley Grange to be greeted by Bill.   Helen had already passed on the news of Philip's award. As he lived on site he spied us arriving and was out into the courtyard in a trice to shake Philip's hand, to say well done and to give him an affectionate slap on the back.   Philip purred, he hadn't been expecting this.

As he was not given a miniature Eagle Trophy to keep I found a suitable small replica, with a base so that his hero Ian Botham could be engraved on it, along with the other previous winners.   The trophy, from Philip's perception, then became more meaningful.   He decreed the cup should be kept in his bedroom at Wooburn Green.

Life seemed to be moving on apace in 1988.   I had settled easily into my role as a District Manager of the bank, based at Aylesbury. We sold our chalet bungalow at Wooburn Green at the asking price to the first person to view it.

House hunting in the Aylesbury area had also been settled.   A property was found in the nearby village of Bierton, set well back from the busy Aylesbury to Milton Keynes road.   From the particulars in the agent's handout coupled with my added description we spent a night of eager anticipation. As Philip was spending the weekend with us he could be involved from the outset and it was explained to him that we would be leaving Wooburn Green in the summer.   The deal was sealed at that visit.   He was pleased at the prospect of now having new cycling terrain to explore with his Dad. It all appeared to be taken on board.   He was quite relaxed about walking round the house with us and selected a back bedroom as his forthcoming domain.   Alice did likewise on her next visit home.

The Spring '88 Review of Philip's previous year was a more pleasant affair.   He had been on the prescribed drug Tegratol for some six months, and it appeared to be having a beneficial effect on his behaviour.   Whilst there were still too many outbursts and broken bottles for our liking it was recorded that the incidents had lessened both in number and severity.   The aftermath of a misdemeanour also seemed more under control.   The immediate knock-on effect of these improvements helped his quality of life considerably, as the staff now felt more able to approach him if he appeared to be unhappy. Were these at last encouraging signs?

Where he could, Bill was still allocating staff to cycle with Philip as this was seen as a safety valve for his energies. Additionally, he liked the one-to-one attention. If there were no staff available he would be permitted to cycle off on his own jaunts, first ensuring that he was at least equipped with some food and drink to take with him. Where he went and for how long he would be gone only he knew.

He was once seen by Bill at traffic lights at a road junction some fifteen miles away from Downley Grange. Bill was concerned finding him this distance from base. His dilemma was whether to interfere by letting him know he had seen him, or leave him to carry on and make his own way back, when he was ready. As Philip was heading in the direction of Downley Grange and Bill could see the label giving his personal details intact on his saddle, he decided to take the latter course of action. Soon after Bill's return to Downley Grange who should cycle down the approach road to the house but Philip Childs, blissfully unaware that anyone should have been in the slightest bit concerned about his ability to find his way back. He either had a built in compass or could read and interpret the signposts to make his way around. He certainly didn't use a map!

There were obviously risks attached to letting Philip express himself in this way and had we known when he was out on his own we would have lived a nightmare existence. HFT, through Bill, were sensible in their attitude to his way of life. They ensured as far as possible that his bike was serviced, with good tyres, and then had to let fate take its course. How lucky we were to have chosen a charity with such a realistic approach to Philip's needs, with a manager of Bill's calibre to supervise him with such understanding flexibility.

Although cycling was still number one in Philip's leisure activities, swimming on an organised basis was becoming a further pastime he enjoyed. He would attend once or twice a week and was becoming a strong swimmer. He was habitual in his actions in the pool. This did not matter as he was getting further exercise and was being occupied.

Whilst still rather aloof with other residents he seemed to select Cedric, another far from tranquil young man, for reassuring words if he had misbehaved. It was as if he was trying to mimic the likely reaction towards Cedric of a member of staff. He was selective in his relationships with staff, appearing to respond to male members more favourably, but he also had respect for the more authoritative females. He liked to know where he stood and reacted accordingly.

Dr. Hughes was still monitoring Philip's behaviour and commented that it could be a further five years before he would settle down. In the meantime, she warned, as one area of his personality stabilised another area could erupt! Were there new upsets, so far not experienced, round the corner to be contended with? We certainly hoped not.

Philip's was still a Jekyl and Hyde existence. Clean at home in Wooburn Green, without supervision he was a vagrant at Downley Grange. In addition to being destructive and uncompromising he could be bossy, a mimic, friendly and helpful with certain members of staff. Within the 'rounded picture' were there signs, despite the ongoing problems, that progress was being made? We so desperately hoped so.

Philip was no doubt a troublesome resident and a challenge to everyone at Downley Grange, and he was lucky in the extreme to have Bill as his manager. Bill, for his part, was thrilled with Philip's fundraising endeavours on behalf of the Trust, which, in turn, benefited the home.

As a tuba-playing member of the Co-operative Brass Band, Bill organised concerts, with HFT as the beneficiary. At one such event the previous year he had concluded the evening by apologising that the audience were having to sit on hard wooden chairs, and had then drawn an analogy of their plight and that of Philip's 'bum', as he was at that moment in Bodmin undertaking his epic cycling journey from Lands End to John O'Groats!

The following year Bill invited us, along with Philip, to a similar concert. Philip loved his music and sat enthralled. The chairs were still hard but it didn't matter! Bill had arranged for Peter Skellen, who regularly performed with Richard Stilgoe, to be the guest artist for the evening. A heart-throb for the ladies, Peter, resplendent in his maroon corduroy jacket, concluded his final seductive rendering of 'You're a Lady' to his own accompaniment at the piano.

After the applause for Peter had died down Bill took centre stage and reminded the audience of his words twelve months previously and how he had referred to Philip and his epic cycle ride. He continued,

"I am pleased to be able to report the ride was successfully completed and raised £53,540 for HFT." At this point Helen nudged Philip as if to say "he's talking about you," to be told to "shush." in an irritated tone! He knew full well Bill was referring to him and didn't need to be told! Bill continued, "In recognition of Philip's achievement could I ask Peter if he would present him with a small commemorative trophy on behalf of us all."

Philip who had listened intently to every word uttered by his mate Bill was out of his aisle chair and making his way to the stage before Peter had time to leave the piano stool and pick up the trophy. With Philip, by this time, already standing anxiously beside him, Peter congratulated him on what he had done and handed the trophy over. The pleasure on Philip's face was there for all to see and now, with his customary aplomb, he lofted the trophy over his head. He stood milking the applause for all he was worth. Again, he deserved his recognition, which continued into the darkened car park with complete strangers coming over to shake his hand. Once more he was the complete ambassador for HFT.

A few days before moving to Bierton we met Cyril and Miriam Quartermain in Maidenhead. We were pleased to see each other for the first time in almost five years, during which time Miriam had retired as head of Vinio House School. Pleasantries over Miriam said, "How is Philip getting on with HFT? We have followed his cycling exploits in the local newspapers. I always say to Cyril look what our Philip has done now! He is such an inspiration to others. He has achieved so much more than I ever thought he was capable of and his ability to concentrate over those long distances is amazing."

We related the behavioural problems, which had continued and intensified after Philip left Vinio House. She looked thoughtful and said, "I think he may well grow out of it as he matures but it may take some time: he is not a naturally aggressive person, far from it. It is a very lonely path that anyone in your position treads. Few people have any understanding of just how difficult your life can be. I admire what you have achieved with Philip." These were not cheap words, coming from a person such as Mrs. Quartermain - we had great respect for her, and her judgement. Sadly that was the last time we would see her as she died shortly afterwards.

The move to Bierton went smoothly. As always we kept Philip in the picture. On looking back he took each house move in his stride but moves or changes in his environment at Downley Grange were not so easily accepted. This was further evidence of the two worlds in which he appeared to live.

Philip busily took his belongings down the stairs and left them outside the front door for the removal men to load into the lorry. Everything packed, we moved off and he witnessed his possessions passing safely into Ransome House.

We left the house in chaos and headed for the 'French Horn' at Whitchurch, a smart, expensive establishment where the bank had agreed we could stay the night. It was very comfortable and, smartly dressed, we took our places for dinner. We were quietly studying the menu in anticipation of helping Philip to make his selections, when having taken in what was on offer he said with great purpose, "I haven't had smoked salmon lately." We were astounded, where did those most unexpected 'pearls of wisdom' come from? Much to his delight the smoked salmon was ordered and devoured with great relish.

Within days of the move to Ransome House, Grandma, who had been in hospital with heart problems, died. Despite having to bring up three young children after the death of my father when I was four and my brother and sister nine and two respectively, she had retained an infectious zest for life. The children always looked forward to her visits, especially as, in their younger days, she always concluded her stay by taking us all out for a meal. Both Philip and Alice were greatly saddened by this loss. One of the legacies from her life, of which we had to ensure HFT were aware, was that she had suffered from Glaucoma, and regular eye tests were required for Philip as the disease could be hereditary.

However we phrased it, Philip declined to attend the funeral and, as Alice was taking her final exams in Newark, she was also missing. Philip had great respect for Grandma and, to this day, still parrots, if asked, her tea and coffee habits. "No sugar in tea please and two spoons in coffee!"

In the summer Alice successfully completed her course at Newark College. It had been the right decision to let her opt out of the 'A-level' stream at the grammar school to pursue studies more akin to her interests and ability. She received glowing reports on both her equine and commercial studies. She decided to follow her love of horses by joining a showing stable in Sussex.

During her time at Newark Alice had passed her driving test but there was no gift of a car - far from it. In my mind passing her test was acceptable away from the envious eyes of Philip but it did raise one of the points in my life which I had been dreading.

Philip had incredible road sense. He had been able to cope with driving a lawn mower at Downley Grange and I was sure that given the opportunity, he would also be able to drive a car. What a potential liability that would create! If he had an accident and seriously hurt or killed someone we would never be able to forgive ourselves, even if it wasn't his fault. In such circumstances, not being able to explain what happened and upon a third party seeing his predicament, he would soon be taking the blame and would not be listened to. It was a risk we could not take. It was for me heartbreaking to have this dilemma. How would he and we cope when the time came, as it inevitably would, for Alice to possess a car. It was the most daunting prospect I had ever faced.

As soon as Bucks C.C. heard Helen was moving to Aylesbury she was offered a Welfare position at an Aylesbury school helping a young lad who had a problem-family background. She enjoyed the work and agreed to start her duties in September.

Where had the last twenty-five years gone? Plenty of water had flowed under the bridge since our marriage in 1963. We held the Silver Wedding celebrations in the garden of Ransome House, complete with a big marquee. It was an ideal venue. Philip was in his element busying himself helping to set up the tables and welcoming the family to his new home. It was a wonderfully relaxed occasion and as usual with the family, he was the perfect host.

Immediately after our celebrations we left for a further holiday in Portugal. It was a defining holiday in that we bought a quarter-share in a modest villa. We could not get Philip to join us in Portugal during the fifteen years we owned it. Having had our invitation declined enabled us to break the secret of going on holiday without him. When this happened, in addition to our weekly telephone calls from wherever we may have been in the world, he enjoyed the additional calls he received from his cousin Philip, Aunty Lavy (short for Lavender) and Alice during our absence.

Knowing the horsey world it was not a surprise to us to get a telephone call from Alice advising she was already disenchanted with life at the stables. The lady owner was a spinster, who herself lived in a large house, but who treated the stable girls like dirt, paid them poorly, yet expected them to work long hours, especially when her animals were attending shows. It was 'all take and no give' as far as Alice was concerned. She returned home to Bierton a pauper but a much wiser young lady concerning the vagaries of a career in the world of horses.

Holidays for Philip were now group affairs with other residents from Downley Grange. He was usually given three options to choose from. These were not easy occasions for the staff, as he would prefer to be undertaking activities on his own. Alan, one of the Team Leaders, was an outdoor type and would get Philip walking or cycling to use up some of his restless energy. Despite needing to be kept occupied, Philip was still not a hyper-active person and could be very quiet and still given the right surroundings.

Whilst each Review, as far as Philip was concerned, seemed to centre largely on his behaviour, it did, along with that topic, cover each Downley Grange activity in which he was involved. The report from each person responsible always concluded that, with each task, he needed close supervision. What a surprise!

Craft Shop – For some reason Philip opted out of working here.

Kitchen/Dining Room - Residents and staff all took their breaks at fixed times together in the central dining room. This was attached to the kitchens. Philip would be involved in the preparation of vegetables, laying up and clearing the tables and stacking the dishwasher. He was remarkably careful with this task when it could so easily have been a disaster area.

Gardens - These were extensive and needed lots of work to keep them in reasonable order. Philip was capable of using the ride-on mower but without close supervision would make his own patterns on the lawn by going round and round in circles. Was he the founder of the mysterious crop circles appearing from time to time in corn fields? Sadly the use of the mower by the residents did not last too long as its gears and clutch took a bashing from the continual rough handling, though in this respect Philip, being blameless, was for a change not the problem!

Woodworking Shop - Philip was no craftsman, not unlike his Father! Unless instructed specifically on what he had to do, with an eye kept on him, he would get carried away with his sawing or whittling to a destructive extent! Rather surprisingly he seemed more adept at painting or staining.

Bill, who had been such a stunning influence on Philip during the past five years, advised us that the Trust had called upon him to use his expertise in pastures new. This we could well understand. We knew that sooner or later he would be moving on. This would be a change nobody looked forward to, especially Philip, who had the utmost respect for his friend in the good, bad, and very bad times.

David, who was already the Deputy Manager and a person Philip had known for some time, would be the new Manager. We hoped the loss of Bill and Jill, his wife, would not create more behaviour problems just when it appeared they could be abating. Only time would tell what Philip's reaction would be.

At Annual Reviews rather than, as previously, the six-monthly assessments of Philip's progress, we were relieved to hear at first hand that the reduction in tensions and incidents had continued. Problems still occurred but with the added discipline from Bill, followed up by David, that damage would in future have to be paid for, Philip appeared to become more aware of the consequences of his actions, particularly as he was very careful with his money! With this threat his moods appeared more controlled and could be managed by the staff. Were the earlier predictions at long last coming to pass? We sincerely hoped so.

The move into a single occupancy, large ground-floor room at Downley Grange had certainly helped to satisfy Philip's thirst for independence. He now had a room which was his where he could occupy himself as he chose, rather than having to consider others. He could also, if he chose, get away from the noisier elements of the home and into his own solitude.

The further good news which would take this transition another step forward was that, on the site of Downley Grange, a new purpose-built building was in an advanced stage of planning. Philip had been identified as one of the residents likely to benefit from this accommodation. It sounded ideal as he would have his own modern bedroom, and a good sized lounge/kitchen and bathroom. The last two areas would be shared with only one other resident.

As building would start shortly, David was happy for us to talk to Philip about these plans and where he fitted into the scheme of things. The staff at Downley Grange did not feel he fully understood what was likely to happen. To us it was not surprising that he appeared unable to interpret a drawing into a future building. The appearance of bricks and mortar would be more meaningful. It at least gave us something positive to enthuse about with him, even if the actual comprehension was limited. It could be just the tonic we all needed. We sincerely hoped so.

Chapter 22 - A New World Starts to Emerge

The transition from Bill's style of management to David's, with Rose as his new assistant, seemed to be taken in his stride by Philip. He had seen others leave Downley Grange so his attitude appeared to be 'what's the big deal?' Was it only in our minds that the change would create more chaos? We could not overlook how important and supportive a person Bill had been in Philips early years with HFT. No doubt Philip, in his distorted world, would be incapable of recognising this.

The next change in the management of Philip and his problems was the not unexpected loss of Dr. Hughes and her wise council. She had become embroiled in county politics and had been told she could no longer cross the county boundary to sit in or advise on another county's clients. We had certainly been privileged to have benefitted from her experience, both for Philip's sake and also to enable Helen, myself and the staff at Downley Grange to become more aware of the complexities in the life of an autistic person.

No sooner had the better news of Philip's behaviour been digested than Debbie telephoned to let us know he was having noticeable problems with his teeth. We had questioned him earlier about apparent discomfort but had not taken it further. We arranged with Debbie to collect him and to take him to our dentist in Aylesbury as, if there had to be some unpleasant treatment, he would probably be better able to cope with it within our home environment.

A local inspection of his teeth was arranged with some urgency. The Aylesbury dentist referred him on to Stoke Mandeville hospital as he had seriously impacted wisdom teeth. An urgent operation was needed to extract all four of them.

We had to tell Philip the truth as he would have overheard our conversation with the dentist. He was petrified, as this would be the first time he would be admitted to hospital on a planned basis. Thankfully, on explaining his mental handicap to the hospital his admission was treated as urgent, which indeed it was, on medical grounds alone.

On the morning of admission to Stoke Mandeville, Philip was visibly terrified, knowing that he would be put to sleep to have four teeth extracted and would need to stay one night in hospital - not a happy prospect for anyone let alone a mentally handicapped young man.

The operation, which was delayed by two hours, was conducted without undue problems.   Helen called to see him but the timing delay meant he was not feeling at all well, having just come round from the anaesthetic.   He was well enough, however, to know he desperately wanted to get out of that place, sooner rather than later.

Upon seeing his distress, Helen went to see the Sister in charge to ask, bearing in mind Philip's desperation to get out of the hospital, whether he could be discharged.   Sister was initially reluctant for this to happen and then decreed that if, after a further hour, he seemed O.K. and had eaten some food he could go home.

What did the food consist of?   A large bowl of soup complete with a good smattering of toasted croutons floating on the top.   Knowing his release hinged on eating this unappetising fare, Philip battled gamely on to empty the dish.   He wasn't going to be beaten.   There was no look of triumph on his face as he finished it, just a readiness to leave that dreaded place.

Shakily he got out of bed.   It took Helen some time to dress him. As he tottered out of the ward, and off down the corridor he was walking as if he was an old man.   He was a dead weight on Helen's arm.   He kept gamely on to the exit.   He was determined to get home to the comfort of his own bed.

Alice, who was living back with us, was taking any agency work she could get.   This included washing up at the local police station. She could not understand how someone who had been brought into the station drunk the night before was still drunk in the morning! This was a side of life she had never previously experienced.   She then joined Grant Thornton which brought forward my long term dread. She wanted to buy a car.   The thought of this filled me with terrible worries of disappointment on Philip's behalf.   He would never be able to own a car, even if he learnt to drive one, which I felt he probably could.   This nightmare, as Alice knew, had haunted me for years and was now upon us, but I could only concur with her wishes.

By the time Philip next came home Alice's car had been purchased. As we did not wish to chance upsetting him it was left out of sight. During the weekend we started to enlighten him by telling him that Alice had passed her driving test and was thinking of buying a car and, when she did, she would be able to collect him from Downley Grange. We didn't expect any obvious reaction to this news but could tell it was being digested. During the same weekend I knew that I had to deal with the problem head on. I could not bottle it up any longer.

I chose a time when he was writing in his bedroom as I felt that having anyone else present would be a distraction from the news I was to impart. To have Helen also trying to say the right things would have only confused what was an already delicate and, for me, extremely emotional situation.

With no joy whatsoever, and no preconceived idea on how I would break the news, I climbed the stairs. As I entered the room Philip looked up and said, "Hello dad, I am busy writing." It helped that he had spoken the first words of greeting.

I simply said, nearly in tears, "Hello sweetheart, Dad wants to have a chat as he has some news. As you know Alice has passed her driving test and wants to buy a car. She will probably have the car the next time you are home." There was a deafening silence. I had to continue, I couldn't just walk away. I continued, "If you could pass a test (not mentioning lessons) perhaps you could also drive a car one day."

He just replied, "No test." Was he already ahead of me in my hour of desperate personal emotions?

The next time he came to Bierton Alice's car stood in the drive and still with a heavy heart I introduced him to it. As ever, Alice was quick to help, asking him if he would like a ride, to which an eager "yes" was forthcoming. Off they went, with no look of contempt from Philip towards Alice as there used to be some years earlier. He seemed pleased to be part of her new car. As they left he raised his hand as if to say, 'this is O.K.' To see this reaction helped to ease my twanging heart strings. The immediate problem was over!

The disappointment for him has still not been fully 'put to bed' in my mind. Unexpectedly, and without planning, a solution to the problem has emerged. He now, very efficiently, works my indicators, flashes the lights to let people through or to cross our stream of traffic, and efficiently regulates the dipping of the headlights at night. He is as alert to the traffic around us as I am. This help to me, and only me, seems to have satisfied any desire he may have had to actually get behind the steering wheel. Another problem solved!

The building of the cottages at Downley Grange was proceeding at quite a pace. Whilst we did not know which of the developing rooms would be earmarked for Philip and Christopher, the young man who had been identified as Philip's flatmate, it was nevertheless becoming an exciting exercise to watch progress, at least for us if not for Philip, who was still not completely sure what was happening and how it would affect him. For safety reasons, we were not permitted to go inside the building.

Christopher, who was a high grade Downs Syndrome lad, was small in stature compared to Philip who was now a well built six-footer. Seen together they looked a bit like 'Little and Large'. Christopher, who had been with HFT at a home in Cheshire before transferring to Downley Grange, was a quiet well-mannered young man and we were pleased he would be joining Philip. We anticipated they would gel as long as our young man behaved himself in his new surroundings.

David was of the opinion that Philip wasn't prepared to think through the changes which the opening of Swallow Cottages, as they were to be called, would bring, and was tending to dodge the issue! Helen thought this was the way he faced issues and defended himself from the threat of change. She was confident that, once the building became more advanced, his attitude could well change. Her thoughts were one-hundred per cent correct.

As soon as Philip's bedroom was allocated, despite being in a bare brickwork state, the first signs of real recognition and interest became apparent. It was also possible to define his lounge/kitchen windows and those of his bathroom. As the building came alive with paint we were able to talk positively about his new home and how nice it would be to get away from the hurly-burly of the big old house and to move into a new modern building. He would still be able to return to work in the main kitchen and go to the old house for meals and coffee. Whilst not expressive, his interest was obviously now being heightened. Despite every now and again uttering what to us was an amazing statement it would help so much with his communication if he could say what he really thought, rather than just giving a stilted mirrored type answer to any questions posed.

Debbie, Philip's long-standing and long-suffering Key Worker who had dealt with him extremely loyally at his most disruptive times, advised she would be leaving. Ceri, a young man who had recently joined the Trust would be her replacement. Philip did not seem at all worried by this news. His philosophy appeared to be, now I have two Key Workers," and to let the future look after itself. When the time came for Debbie to leave, her loss seemed to him a routine event as he still had Ceri. Was it a case of routines being more important than people? It began to appear so.

At the review following Philip's occupation of his flat in Swallow Cottages it was reported that the move had involved a major change in lifestyle for Philip, to which he reacted very favourably. From day one he showed a great pride in his new house, helping to hang pictures and choosing furnishings. Suddenly his aggravated moods had largely evaporated. He was pleased to show visitors his new home. It appeared he was happy as he could make decisions about the structure of his day and, probably most of all, he felt in control of large areas of his life, a major step forward. He still had his foibles but these were insignificant, balanced against his mental progress and behaviour. Over the following years as he suffered fewer tensions, his reward was a markedly improved quality of life and relationships! He became much easier to manage.

Regrettably, Dr. Hughes had already received her edict not to cross county boundaries before Philip moved into his new home. It would have been very rewarding for her to have seen, at first hand, how her earlier prognosis and time-scales for his behaviour to improve had started to fall into place. I hope David updated her, as she had been of great support to Philip, and also to HFT.

Having moved from Regional Office to Bletchley and then having been asked to front up a new Debt Recovery Unit covering the Milton Keynes area, there were not too many positives in my work. It was a depressing job continually trying to deal with delinquent borrowers. I made it known that I would be prepared to take early retirement, and when it was offered, it was gratefully accepted.

Moving back to East Anglia was an easy decision to make. We still considered it 'home', despite having lived in Bucks for almost twenty-five years. After a very indifferent start Bucks had been a good county to us through its continuing support for Philip.

We sold Ransome House and found a plot of land which we developed. Most of our furniture went into store and during the six months of building we rented superb accommodation on the East Coast at Orford. Philip never seemed at ease there, probably as the bulk of his belongings were not available to him. He was, as previously, interested in visiting the new site to see the bungalow and his allocated bedroom developing. The final move went well and Philip immediately appeared settled and accepted the change. We were into another stage of the family's life.

Philip and Christopher gelled quite well in an unobtrusive way. They coexisted and shared their lounge area and were friendly to each other but that was it. They were encouraged to eat together but, as Christopher remained in his bedroom for long periods, Philip had the run of the lounge and had no competition over which programme to watch on television.

Socially, while Philip was polite and friendly to everyone, despite being associated with some residents for ten years, he did not have anyone to call a friend. He was happy with his own company. To us this was sad, but that was Philip! He could, however, when the mood suited him, be quite an extrovert. At Downley Grange he remained a complex character needing regular support and monitoring.

Although Philip's social behaviour was unrecognisable from a few years earlier he nevertheless still retained his obsessive traits. Hours were spent in repetitive, largely statistics related writing. He hoarded large quantities of his daily newspapers and used computer paper in his bedroom. This got to such a ridiculous level he had to be told it was a fire hazard. Very reluctantly he relented and a wheelbarrow was required to reduce the accumulation to more manageable proportions, ready for the cycle to start all over again!!!

Part of his self-help training included using the laundry washing machines. He took to storing the wet washing in his bedroom. To stop this, closer supervision of his room was needed and what a sight it was to behold - old newspapers on the floor and in every available drawer with wet washing under the bed - it resembled a pigsty! This was made possible by his right to privacy, thereby making uninvited access to his bedroom more difficult for the staff.

Money was a precious commodity to Philip. From his weekly allowance, other than buying his newspaper, he spent very little. He would possessively hoard his spare cash in his chest of drawers in a locked cash box, with the key lying on the top of the chest. There was always very great stress in extracting the vast amounts of accumulated loose change and depositing it into his P.O.S.B. account. Having money saved in the Post Office had its advantages when he was at his most voracious in collecting paper. Having the passbook in his possession he had observed how to make withdrawals. He cleared out his account by buying and storing scrap pads and other paper products.

Obsessional phases would dissipate in one area and suddenly erupt into something else. Kept within bounds they had to be tolerated and were preferable to his earlier agitated state of mind.

After a lecture on the merits of recycling at Hatfield College, Philip took the advice literally and started going through the waste bins, without gloves, at Downley Grange, sorting out their rubbish. This had to be stopped before it got out of hand. It however highlighted how vulnerable he was and why he needed the residential care he was receiving. Quite incredibly despite the potential hazards of his conduct he survives unscathed and enjoys robust health.

After the stability of management and staff at Downley Grange in the early 90's it was all change yet again. David, like Bill before him, was asked to take on a management position at pastures new. Rose, his assistant, was promoted to manager but sadly soon afterwards became terminally ill and Margaret, a new face at Downley Grange, took over. At the same time Ceri left the Trust and a series of Key Workers were allocated to Philip. Thankfully, with him now in a more tranquil frame of mind, the constant changes did not upset him too much. As long as he had his one-to-one time he was largely content.

The ever changing Key Workers all helped Philip in different ways but one in particular, namely Jackie, was just what he needed. She was a mature lady who was a non-stop talker, to Philip, and not at him. Her good natured nattering seemed to make his brain aware that talking was a way of communicating. Jackie's banter and cajoling helped to develop his talking and self-esteem. He still did not have the ability to originate meaningful conversation but, as long as he was not exposed to pressure he was more able to express himself. Under pressure the result would be utterances of gobbledegoop.

It was noted that, notwithstanding the improved communication ability and closeness to Jackie through his new found gift of speech, there were no apparent sexual connotations. He would put his arm round her shoulders in a simple acknowledgement of friendship and nothing else. For him physical contact was a big step forward in relationships. The loss of Jackie to the Trust was also to be Philip's loss.

Whilst swimming twice a week and cycling were still playing an important part in his life, the need to 'escape' on his own lessened. This was so much so that he was given a key to the shed where his bike was housed.

With Philip's improved behaviour patterns, in addition to his on-site activities, which now included maintenance with Ray, he said he wished to attend college day-courses. He tried courses at both Hatfield and Welwyn, but decreed he no longer wished to go to the latter. Although a member of staff went and stayed with him, something probably happened via a fellow student or tutor to upset his sensitive and fragile outlook on life. He needed to be dealt with sympathetically and to be kept involved. A sharp word out of place or a callus comment would undermine him and he would take the easy way out.

The courses he attended included, Construction, Adult Literacy, Woodworking and Sport. He thoroughly enjoyed his sport, no doubt copying the actions of those he had watched on television. At the Woodworking course, with help, he created a set of cricket stumps, bat, bails and half a ball. He was very pleased with his endeavours and they have adorned the walls of his bedroom ever since.

Whilst the courses occupied him and gave him a chance to do under supervision what others do, the ability to translate the instruction into practical meaningful living-skills was open to doubt. With Philip, even routine daily lifestyle norms such as eating, shaving, changing clothes and taking medicine all needed close monitoring. Without one-to-one help, which he willingly accepted, he would never think of cleaning his flat or, for that matter, originating new routines. Even if he thought about them, his speech capabilities, whilst improved, did not allow him to convey his thoughts to others in a logical way.   He responded better to questions, but other than a repetitive greeting on meeting someone his conversation had to be originated by third parties.   An example of this is that he would never ask for or take his medication if it was not dispensed.   These points were highlighted on his Personal and Social Assessment charts which showed progress but on a very spiky basis.

Other interests came and went.   He enjoyed, for a time, using the local Dry Ski Slope and got quite proficient.   One of the staff members took a group to the local golf club to use their driving range. Philip had a good eye for the ball and enjoyed his visits.   Both of these pastimes seemed to lapse when particular members of staff left Downley Grange, which was a shame.

There was improved interaction with other residents but always on Philip's own terms.   If, however, a fellow resident had an emotional problem he was very much to the fore in offering his reassurances. Was this genuine concern or was he mimicking the reaction of the staff?

To widen Philip's horizons further the local CTC club Weeley Wheeler's were approached to enquire if he could become a member. On hearing of his cycling pedigree Ken Rands and Paddy Logan, two senior club members came to be vetted by HFT and to take Philip out to see for themselves if his cycling was up to the required standard. All tests were passed and he became a member of the club, which rode out every two weeks on a Sunday morning.   He received his event programme and the staff of HFT drove him, along with bike, to the scheduled starting point.   At the end of the morning, he would make his own way back to Downley Grange, with a call from Ken to let the staff know he was on his way.   Having had his ride he never delayed his return to cause the staff any worries.

This worked well, to the extent that he prized his rides out with the club so highly that he would not come home if it meant missing a club morning.   To counter this I would promise to drive the sixty miles to the assembly point with him for an 8 o'clock start and would ride out with the group. He liked having his Dad along but it was, to me, very obvious that whilst the older members such as Ken and Paddy were around he was welcome but the younger members appeared to have little feeling towards Philip.   Perhaps they just didn't know how to cope with a young man with a problem which was now termed a learning disability in their midst. Philip could cycle as well as they could but would not get involved in conversations; it was something he was unable to do.

Surprisingly, he agreed to attend the club's annual Christmas Dinner. On return to Downley Grange he said he did not want to go again. His presence would have been hard work for members, who would have to go out of their way to involve him, and then it would all be one-sided. Philip could not originate or continue conversation so there was a limit to how much sociability others could continue to generate. Sadly this is a fact of his life and he would have been very sensitive to it. What a shame, as it restricts his social life, particularly with strangers.

The CTC cycle rides would cover some thirty-five/forty miles at a fairly leisurely pace. One morning, when I was with the group, I heard the younger members talking of riding further afield to Whipsnade, a distance of some sixty miles, and wishing to do the distance in the same sort of time as they were currently cycling forty miles. The distance would be no problem for Philip but the time element would be. He simply cycled, like Ken and Paddy, for pleasure and not with a 'bums up in the air and off we go as quickly as possible' attitude. He was not a racer.

The upshot of this was that Ken and Paddy lost interest in the club as the youngsters ran it as they wanted. Philip was summarily dropped from the mailing list and that was the end of what had, for a short time, been a very important out-door pursuit for him. It was a bitter pill for him to swallow. He couldn't understand why he was no longer welcome. Sadly, my assessment of the change was that there was no room for Philip in the midst of these younger people who just wanted to cycle as they chose and had no time to consider or accommodate his needs. He was unlucky with the CTC available to him as most of those I have observed consist of mainly staid mature people just like Ken and Paddy. Sadly that's life.

To soften the blow of his loss of CTC cycling I would drive over to Downley Grange, a return trip of one hundred and forty miles and cycle with him. He looked forward to these days where we would be out all day, having lunch in a pub, but I was a poor substitute for his CTC excursions.

Cricket, and in particular the days out at Lords, continued to be eagerly anticipated occasions. A new very kind and welcome routine had developed. Angela and Philip, his namesake cousin, invited Philip and me each summer for the weekend so that on the Saturday we could attend a One Day Final. Despite Angela making us a mouth-watering picnic, the first task on arrival at the ground was to retire to the Harris Gardens and enjoy a large bap filled with freshly grilled bacon complemented with a quantity of tomato sauce oozing from the sides, a potentially very messy breakfast! These are very special excursions for Philip, who has formed a close relationship with both his cousin and Angela. They always make him feel so welcome.

Philip's recall of detail has its uses. The first time we were to visit Philip and Angela at Clavering Avenue in Barnes, as we approached Hammersmith Bridge I realised I knew the road name but had no idea of the number. Getting rather steamed up in the masses of traffic as we crossed Hammersmith Bridge I related my oversight to Philip. Immediately a little voice piped up with an air of 'Oh father' as children do when parents exasperate them, "It's number ten." Of course he was right!

On arrival, his cousin Philip's Wisdens were still like a magnet despite our Philip now having a set of his own covering each year of his life. The rote memory highlighted by Dr. Jack certainly works overtime as far as cricket statistics and the birth dates of the cricketers are concerned. I treat it as useless information but third parties are always amazed at how a person with a learning disability can home in on, and retain so much knowledge. An autistic brain is certainly a complex organ!

During one such weekend Philip realised his cousin no longer read The Daily Telegraph. He had changed his allegiance to The Times. As a result of this, what does our young man do? He also jettisons The Daily Telegraph and starts to buy The Times.

Evidence of Philip's more flexible demeanour was now becoming apparent. It was, however, paramount that any change in routines needed to be talked through with him. Whilst not able to comment to any degree he would take the information on board and usually accepted what he was being told. If it was obvious a proposed change was causing him a problem it could now be discussed. He would not necessarily acquiesce but at least differences could be talked about rather than a table overturned or something close at hand thrown, which would have been the earlier outcome.

An example of this acceptance of change was that for some two years he had walked two miles to get his daily newspaper. The shop he had been using announced it was closing. Knowing what was happening without reference he quite happily took his custom elsewhere despite having to walk much further. For his purchase he preferred to have the correct money so that he could confidently collect the newspaper from the shelf and plonk his money on the counter and march off out of the shop, but not before greeting the staff with "Morning," and leave with a cheery "Thank you."

With behaviour now less of a problem the Annual Reviews were more relaxed affairs. Gone was the foreboding as to what we were about to hear. A common theme was still, however, present in that Philip needed close supervision with his hygiene and eating habits. He retained his two standards - a scruffy, unkempt and sloppy way of life at Downley Grange and a clean, disciplined code at home. He still lived in two different worlds, with the earlier words of Dr. Hughes concerning his difficulty in transferring one way of life to another as true as they were the day they were first uttered. Despite this, his personality at both venues was that of a well mannered, grateful person who was respectful to others.

Holidays with HFT became more selective in that he preferred a one-to-one situation. For staffing reasons this could only be condoned for short periods. He was quite happy to substitute days out, which pandered to a virtual obsession to seek individual attention. Alan would take him away for a couple of days cycling and David took him to Kent, which included a day trip to France.

Day trips to France with us were also popular. We would drive to Dover at breakneck speed in the early morning to catch the 8 o'clock ferry, have lunch at Le Touquet Airport and a long walk on the flat sandy beach before racing back to Calais to load up with booze before heading back to Bierton. In retrospect, it all now seems an exhausting day out but at the time we enjoyed it.

A short while ago on looking through some old photographs, despite racking our brains we could not place where one had been taken, of Philip sitting on the bonnet of the car. From the car in question we knew the photograph was some twenty years old. Quite casually we showed him the photograph and asked if he remembered where it was taken. Without hesitation he disdainfully said "Le Touquet Airport." Of course he was right; what a graphic memory he has – it's such a pity it cannot be put to constructive use!

To complement Philip's love of watching sport on television a Sky subscription was taken out, and a satellite dish installed. Understanding and working this new equipment along with his video presented no problems - quite unlike his Dad! After initially declining computer instruction it suddenly came into favour when he discovered even wider statistical information was available from that source than from his books.

In line with social demands, HFT were seeking to move some Downley Grange residents out to live in the community. Margaret, by this time, had taken over from Rose as manager and felt Philip would respond positively to this initiative. Christopher, his flat mate, said he would like to move but, much to Margaret's surprise, Philip implied he wished to stay where he was. This was further evidence he was much happier with his lot despite more freedom being offered by living in Hatfield. He probably could not appreciate what was on offer, or if he could, was wary over making any move towards independence.

Helen and I were relieved to hear of his decision as we did not feel he would cope and preferred for him to have the closer support of the staff at Downley Grange. Each review still suggested he needed this support, so to our minds he would be staying in the right place for his needs. However, this incident made it very apparent that he knew his own mind when offered choices.

Our longer holidays with Philip included twice flying to Jersey to visit John and Chris Parker. He was reluctant to fly but did it to see 'his friend' John, whom he still held in great esteem from 1987 when he cycled with us from Lands End to John O'Groats. John had hired bikes and the three of us cycled round Jersey. It took us all day.

On the Sunday we were booked into a very swish hotel for lunch overlooking the bay below. The waiter took the food order and, without consulting Philip we ordered the wine assuming he would have his customary shandy, to which he retorted, "I'll have wine." Never before or since has he proffered those words. He was being taken for granted? It was a lesson to ensure he is asked what he wants, rather than assuming we know!

After our first visit to John and Chris we transferred, by ferry, to Guernsey and also visited Sark. Hiring bikes to get around the island introduced Philip to cycling with Helen for the first time. At the conclusion of the day, with a twinkle in his eye, he complimented her on her riding. Cheeky monkey!

On our second visit to Jersey, on the morning of our departure to Heathrow, Philip had watched graphic pictures of a transport plane crashing into a building in Holland. Not surprisingly it worried him and, on arrival back at Heathrow, as he descended the steps from the aeroplane he simply said, "No more flying."

Using the ferry and car Philip enjoyed his holidays with us in Germany visiting cousin Carolyn and family near Essen. He thoroughly approved of taking two bikes, fitted precariously as it appeared on the top of the car. He enjoyed, along with Harald and Martin, cycling on the miles and miles of well maintained and well signed cycle tracks. Full days out with hardly the need to cross a road weren't difficult to achieve.

Philip enjoyed driving 'on the wrong side of the road' and now for short periods he was doing it with his cycling. In those days Martin was a bit of a wayward soul but Philip took great delight in reassuring him in troubled times everything was alright. 'Pot calling the kettle black', from only a few months earlier!

After visiting the family we would transfer to Boppard on the Rhine. Philip enjoyed his room with a balcony overlooking the river. It was an ideal venue for Philip with lengthy goods and passenger trains trundling along on the opposite bank, the numerous barges complete with family and car on the deck, plying up and down the river and the large pleasure passenger boats arriving and leaving the landing stage below. He spent hours just watching the action and sipping a cool beer. This was a very therapeutic break for us all.

With his marked lack of English language we were highly amused to hear Philip, without prompting, using 'morgan' and 'danke' in the right places. He was quite the little linguist!!

Our attendance at a wedding in Ireland was another enjoyable event. The long journey to Fishguard, followed by the rough ferry crossing to Rosslare, created an exciting experience. Mum was queasy but Philip wasn't bothered one little bit.   At the wedding, dressed in his dark blue blazer and light trousers he was, and obviously felt, 'the bee's knees'.   We all loved the casual way of life of the Irish, especially the lack of signposts to tell a stranger where he was!   Philip became quite partial to his halves of Guinness, and so did we all!   He was particularly amused by an old Land Rover which pulled up beside us, its flapping mudguard fixed to the body through neatly drilled holes by means of a length of rusty wire.

The above are all fond memories of the better times which had emerged.   However, throughout even his most disturbed times and now into more tranquil waters, the importance of the family to Philip has always shone through.

There were times when we thought he despised Alice, yet when showing him photographs of her leaving Heathrow for Australia on the first occasion he was obviously very hurt to have missed the send-off as, on viewing a photograph he simply said, "I wasn't there."   On her next, longer trip, we made certain he WAS there and, as she left he said to her, "Look after yourself."   His feelings for her ran deeper than we had realised.   From her numerous cards he plotted her movements on his wall map.

Chapter 23 - Off We Go Again

There I was sitting quietly in our conservatory, minding my own business reading the summer edition of 'HFT Today,' when I came across an article featuring planned adventure activities involving the Trust.   An escorted cycle ride from John O'Groats to Lands End in May 2001 immediately grabbed my attention.   As Philip and I were still regularly cycling fair distances I had been hankering to relive our 1987 adventure.

At that moment Helen came into the conservatory and said "What are you looking so thoughtful about?"

Not really answering as I was still deep in thought I dreamily replied "I wouldn't mind doing that."

"Doing what?" I was asked.

"Cycling from John O'Groats to Lands End next May," I replied.

"You must be off your trolley," I was informed.

"No seriously, it could be a possibility but I would have to ask Philip first," I continued.

"How would you get there?" Helen mused.

An enquiry rather than a put down I thought as I said "We could fly from Stansted to Edinburgh and from Edinburgh to Wick and then get a taxi to Thurso where it looks as though participants will assemble. I'll send for the details and when I have more information I'll ask Philip if he is interested." concluding with, "It's early days and it may not happen."

"**May** not happen!!!" madam replied.   "You know Philip won't fly so it's a non-starter isn't it?   Anyway, how would the aeroplanes take two bikes, have you thought of that?" was the final retort.

By the time Philip came home two weeks later an impressive looking package had arrived from 'Outdoor Adventures.'   It set out a skeleton itinerary, with nightly hotel accommodation to be arranged, and a back-up mechanic escorting the group.   Safety fluorescent jackets would be compulsory but would be provided, and if required, bikes would be supplied.   It sounded a well thought through exercise but the contents of the envelope, although seen were not discussed, Helen no doubt hoping they would 'go away'!

True to form Philip and I were out cycling during his next visit. We had stopped at a pub for refreshment when I posed the question.

Before I asked it I knew the answer had to be an unqualified 'Yes' to be in business. It could not be a case of trying to persuade him to give me the answer I sought.

"Philip," I said, "In 1987, when you were twenty-one, we cycled from Lands End to John O'Groats." His eyes lit up but he let me continue, "Would you fancy doing it again, but the other way round by riding from John O'Groats to Lands End next May?" At this early stage I felt I had to add, "We may have to fly to Scotland from Stansted."

He simply said without hesitation, "Good idea," which in Philip's language is "Yes", but did he really understand what I was asking? You bet he did! On our return home I broke the news to Helen that Philip thought it was a good idea, whereupon Helen, not surprisingly, having no doubt been mulling over my mad-cap scheme since its first airing, fired her next set of questions in rapid succession!

"Who will help you?" was the first question.

"It is organised from start to finish, even down to the hotels and supplying a mechanic," I replied.

"You are sixty-five. Are you fit enough to do this? Cycling round here is one thing, doing it every day for two weeks is entirely different," was the next poser.

Thankfully I had already covered this problem in my mind and replied "I will have an independent medical before I finalise any plans."

"Oh yes, fine, but how much will it all cost?" was the next probe.

"£700 each, all in for fifteen days isn't bad," I countered.

"£1400 in total, you must be mad to consider spending that amount of money and where's it coming from and how much more will it cost to fly to Scotland on top of that I would like to know?" was the next broadside.

"I don't know," I said rather meekly, adding "If we could get free flights it would help." I continued, "Harry (the chairman of the East Suffolk Group of Friends of HFT) has agreed that if we raise £6,000 in sponsorship, any costs of undertaking the trip, which would include a medical, could be borne by the East Suffolk Group."

"Oh so Harry Norris knows more than I do" terminated the exchange!

A few weeks later, Alice had joined Philip and me on the HFT fifty mile annual sponsored cycle ride. With the thought of next May on the horizon and not wishing to ask friends for money twice in a short time, on this occasion we had just paid an entry fee. As usual at lunch time we stopped at a local pub for a snack. Whilst waiting for our food to be served I formally broke the news of our intended new adventure to Alice. I am sure it wasn't news as no doubt the subject had already received a vibrant airing through Helen on the telephone! On hearing it officially she turned to Philip and said "Great news Philip! Are you looking forward to it?"

"Yes," he said, adding "And I'm going to fly."

It was like a breath of fresh air to here those six little words, as at a stroke Philip had removed my final misgivings. In his mind he was already on his way. It was a similar feeling to being in the greenhouses at Downley Grange in 1986 when The Princess Royal gave her seal of approval to the 1987 jaunt. Obviously, Philip had known from the start exactly what was going on, including the flying. His decree of 'no more flying' on return from Jersey some years earlier was summarily pushed aside in his quest to take on this new challenge.

I registered our intent to take part in the event with Outdoor Adventures asking, at the same time, if a lad with a learning disability was welcome to join them. I explained that, despite his problems, he was a competent cyclist and I would be looking after his day to day needs. The reply came back; Philip was welcome.

The next person to advise of our plans was Margaret, the manager of Downley Grange. On hearing the news her eyes opened wide and she exclaimed, "Oh, goodness gracious, you can't be serious! Do you know what you are doing?" After a short pause, to take breath, she continued in more reflective tones, "Of course you do, you've done it before," at which point Helen with eyebrows and head lifted towards the ceiling chipped in with rather resigned tones.

"I've had my say for what little good it did. You know how determined Andy is when he gets a 'bee in his bonnet'. End of story, they start on 5th May."

With seven months to go to 'lift off' and my misgivings all put to bed, a committee of one was hastily formed, as everyone else in the East Suffolk Friends Group was of very senior years with Harry already eighty-five. The first task was to arrange a medical to see if I was 'sound of wind and limb'. No problems were revealed but the doctor did advise that at my age, although not a heavy drinker, my muscle density format would improve if I reduced my intake. With no further ado I decided alcohol would be taboo until I arrived at Lands End.

Using my experience of fourteen years earlier I set about making a skeleton of plans:-

Travel - I wrote to Barbara Cassani the Chief Executive of Go Airlines, who flew to Edinburgh from Stansted, outlining our plans. By return, she personally wrote back, "What a challenge for you and Philip, we will be delighted to help." What a star! I made contact with Hugh Wilson who had previously arranged our 1987 Loganair flights. A telephone call later and we had confirmation they would be pleased to repeat the gesture by flying us from Edinburgh to Wick. What a positive start!

Publicity - The Princess Royal was only too pleased to again offer her backing for our leaflet with the comment, "To cycle from Lands End to John O'Groats once would be considered a remarkable achievement, but to do it again - exceptional. Good luck Philip." As Brian Johnston was no longer with us, more's the pity, I asked Griff Rhys Jones if he would offer a quote, which he did. "This is a really tough undertaking. Philip will need all the support he can get, and not just in the saddle." For good measure Philip made his plea too. "Please help me to help others by replacing my lost lbs with your £££££'s." Once again it was an eye catching array of support.

To my surprise, 'out of the blue' came a call from Bruce Hobbs who lived in the village, and who for twenty years had fashioned the Guinness corporate identity, offering his services with any design features we may require. This was a top man in his profession offering us his services! Of course his offer was taken up and he designed our sponsor form.

Despite now living in a completely different area from when the 1987 ride was undertaken, the requests for help were being responded to just as positively as in 1987. The icing on the publicity cake was that both the East Anglian Daily Times, and The Echo, were pleased to put their names to the event and both ran feature articles. With lots of effort and lots of rewarding, positive responses, we were well underway.

Training - Limited entirely to cycling, to commence on a planned basis, just as in 1987, in February. We would start with twenty-five miles on two consecutive days, rising by five miles every two weeks.

Fund Raising - A quantity of the Commemorative Crowns still remained so these would again be circulated, on an unsolicited basis, to community clubs asking them as previously to multiply their face value of £1.25p by twenty in the hope they would donate a minimum of twenty-five pounds to our cause. As we had moved house during the intervening years we were in a new area of clubs to be contacted.

A March launch for fundraising was planned. Appeal too early and it doesn't seem relevant and by leaving it too late you risk "I wish you had asked earlier." Timing is crucial.

After the initial frenzied activity all went quiet until February when it became obvious that little training help would be forthcoming from the Downley Grange staff. Most were just not athletic and those that were did not have the desire to take Philip out on regular training stints. I contacted Ken Rands, the CTC member, but sadly he no longer cycled. In desperation I contacted Hollie at The Echo, and asked her newspaper to issue an appeal. Sadly there was not a single enquiry, and so with a commitment to enter the event already made training was largely down to me!

Philip would have to come home every two weeks and we would cycle on Saturdays and Sundays, whatever the weather threw at us. During the intervening weeks I would travel to Downley Grange and take him on longer than scheduled rides just to get the mileage on his legs. With a round trip of one hundred and forty miles it was all very tiring and time consuming, but it had to be done, there was no alternative. To supplement my fitness I would continue to play competitive tennis and sometimes cycle without Philip.

The March launch of the fundraising push was scuppered at the first hurdle. Having planned to circulate as many of the Lloyds TSB branches as I could via an appeal as a 'poor eccentric old bank pensioner', my first enquiry brought doom. The bank had just circulated all branches advising that the adopted corporate charity for 2001 was Mencap. Oh dear, £25,000 came from that source in 1987 and now it would be negligible, so fundraising this time was obviously going to be more of a struggle.

Christmas came and went. Griff, after giving us his publicity blurb, continued to be interested in our progress. In February his P.A. telephoned to ask if we would be interested in holding a press call at his home on a Saturday afternoon. It was a great gesture from a very busy man.

Philip and I had planned to arrive by bike but overnight snow and icy roads made the conditions too treacherous to even consider such a mode of transport.

Griff put on a wonderfully informal relaxed occasion. Barbara despatched Julie from Stansted to present us with our airline tickets and everyone attending was made to feel very welcome. The afternoon was ours, which concluded with supping mugs of tea standing round a large wooden table in his breakfast room. A super P.R. job, both for us, and HFT!

February was also the time to pay the final £1,200 to Outdoor Adventures to guarantee our places. With the receipts came copies of the itinerary and joining instructions. If required, the company would supply Saracen bikes. The accompanying picture showed gears on both sides of the handlebars rather than two levers on the cross bar. They advised us if we used our own bikes they could not guarantee to maintain them unless we provided the spares. With our two bikes, which were both quite different there would be a need to take a large package of additional equipment. If on the other hand we used the Saracen Bikes all the spares would be carried by the mechanic in the accompanying van.

Which bike option to use was a very serious dilemma for me to consider. I could not afford to get it wrong. Dare I risk introducing Philip to a new bike on the eve of the ride? Establishing that the bikes would be supplied by Halfords, Philip and I visited their local store in Ipswich. Philip sat on a similar machine and seemed quite impressed but taking one out on the road was not an option.

The group would assemble at Thurso on the Friday evening, when the fluorescent safety jackets would be issued. Cycling helmets had to be worn and a mobile telephone carried at all times. We would be given an emergency number to call in the event of problems on the road.

Subsequently, on reading through the joining instructions again, it occurred to me, what a 'Rag Tag and Bobtail' outfit we must have looked in 1987!   Back then we had no helmets, no fluorescent jackets, no mobile phones and we were cycling in an assortment of trainers, whereas we were now the proud owners of our first leather black cycling shoes. I drew the line at lycra shorts; our cloth versions with their padded bums were quite good enough.   I couldn't see myself or Philip for that matter, prancing around in skin tight lycra with its embarrassing bulges!!!

Details of the route were already fixed and it would be quite different from 1987.   After Inverness, instead of passing through the Grampians we would travel west along Loch Ness to Fort William and up through Glen Coe to Glasgow and on to Carlisle.   North of Shrewsbury the 2001 route would go south via Ludlow, Hereford and Chepstow, linking up with the previous route again after crossing the Severn Bridge on leaving Bristol.   The hotels had been reserved for an estimated party of thirty.

For Philip to understand the journey I plotted on a U.K. map both the earlier ride north and the proposed route south along with the miles to be covered each day. These varied from a minimum of 47.8 to a maximum of 73.2.   He showed more interest in the daily mileage figures than the route.

To keep the finances of the event at 'arms length,' our cousin Mary agreed she would act as our Treasurer.   I had enough to do without concerning myself with money, although at that point there was but a mere £1,700 at stake from the family coffers!

By early April, with training going well and donations coming in quite steadily, helped considerably by a most generous donation of £1,000 from Woodbridge Round Table, I advised, on request from Outdoor Adventures, that our estimated fundraising would be £10/12,500.   In response to this information Lisa telephoned to ask if I was sure we would raise that amount as we were quoting a figure very much higher than anyone else.   I confirmed the figure, hoping that that would be the minimum, despite the loss of the Lloyds TSB staff.   As previously Philip showed no interest in the fundraising, his only interest was getting out on his bike in readiness for the big adventure.

Two weeks before the event the final details of the other twenty-five participants came through.

As he lived locally I contacted John, a participant who lived in Ipswich. We met and he divulged to me that during the previous year he had had a heart attack when out cycling. He had nevertheless been passed fit to take part. On hearing this news, Alice was very quick to retort, "Dad keep clear of him you have enough on your plate looking after Philip." As ever, wise words from daughter!

After much heart-searching I decided that we would use the Saracen bikes which were on offer. We would already have enough baggage to carry with a case and two panniers each, without taking spares to try to cover all eventualities. As soon as I made the decision I told Philip who seemed quite pleased he would be riding a new bike. Only time would tell if it was a foolish decision!

To enable us to settle into the task ahead I had arranged that we would leave home on the Thursday and spend two nights at Thurso before starting our journey on the Saturday. As the escort van would be arriving with the bikes during Friday afternoon I arranged with Lisa for our two bikes to be set up first.

In view of Philip's participation, Lisa had taken more than a passing interest in his entry and was committed to doing whatever she could to help. The early collection of the bikes would enable me to get Philip out on the road for a few miles of quiet practice before the hubbub started with the arrival of the other participants. In their nervous state they would all think they were the most important entrant around and demand attention. I wished to keep Philip calm as I guessed their interests would all be of a selfish nature. I was only too right in my thinking!

Having worked hard and cycled in some atrocious conditions, May was suddenly upon us. In training I had cycled some one thousand miles and Philip seven hundred. We were as ready as we could be for the days ahead.

During the past weeks I had been trying to interest BBC T.V. (Look East) and Radio Suffolk in our plans. The BBC wanted to issue me with a small camera to do their work for them. I declined the offer as I had enough to worry about without getting to know how the camera worked, and then using it!

Everyone we knew was made very well aware of what Philip and I were setting out to achieve. We don't have too many friends left after over twenty-five years of holding out the 'begging bowl' but they are, without exception, always generously supportive, and this time around was no exception.

Malcolm, a friend in Bourne End, had let Terry Wogan know about our May jaunt. What a pleasant surprise to hear him, on his Breakfast Show, commending and wishing Philip well on his cycling adventure which was starting the following Saturday.

Via Radio Suffolk I had appealed for local pubs to have collecting boxes on their counters for just the two weeks of our exertions, but we received only two replies. The station retained its interest and wished to monitor our progress for their listeners. They set me up for a call on the first Tuesday morning.

I collected Philip from Downley Grange on the Wednesday. Margaret had assembled all the residents on site to see us off and to wish Philip good luck via an array of balloons. Embarrassingly, he seemed quite unmoved by this gesture and was reluctant to have a group photograph taken. He couldn't get away quick enough and was quite a different person once we were on our way home. It appeared he couldn't wait to get going, and leaving Downley Grange was part of that urge.

Philip's attitude concerned me as I will openly admit to the increasing worries which had built up in my mind over the previous few days which had turned to near panic. There was no turning back. Would my health survive the rigours of nine hundred miles in fourteen days, in all weathers? Would Philip become intolerably difficult? Would one of us have an accident? Any one of these, and other fears, could change/ruin the rest of our lives, and our families' lives, and I would be responsible. These were sobering thoughts, hence from me at this late stage there was no excited anticipation.

Previously I had been too wrapped up in what we were doing to give time to any personal thoughts or fears. Now it was too late to do so. Even now, on looking back nine years it still scares me to think about what we were at that time setting out to do. I must have been crazy!

With cases packed and seemingly more than enough luggage, we left home at 5.30 a.m. for Stansted Airport, as ever accompanied by our trusty escort, Helen.

We said our emotional good-byes in the airport lounge, with Philip adding for good measure "Don't worry Mum, see you in two weeks."

In Mum's case, not worrying was easier said than done. She had not one loved one out on the road for fourteen days, but two. Helen would be welcoming us again at Lands End.

She had made the decision, to drive some four hundred miles on her own, to be there at the end of the journey on learning that Philip and I would be staying on for two days. Some weeks before our departure I had said, no doubt already getting stressed, that I could not face the thought of on completion on the Sunday morning rushing around, with Philip in tow, hurriedly getting ready to be transported back to Bristol, as there were no suitable trains from Penzance to London and onwards to Ipswich. I knew I would just want peace and quiet.

Having checked in at the 'Go' desk, Philip was ready for a Full English Breakfast, which he devoured with great relish. There was no nervous apprehension in his make up! He was raring to go.

Having boarded the aeroplane I saw the hostess, who was reading a memo, glance over towards us from her seat. She leaned across and said, "You must be considered important cargo as the boss (Barbara Cassani) has sent me a note letting me know what you are doing." How important could we get? She then went up onto the flight deck.

As we approached Edinburgh, the distinguished looking tall captain in his smart uniform came out of the cockpit. He was also well briefed, asking Philip if he would like to go onto the flight deck to watch the aeroplane landing at Edinburgh. Philip declined: the flight for him was an ordeal in itself. This would not be allowed today. How the world has changed in the short time since then!!!

Philip was quite relaxed as we waited to be called for the Loganair flight to Wick. On the dot of 11.30, our flight time, we boarded, with Philip still clutching his copy of The Times. We made ourselves comfortable, both having window seats. No sooner had we done this than a head popped round the door to announce, "You'll all have to get off; the crew were held up getting out of Glasgow; they will be late." Thankfully Philip saw the funny side of this, in a nervous sort of way.

We duly arrived at Wick to a warm sunny day. We took a taxi to Thurso. In the early morning rush, on arrival I realised I had completely forgotten where we were staying. The taxi driver was very patient whilst I telephoned Helen, who was not best pleased. What a good start to my being responsible for Philip's welfare for fifteen days. I had fallen at the first hurdle! Surely though, it could only get better. The Thursday afternoon was spent just settling down and getting acquainted with Thurso.

With the weather still superb on the Friday morning we took a taxi to John O'Groats calling on the way at the most northerly part of the UK mainland, the spectacular Dunnett Head. We strolled through the grassy expanse to view the 400 foot craggy cliffs falling away into the Pentland Firth, which was guarded by a pristine white lighthouse perched some 300 feet above the lapping waves. Even from that height one could see the vicious tides ripping the water between the rocks below.

To add to the drama thousands of seabirds were squawking and making a terrific din as they circled above us before alighting onto their precarious rock face nesting sites. The views to the Orkney Isles and beyond were crystal clear, they looked but a stones throw away.

It was certainly 'good to be alive' type weather and with Philip totally relaxed and enjoying the day out with his Dad we walked from John O'Groats to Duncansby Head. Rather than walking on the road we took the paths zigzagging over the meadows being grazed by sturdy looking Highland beasts. In the sky above us another treat unfolded as we watched a number of lapwings/green plovers (peewits) wheeling, diving and displaying their prowess to an admiring prospective mate. It was captivating to just stand and watch their antics, including their shrill call of 'peewit' to anyone who wanted to listen. It was such a spectacular sight and one never to be forgotten.

As we stood watching the birds, a small white twin-engined aeroplane with a red stripe around the body passed overhead. The ever observant Philip exclaimed "That's our plane," and of course he was right, it was the same plane we had boarded in Edinburgh and it was now on its way, a day later, flying from Wick to Kirkwall on the Orkney Isles.

Duncansby Head was awe inspiring in a completely different way from Dunnett Head. The cliffs were not quite as high but even with calm seas it was not difficult to imagine the times when raging seas would have carved the cliffs into the series of black chasms, arches and castle-like stacks which now tower anything up to 300 feet above the water below.

With not too much time to linger we retraced our steps over the grassy meadows back to John O'Groats. A quick snack lunch and we caught a service bus back to Thurso. What a leisurely, glorious few hours we had enjoyed. It was certainly right to have arrived a day early.

As we walked into the hotel we met Buzz, who had a special badge emblazoned on his cap. We introduced ourselves and he took us out to the car park to be sized up for our bikes. Philip by this time was overawed by the activity and near bedlam as the van was being unloaded and people were running hither and thither with partly assembled bikes, wheels and saddles.

Buzz soon had our bikes ready for action so I took Philip away from the organised chaos to enable him to concentrate on my instructions regarding the use of the gears. Riding, balance, and stopping via the different type of brakes posed no problems, but if he was to be efficient he needed to get the hang of the gear changing. There were three numbered options on the left and eight on the right (twenty four gears). He seemed bemused, and so was I!

I suggested we went for a ride. "Good idea," was Philip's reply. Off we went to the large esplanade and car park. As soon as I was confident he had settled into his riding I suggested the gear ratios. He could use gears 1 or 2 on the left and up to 5 on the right, but more if he chose as it was important he appeared to making his own decisions on use. He soon realised 1 was for climbing hills and 2 for use on the flat. He enjoyed fiddling with the gear options and adapting to the ratios as we circled around, and rode up and down the esplanade.

Within twenty minutes he was ready for the challenge and had adopted his trusty steed for the next two weeks. The first worry had been happily put to bed!

Before dinner, the group of twenty-seven cyclists, comprising four females and twenty-three males of all sorts of shapes and sizes and varying ages assembled in the hotel lounge. Jokingly it was soon established that at sixty-five I was the oldest participant. This did not worry me as I had trained conscientiously, knew what was involved and, barring accidents, was confident I could complete the task.

Philip, on being thrust in amongst so many chattering strangers, was completely overawed and could only stand and stare at the noisy throng. I tried to reassure him, telling him everyone was very nervous and making such a noise as, unlike him they had not been on a big cycle ride before. He didn't react; he just had a glazed look in his eyes.

At dinner the conversation became more intense. I suggested to Philip he sat at the end of the table so that I could help him by deflecting any direct approaches which he could not cope with. It worked and he had a good supper, but without doubt he was still bewildered by suddenly being thrown in amongst so many strangers who had no knowledge of him or his background, and who were largely individuals whose one aim was to get to Lands End. They talked to me and portrayed potential problems as if Philip did not exist. All he could do was to listen and worry about what was ahead, in other people's minds.

As soon as possible after the event briefing from Kenny, our tour leader, and a mechanical resumé by Buzz, I took Philip away into the peace and quiet of our bedroom. We were ready for Saturday!

Chapter 24 - Heading South

After an apparently good night's sleep Philip arose bright and breezy. I had not been so fortunate, mulling over, in my mind, what the next fifteen days could entail. Of course the thoughts were all negative. Nothing positive was ascertained at this stage of the operation.

Breakfast was soon finished and appropriately dressed the group boarded the coach for John O'Groats. Along the way there was more nervous chatter but suddenly this turned to admiration for Philip, as Kenny announced that Philip and I had completed the trip fourteen years earlier.

We alighted from the coach clutching our four heavy panniers, which contained our wet weather gear, lunch, bananas, tool kits and litre bottles of water. Having collected our bikes, with front wheels detached (there was insufficient room in the van to house twenty-seven fully assembled bikes) from Kenny and Buzz, we retired to a quiet spot.

Assembling bikes for the two of us with most people already set to go heaped pressure on me. The title of this book was certainly inappropriate at that particular time; it felt just the opposite! I was very much alone in supporting Philip. I would be fending for two people and in particular ensuring I had made provisions for trouble through the label fixed firmly to the saddle of Philip's bike to say who he was, his medication, what he was doing and where he was destined for each evening. If I lost him, or I became ill, he most certainly would not have been able to cope. Although there was a group of twenty-seven of us, once we were under way everyone cycled at their own speed and would soon spread out into a remote crocodile of people whose only aim was to get safely to their destination each day. The lairy way some people rode one wondered if the safety aspect even crossed their minds!

In our moment of triumph in 1987 we had been thrilled to see the signpost showing Lands End 874 miles. It was now a chilling sight, what would the days ahead have in store?

At 9.20 we were all set and headed south along the coast towards Wick into a fresh and chilly breeze. Gone was the sunshine of the previous day. Rather disconcertingly, soon after our departure, three cyclists came easily towards us, nearing the completion of their adventure.

I knew the sixty-three mile journey to Brora would be a hard slog, and so it proved. Long stretches of open, exposed barren roads encompassing long gradients and short steep falls ensued. There would be little chance of refreshments along the way. There were no wayside catering vans in this part of the world!

Towards the end of the day we would be faced with the notorious climbs posed by Berriedale and Helmsdale. Their negotiation was no easier than in 1987 but we arrived safely in Brora. The last ten miles seemed never ending as we could see the town clearly jutting out into the North Sea from Helmsdale but, as we traversed the coastal roads, it only very slowly appeared to get any closer.

Having arrived in the hotel car park for what was to be a daily routine I lowered the saddles on our bikes and removed the front wheels along with the pannier bags. Carrying the retained wheels and panniers we trudged off to find our bedroom.

The first priority, after ensuring the television worked, was a shower for Philip and to prepare his clothes for the evening. To lessen any risk of chafing from soiled clothes clean pants, vest and socks were worn each day. I would then sort myself out and finally prepare for the next day by repacking the cases and panniers before bed. There had to be a daily routine as I could not risk a 'panic stations' start to the day as that would have been counter productive in dealing with Philip. At all costs I had to keep him calm and on an even keel.

With this in mind, tired as we both were at the end of each day, I would not decree when the television had to be switched off. After watching the weather forecast for the following day I would just say good night and well done to him and lie down. Within minutes Philip would switch the television off. He was making the decision and not, aged thirty-five, being told what to do. I knew that this approach would suit his disposition.

Sunday 6th May Brora to Inverness, 60 miles - Rising at 6.30, the first task was to peer through the curtains for a check on the weather. Thankfully it was fine but the cold wind was still in the southeast. It was final packing and cases downstairs for a 7.30 breakfast. Philip had not been particularly pleased to share a room with me but I tried to explain the alternatives, of which there were none, and the pattern for the future was thus established. To have had a separate bedroom would have been a nightmare in trying to organise him into getting up, dressing and being ready for breakfast. By sharing a room I could disturb him by just getting up and brewing the first cup of tea.

In setting up the bikes for the day ahead Philip, other than being a 'beast of burden', could not help. It was down to me to ensure we had everything we were likely to need and that the wheels were fixed, seats at the correct height, label amended and the panniers securely attached.

The highways were still open and barren as we headed towards the Solway Firth with its many anchored, redundant oil rigs. At last, as we turned to head in a westerly direction we were getting some wind assistance.

The Black Isle could have spelled disaster. When we had earlier stopped for a snack, as I did not possess a chain I had had to remove our front wheels, yet again, to stop our shiny new bikes going walkabouts. Carelessly, probably being distracted, I had not fully tightened Philip's front wheel nut. It then worked lose and, thankfully, just before we were to start a sharp descent he called out from behind "Dad I've got a wobbly wheel." Perish the thought what could have happened!

As we crossed the Black Isle the sun, for the first time, suddenly broke from behind the clouds and we were soon into clear blue skies. Everything looked so bright and attractive.

By the time of our arrival in Inverness the saddle on my supplied bike was becoming uncomfortable. It was 'reaching the parts other saddles couldn't, or hadn't, reached!' Philip also appeared to be easing himself around on his seat more than I would have expected. With showers and routines complete I hailed a taxi to Halfords, just getting into the store before it closed, to buy two gel saddles and two chains with locks. I could not take the risk of a sore 'bum' at this early stage. Philip was not too impressed by me inspecting and creaming his most vulnerable parts!

Whilst most of the fellow cyclists made little effort to communicate with Philip, either not knowing what to say or do, I was pleased that Paul and Malcolm at Brora and again at Inverness made an effort to welcome Philip into their midst. He responded very positively and soon established when their birthdays were. This helped him enormously to feel part of the group. They, in turn, without being intrusive, were interested in Philip's background.

On the nightly update to Helen I reported why we now had new saddles but the 'wobbly wheel' was an event best forgotten. The fact we were where we were was enough drama for her. After the call Helen would report our position to Margaret at Downley Grange so that she could plot onto the map where we were for the other residents.

Monday – Inverness to Fort William, 64 miles – It was a glorious sunny morning of blue skies with a light nippy breeze. A long, yet spectacular day beckoned, as we were scheduled to pass along Loch Ness.

Within the group, allocated by Outdoor Adventures, was a fitness trainer. She encouraged us to tone down when we had concluded the activity of the day and insisted on holding a 'warming up' session each morning before setting off. The former was something neither Philip nor I had ever entertained, and as for the latter, whilst attending, as we had to do, the daily roll call, for peace and quiet I would go through the motions of warming up. Philip would have none of it and steadfastly stood aloof from the group, with his hands in his pockets. He was not prepared to waste energy he may need later in the day. The morning warm-up sessions were often the subject of great mirth to the passing public as they were usually performed in an open area. Twenty-odd mature people of various proportions going through their daily contortions could not have been a pretty sight!

Having the previous evening explained to Philip why I was creaming his bottom it was rewarding the next morning, when he first sat on his new saddle to hear him quietly say "That's better." He had obviously been in some discomfort but would not have said of his own accord until it was too late. A future problem averted!

On leaving Inverness we diverged from the 1987 route and headed for Loch Ness via Glen More rather than along the A82. What a reward to have taken the more southerly quieter route. The scenery was magnificent but the going was tough. We climbed to spectacular views before descending to Fort Augustus. Sadly my camera had jammed earlier in the morning. I lost the opportunity to take what would have been very picturesque photographs!

Thankfully, Philip took the steep downward gradients very carefully before we stopped for coffee at Fort Augustus. We rested and relaxed for a few minutes, watching the pleasure boats manoeuvring through a series of locks.

We then joined the A82, with its heavy volume of holiday traffic. Philip stuck manfully to his task on a very tiring day, no doubt spurred on by the promise of a coffee and a pancake at the Speen Bridge Little Chef, some ten miles out from Fort William.

Ben Nevis, all 4406 feet of it, looked a picture against the bright blue sky. There were just a few wispy clouds hanging around its summit – again I lamented not having a working camera.

On our arrival at Brora two days earlier I had seen Buzz read the label on Philip's saddle. He said nothing, but on arrival at Fort William he was quickly out of the escorting van to greet us, and with his marker pen drew a line on the stalk of our saddles where they joined the frame. Each morning thereafter, when collecting our bikes off their stands the saddles had already been set at the correct height. Any time saved in the morning was of great help.

Tuesday – Fort William to Arrochar, 68 miles - A day I had not been looking forward to before we started this adventure. I'd known Monday would be a tough assignment and would be followed by this leg through Glen Coe. My only previous recollections of the place were of a stormy day some years previously and I remembered it being dark, foreboding and eerie. Was I physically up to the challenge it posed? How would Philip set about the long gradients, the first being eight miles?

An early start was scheduled and, having persuaded Philip to shave in the evenings so that I didn't have to chivvy him in the morning, we rose at 6.00. Bikes prepared, three litres of liquid in the panniers, an early breakfast and after the customary physical jerks we were on the road at 8.00 in benign, chilly conditions. This was ideal for the task ahead. The first eighteen miles were comfortably flat, after which we entered Glen Coe, which presented a forbidding, overcast sight.

We made remarkably steady progress as we pedalled up the long climb towards the summit of the pass. Our endeavours were certainly rewarded as the sun broke through and revealed blue skies with light cloud hanging around the snow-covered peaks. We were now cycling just below the snow-line as we looked back into the stunning valley below.

During the climb Philip was far from happy on being told by me to drink as otherwise he would get dehydrated and feel ill. Fortunately Eric, one of our group, was nearby and chipped in "Come on Phil you must drink as dad says." With no more ado the bottle attached to his cross bar was uncorked and the contents downed!

Bang on cue at 10.25, my mobile telephone rang. "BBC Radio Suffolk here, you will be on air in five minutes," said the caller.

"Oh good gracious," I replied, "Philip is ahead of me I must catch him up to stop him so I can talk." Having hardly managed to catch him we went live. I was asked for an update on our progress and, as I was breathless from the chase, I probably sounded as though we were having a hard time of it. In a nutshell I said all was well and Philip was doing fine. He declined to get involved in the conversation.

After Glen Coe we passed over Rannoch Moor and other open, remote areas of moorland, before reaching Loch Lomond on our way to Arrochar, on the shores of Loch Long. As Arrochar was three difficult miles off our route we rested at Tarbet to await a lift to the hotel. A group of us had assembled, awaiting the transport, but Philip remained aloof, watching the boats on Loch Lomond. Perhaps he fancied a cruise more than a bike ride!

Arriving at Arrochar to a glorious balmy evening, having showered and feeling refreshed, Philip and I sat in the hotel gardens in the warm sunshine, Philip with his pint of shandy and me with my lemonade and lime. Oh for a beer, but I was not going to break my non-alcoholic pledge at this late stage. In the warmth of the sun I fell asleep, not an unusual pastime as those who know me will confirm! It was soporific bliss just gazing up at The Cobbler on the far side of Loch Long.

Wednesday – Arrochar to Stonehouse, 64 miles – This was another potentially difficult day as we would be cycling around the outskirts of central Glasgow. It had been suggested by Kenny that to minimise mistakes en-route single cycling was not advised on the busy A82, particularly as we moved towards the Erskin Bridge.

Paul and Malcolm suggested Philip and I should cycle with them, with Philip always No. 3 in the crocodile so that nobody had to turn round to see if he was O.K. In the traffic one could not relax for a moment. We got through unscathed, skirting Glasgow Airport and cycling on until 13.45. Back on the road at 14.10 with only twenty miles to go, we expected an early finish. How wrong can you be? Those last few miles were unexpectedly difficult, undulating and with buffeting strong winds. It was 16.45 before we arrived at our destination. Philip stuck to his task in difficult conditions, and the four of us helped each other along - it was a long tiring day, all things considered.

Thursday – Stonehouse to Gretna, 70 miles - We were making steady progress as we headed south for Gretna Green. The weather was getting hotter by the hour tempered by the fresh gusting easterly wind, which made for uncomfortable riding. Philip was still finding the masses of new faces and the general hubbub around him rather bewildering, so he remained aloof. Not too many of the group, and in particular the ladies, made any effort to get to know him, but he was coping.

On the road I had found letting him lead me gave him a feeling of importance. He then rode with great gusto. Such was his strength it was also a chance to cycle in his slipstream and to take advantage of the thirty-year age difference. As long as he was in sight, even if he was two hundred yards ahead, it was not a problem as I knew that, if he came to a junction, he would wait for me to see if he should turn left or right.

We made good progress through the picturesque Border Country, but the tiresome wind again made the last few miles of our journey rather difficult. One could only describe our hotel at Gretna Green as an ancillary part of a wedding factory. There were wedding parties everywhere and as a result we felt rather out of place!

Today saw the first casualty of the group. Geoffrey who at sixty-three was the second eldest had to quit. He was obviously feeling the strain after the second day, as prior to leaving Inverness he had approached me and said "You are the oldest here yet you look as 'fit as flea' and in much better shape than many others, how come?" I related the training Philip and I had undertaken and he looked at me rather wistfully and continued, "I should have done more but somehow I never got round to it." Mistakenly he thought fitness would come as he went along. Being accompanied by two younger relations they should have been able to help him more than they did. Whenever we saw them out on the road they always seemed to be going 'hell for leather' with Geoffrey struggling to keep up. My sole aim each day of getting Philip safely from A to B should have been theirs, but not so, and Geoffrey was paying the ultimate price of disappointment – I felt for him!

Friday – Gretna to Shap, 48 miles - Within minutes of departing from our hotel in warm humid conditions, we were leaving Scotland. How lucky can you be? On both the 1987 ride and on this one we had not had a single drop of rain whilst traversing Scotland, although there had been plenty of wind. Fortunately our wet weather gear had stayed in the panniers.

Soon the sun was burning down and dehydration, without care, would be a real possibility. When conditions permitted Philip, who had been watching others, now had the hang of drinking from his water bottle as he rode along.

We quickly passed through Carlisle and were heading along the A6 towards Penrith and The Lake District. We were making good progress with Philip leading the way when a potential disaster struck. On a long gradient some six miles south of Carlisle I urged Philip to overtake a grey haired old gentleman (not me) who was struggling to make progress into the headwind. He did as I asked but, due to the unsteady path our decrepit friend was ploughing, coupled with the passing traffic, I could not immediately follow. No doubt with an element of frustration I changed my ratios to a lower gear and off flew my chain and wrapped itself round the gear cogs of the back wheel. Suddenly I was in limbo: Philip was getting ever further away and could not hear my calls to stop through the wind and traffic. 'More haste less speed' was certainly the order of the day as I tried to quickly fix my problem. Twice more the chain flew off as I put too much pressure on it in trying to start off again going up hill. With no alternative but to ride down the hill I got going again, but by this time Philip was out of sight.

Suddenly it was panic stations.   Although I am not an admirer of mobile phones they have their uses.   With black, greasy, trembling hands and sweating profusely, I managed to extract the emergency number of the escort van from my pocket.   I knew the van was somewhere ahead as it had previously passed us and had given the customary toot.

Fortunately, the van was parked up only a mile ahead.   In reply to advising the crew of my plight and concern about Philip's whereabouts, came the unexpected reply, "Oh yes he's passed us and is heading off towards Penrith."   I will not try to put into words my frustration that on seeing him and knowing his problems nobody sitting in that van had had the nous to think, 'There's Philip, but where's his Dad'?   Not particularly politely I asked them to go and stop him and ask that he wait for me.

Cycling hard for a couple of miles to catch up with him, I suffered for the rest of the day.   Philip had had no idea that I was not following on behind him.   He was somewhat bemused and distressed by the time I rejoined him, sitting on a grassy bank by the roadside.   It was fortunate that the van, in those circumstances, was near at hand.

As we progressed through Cumbria we were seeing palls of black smoke.   They came from the fires burning the carcasses of the condemned animals affected by the Foot and Mouth epidemic which was sweeping the country.   In total six million cattle had to be slaughtered.   Attempting to alleviate the necessity of creating pyres everywhere Tony Blair, the Prime Minister summoned senior army officers and gave them the task of finding a way of disposing of the culled animals.   Within a short time vast pits had been dug and no less than half a million head of cattle were buried by the army.   What a heartbreaking disaster, not only for the animals but for the livestock farmers who had seen their cherished herds sentenced to death in such cruel and sudden circumstances.

In an attempt to control the disease, as our hotel was at the end of a long approach drive we were precluded from leaving it that evening.

Having to stay put was not all bad news!   As we supped our well-earned drinks, there was an unexpected thrill.   Suddenly two red squirrels bounded out of the trees.   They were my first sighting of the animal - they were beautiful.   Their sole objective was to nick nuts from the bird table.   Another photograph opportunity missed!

As we sat in the hotel lounge waiting for our dinner I could see Paul and Malcolm in animated discussion with a middle aged, rather portly, brassy blond. All in all she looked a rather unpleasant lady. Suddenly Paul came over and indignantly said, "Will you introduce Philip to 'madam' over there as she refuses to believe Philip is undertaking this ride". Just from her appearance she looked a 'know all'! Initially I was reluctant, but then obliged. Her face was a picture of disbelief to be confronted by Philip who immediately after he had been introduced asked her when her birthday was. She spluttered a reply and we speedily left her with her mouth wide open. As we walked away I could hear her being rebuked by her husband. He made a point of meekly apologising for his wife's behaviour as we went into dinner - that's life!

Saturday – Shap to Preston, 62 miles - On the Friday morning as we dressed I had told Philip that as it was so hot I was not going to wear my tracksuit bottoms, just shorts. He insisted on wearing his full tracksuit. Without further comment I had laid his clothes out for the day ahead. On leaving Shap, I found his tracksuit bottoms neatly folded on the back of a chair. Philip was outside bouncing about in his shorts! He was going to make his own decisions!

Returning to the A6, before departing we were instructed to wheel our bikes through a deep trough of disinfectant.

With rested legs the ascent of Shap passed quickly and we arrived in Kendal. Our progress had been too swift and I had got over-confident and careless. Missing a turning onto a minor road out of town I suddenly realised we were heading for Barrow-in-Furness and not Lancaster as planned. With only the daily route instructions with us I hailed a passing camper-van. The occupants quickly put us back on the right road. In the intense heat going six miles out of our way was not a welcome detour, with liquid refreshments becoming increasingly important as the day progressed.

The final miles of the journey included skirting Preston and heading towards Chorley along the A6. Having been exposed to the searing heat all day I was concerned that Philip's concentration may waver. Being tired and hot after cycling sixty miles, a small error of judgement on that busy, noisy road could spell disaster for either of us. I knew being extra vigilant and fussing would have been counter-productive so I had to leave him to negotiate the busy roundabouts and junctions. With great aplomb he survived.

During the evening John of heart attack fame who was by far the most energetic person in the group, showed us his photographs on his laptop. He promised us copies when we got home.

After completing his daily diary he asked if he should send a report to our local newspaper. He quickly compiled a story, with a stunning photograph of us passing through the Lake District. Helen was thrilled to see evidence of our well-being in the newspaper on the Monday morning.

Sunday - A day of rest!! With the weather so settled and rain on its way I wished we had continued cycling. However, it was not to be, and in trying to relax, it was 8.30 before we arose. After breakfast we caught a bus into Preston to purchase a new camera.

Our free day continued with Philip staying at the hotel whilst I had the experience of a lifetime! Setting off with a bag of eighteen sets of underclothes which when we left home were all 'Persil White' it was time to visit the local launderette. The rather large, but friendly lady who was supervising the place knew exactly what I was about as other participants had earlier visited her establishment. As I entered the door I must have looked bewildered as she greeted me with "Hello love, do you need some help?" Having established that I did she continued "The powder is over there, it's 20p a shot and the dryer is in the corner." What a nonplussed spectacle I must have presented as without further ado she declared, "I'll tell you what, you go round to the pub for a pint; I'll sort out your washing and it will be ready when you come back, how's that?" I needed no second bidding to accept her offer and when I returned everything was neatly folded and back in my large plastic bag. What a star that lady was to a tired, easily bewildered old man!!!

Monday – Preston to Beeston, 48 miles - Our luck had to change and the wet weather forecast was correct. We arose to low cloud and drizzle.

After the usual preparation, Philip was none too keen to start cycling but, once out on the road, he stuck to his task. Fortunately it was a short day, but the roads were sodden and dangerous. Most of the time we were on the busy A49, coping with spray and potholes full of water which invited either smashed spokes or a buckled wheel.

In addition to passing through Warrington and Wigan, the journey, just as in 1987, included negotiating the busy east-west cross routes linking Manchester and Sheffield with Liverpool. Sitting beside and virtually underneath vast lorries at traffic lights, we felt insignificant and vulnerable, especially as the visibility was so wretched in the dark, wet conditions. The riding was so fraught that I told Radio Suffolk I could not take their call when they telephoned.

Whilst traversing Warrington we had been invited to call at the Head Office of Outdoor Adventures for refreshments. Rather rudely, Philip and I continued cycling as I did not wish to get cold and then have to turn out again into the incessant rain. My sole aim each day was to get Philip safely to his destination with as little fuss as possible.

We duly arrived at Beeston with our shoes full of water and gloves and socks having to be rung out. It was with huge relief we were able to don dry clothes. We were quite drained by the concentration exerted over the previous five hours. Fortunately, the hotel was warm and comfortable and provided a welcome hot snack lunch. Philip appeared none the worse for the day's ordeal but I could not get warm.

Sadly, although Philip was coping comfortably physically, the social side of the adventure was still quite stressful. Few people, even after ten days, were making any attempt to even pass the time of day with him. Perhaps they didn't know how to cope themselves. Paul, John and Malcolm were however always ready to help in putting him at ease. John had become Philip's hero after he'd watched him compiling and sending his report to the newspaper on the previous Saturday evening. He was fascinated by John's explanation of what was going to happen and seeing himself on his laptop.

Tuesday – Beeston to Ludlow, 65 miles - After the rigours of the previous day, Philip arose in a peculiar mood. He was unhelpful, awkward and very withdrawn, especially after breakfast – it was clear something was annoying him. This could not continue. I had a few sharp words in private which led to him stomping off back into the hotel. Oh dear I thought, now what? I was soon to find out. Within a few minutes he returned in a completely different frame of mind. Perhaps it was the music in the car park which had grabbed his attention.

Suddenly as everyone assembled for their 'physical jerks' in the hotel car park the tune 'The Stripper' blared out from the escort van as lively accompaniment for the groaning contorted bodies of the group who were trying to move lithely around in time with its seductive tones. Hotel windows opened as the music blared and the cavorting about caused much mirth with resident guests. It really was a sight for sore eyes!

Despite the bad start to the day, Philip was a pleasure to be with whilst cycling. Paul joined us as we pushed along into the breeze. This weather was accepted with an element of relief, as the forecast for the day had been poor. Starting off in heavy cloud, and with the threat of rain which did not materialise, we had a dry run which finished in sunshine.

Wednesday - Ludlow to Chepstow, 55 miles - On the face of it this would be a fairly easy day. The hilly terrain therefore came as a bit of a shock, particularly the climb from Tintern, just before we dropped down into Chepstow.

We were again fortunate with the weather. We missed the worst of the downpours but it didn't stop us from getting covered in spray from passing lorries on the wet roads. Philip was not in the mood to be hurried, but, as soon as he came to a hill (and there were plenty of them) he seemed to power forward with the greatest of ease, or was it a cussed case of, "I'll show 'em." I will never know!

As radio contact had been impossible in Shropshire, Radio Suffolk reached me for an update. When they telephoned eight of us were, unusually, cycling together. I suggested to Philip that he should cycle on with the group and I would catch him up after stopping for a few minutes. He thought this was a good idea and, pleased as punch no doubt to get away from Dad, cycled off into the distance whilst I waited to go on air. Although I didn't stop until just before going live, by the time I was back on the road five or six minutes had passed and everyone else was well out of sight. Cycling at only ten miles per hour one covers a mile in six minutes and this, I decided, was probably the distance I was now adrift of the group.

To put into perspective the task I now faced I had to cycle two miles per hour faster than the group, on my own, for some thirty minutes to make contact with them again. I expended so much energy doing this I felt queasy. I had become dehydrated through my exertions and it was not a pleasant feeling. Fortunately, it was nearing lunch time so I could rest for longer than usual and take on board plenty of liquid.

Despite this it was an enjoyable day cycling through the splendour of the Wye Valley as the river made its way to the River Severn, which we would be crossing the next day. Helen, in our nightly call, referred to the foreboding weather forecast of strong winds and rain overnight and into Thursday, particularly in the West Country. This was just what we needed!!!!

Thursday – Chepstow to Taunton, 64 miles – Overnight, as I lay in bed, I could hear the winds freshening and the rain beating down on the windows. Oh dear, I thought as I fell asleep, consoling myself that the worst may have passed through by the morning. Not a bit of it! Rising at 6.30, the strong wind was in the north-west and heavy rain was still falling. What a day was in prospect. We had come prepared for all weathers, and this was it.

At breakfast, Kenny called everyone together to warn of the conditions to be faced and that, unless we were sensible, hypothermia was a real risk. With the wet and windy conditions and the air temperature only eight degrees, when stopping for breaks we should ensure we got off the road and into warm cafes or pubs. We would not be protected by sitting in bus shelters. This advice was good enough reason to get re-dressed after breakfast with another layer of clothes. Having to undress and be supervised in dressing again, did not please Philip but I tried to explain the problems we were likely to face. He was still not impressed!

With every item of wet weather gear we possessed adorning our bulked up bodies we left at 8.40 to cross the Severn Bridge. No 'physical jerks' today, everyone was too cumbersome in their additional gear to even consider it.

Hardly had we got started than 'Oh good gracious me' was the lament as Kenny wished to take photographs of us leaving Wales before we crossed the bridge. Already cold and shivering, as we had yet to warm up, everyone grudgingly obliged.

Thankfully as we crossed the bridge, the wind was more or less behind us. Had it not been it would have been an impossible task!

As we were about to leave the bridge complex on a cycle track heading for the Avonmouth area of Bristol there was a raucous call - "Smile please," it was John, of heart attack fame, standing on the bridge gantry, busily snapping everyone as they made their sodden windswept way below. Unbeknown to me he had left the group the previous day to cycle to Gloucester to spend the night visiting his parents. I dread to think, given the conditions we faced, what time he left them to be in place on that bridge awaiting our arrival. That was John, a through-and-through bundle of unrepressible energy!

It was absolute hell riding through Avonmouth. The gusting winds were funnelling between the warehouses and riders were getting physically blown off their bikes. One minute they were in front of you and the next they were in the hedge or gutter. As soon as we hit those conditions I stopped to have a word with Philip. I told him to follow as close to me as he could and to cycle crouched down, just like Dad, and by doing so I would protect him from the wind. He just replied "Good idea." He understood and did exactly what I asked. His endeavour, application, and concentration, were incredible.

In these uncharted conditions we were proceeding very carefully when suddenly I was beset by a moment of sudden, absolute helpless panic. As we skirted Bristol and were coasting down a sweeping dual carriageway gradient and were about to pass under the Clifton Suspension Bridge, with the wind unusually in our favour, a tipper lorry sped past me and, through the turbulence following behind it, I momentarily completely lost control of my bike. It was as if I was a feather being tossed around in the wind. It was scary and I can still relive the feeling of having, for a split second, no control over my destiny. With equilibrium restored I glanced back and was mightily relieved to find Philip still behind me.

We cycled on in the wind and driving rain. Having left Bristol we were in open terrain, which was more exposed to the conditions. At least in that environment, unpleasant as they were, the elements were more consistent and easier to contend with.

It was 11 o'clock before we found a warm welcoming roadside cafe. We certainly appreciated a hot drink, even though it was excruciatingly painful getting the circulation back into the wet gloved fingers. At that point we heard the first stories that some of the group had been in some distress as they traversed Bristol. It could easily have been us. We had trained in poor weather, but these were by far the worst conditions we had ever encountered; our training was paying off! There was not a word of complaint from Philip, and I wondered if he was enjoying the adversity?

By the time we found a pub for lunch both the wind and rain were abating. I persuaded Philip to have a large bowl of soup so that he could warm his hands by holding it ahead of it warming his insides. It was a welcome longer-than-usual break, and we certainly needed it.

The sun was breaking through the cloud as we left the pub for our onward journey. At Bridgewater, having led Philip all day, I was shattered. I told him how tired I was and asked if he would lead. Incredibly, he dragged me in his slipstream all the way to Taunton, a distance of some fifteen miles. Our journey had taken over eight hours at less than eight miles per hour!

On completion of the leg we learned that 25% of the party had had to give up and be recovered by Buzz in the escort van. No wonder we had seen little of the van during the day, it had been busy collecting distressed colleagues! Given the chance, Philip would probably have opted for a warm van but not once during the day did he complain. He had, at a stroke, through his strength and fortitude gained the respect of both the organisers and colleagues. He had earned his spurs, or cycle clips!! A letter from the organisers to Philip's sponsors after we had returned home is worthy of a mention:-

'What more could Philip have done today to deserve your support? Nothing I would suggest. He cycled sixty-four miles from Chepstow to Taunton in cold, strong winds with rain pelting into his face most of the way. The temperature only reached 8 degrees during the day.

Philip stuck to his task, with his dad, with commendable spirit, when 25% of our party failed to complete their journey, such were the conditions faced by our group. I thought you would like to know of Philip's outstanding endeavour today. 8½ hours to cover 64 miles says it all!'

Having arrived at the hotel, with clothes wet both inside and out, the former through sweat and the latter through the elements, it was time to see about getting shoes and everything else dry. This vast amount of sodden gear could not be hung up in our bedroom. The hotel porter came to our rescue. "Tell you what," he said, "we have a small conference room which isn't being used. I'll put the caged radiator on and give you the key." Superb, just what was needed. It was a large radiator with an equally large cage, just right for laying out our wet clothes. The shoes dried out gradually and were ready for the next morning. It's one thing getting wet during the day but putting on already wet cold gear is no joke, ugh!

Friday – Taunton to Okehampton, 54 miles – Thankfully, the sun was back in the sky. I felt a bit 'leggy' from the previous day's exertions but Philip seemed in fine fettle. Paul cycled with us and Philip led us with great gusto for the first twenty-seven miles. Paul said "I don't know if I can keep up with him."

Where were those Devon hills I remembered so well from 1987? We soon found out at Bickleigh, where a long 1 in 7 met us. The steep incline went on for ½ mile followed by a further 1½ miles of a lesser but still steep gradient – it was tough cycling! On reflection I remembered this being the very welcome last hill in Devon in 1987 but now it was an unwelcome sight. The next thirteen miles took two hours!

During late morning I had my second bout of feeling queasy. It was nothing to worry about, probably dehydration from the exertions of the previous day and being careless with my liquid intake during the strenuous cycling terrain we were now in. Another long liquid lunch sorted me out but the last fourteen miles of the days took a further two hours to complete. It had been a hard day's cycling especially following the exertions of the previous day but the strength and stamina Philip was displaying were very heartening. By this time he was drinking frequently, of his own accord, to counter the deceptive levels of fluid loss.

The evening in Okehampton appeared to be going along as normal, until after dinner. Philip, for some reason, was in a peculiar mood which I put down to someone having said something which offended him, or had said nothing at all to him, so immersed were they in their own conversation during the meal.

We went up to the bedroom but he would not enter saying "I don't want to live with Mum and Dad anymore or at Downley Grange with Margaret." As usual, when such problems get in his mind he has no idea of a solution or where he wants to live, but it certainly grabs ones attention! Sitting on the staircase with him somewhat distressed, I tried to reason with him.

After a while I said "O.K., let's finish the ride and see Mum on Saturday and then we will see what we can do." This placated him. He went to bed and that was that!

I lay awake for some time that night wondering what the morning would bring but he arose in a stable frame of mind and the issue was not raised again. Was he tired, exhausted or not feeling well? I will never know, but he had worked extremely hard during the previous two days.

Saturday – Okehampton to Redruth, 73 miles - Knowing how at times I had struggled during the previous two days, we were about to set out on our longest ever journey in a day. The terrain would be a series of long gradients/hills, including Bodmin Moor. It was not a day I was relishing. We would be exposed to the busy A30 all day with an estimated time of arrival of five o'clock.

Philip, when asked, was now quite happily leading the way along the noisy busy road full of holiday traffic, pleasingly without too many lorries. A lay-by snack at twenty-three miles and on we pedalled, having been told there was a Little Chef at thirty-seven miles which turned out to be forty-seven miles. Annoying as it was at the time it left only, yes, only twenty-six miles to cycle at 14.00 hours, such had been our progress.

We had had a pleasant surprise during the morning from a 'little old lady' sitting on a lay-by crash-barrier taking photographs. Being polite, I put my hand up to acknowledge her. Surprise, surprise, she spoke to me! It was Helen who, without us realising, had overtaken us on the road a few miles earlier on her way from High Wycombe, where she had stayed with Alice on her way to Redruth!

Had Helen not spoken to me I would have cycled on without even recognising her, or my car, standing in the lay-by! That incident shows just how much concentration one puts into the journey ahead, particularly on trunk roads, in trying to avoid the roadside debris which is waiting to knock you off course! Large stones and glass are a menace.

Philip was thrilled to see Helen. As we started off after lunch, he was still visibly excited. I had to tell him to calm down, and to get back to concentrating over the last few miles. We didn't want any slip ups so close to our destination. Although we were tiring, by the time we reached Redruth at 16.15 hours, well ahead of expectation, the peace and tranquillity which greeted us as we turned off the A30 after the hours of constant noise, and into the deserted streets of the town, was quite unbelievable. It was so peaceful it was like moving into another world after the earlier noise and bustle.

Subsequently when Alice saw photographs of Philip and me sitting outside the Redruth hotel in the Saturday evening sunshine with our customary drinks she remarked how smart we looked. I reminded her Mum had arrived on the scene and our evening attire had therefore been laid out on our beds before we arrived! Helen, not being able to get accommodation at the hotel, had by this time gone off to her B & B, before returning for the evening dinner.

After dinner, as time would be at a premium on the Sunday morning, the certificates for completing the marathon journey were to be presented to each participant at the hotel entrance. Philip, on hearing his name being announced, proudly strode up the steps to the loudest applause of the evening. He realised the significance of his achievement and, with beaming face and proudly clutching his certificate, returned to us. He had certainly earned his recognition.

It was not until later, when I saw the photographs of us watching the presentations, that I realised how gaunt and thin in the face I had become. The strain of the previous two weeks had taken its toll and so had the chesty cough and cold I had inherited from our soakings earlier in the week.

Sunday – Redruth to Lands End, 29 miles - We were both up bright and early with less than three hours cycling to go to complete this epic journey. There were no physical jerks before departure but there were plenty of high jinks in the car park. John, who had cycled every scheduled mile, and more, was busy riding around with two others perched on his bike, one on the handle bars and one on his seat as he stood up on his pedals. Who would have thought that only months previously he had been lying in a hospital bed, seriously ill! Philip stood aloof from the frivolous goings on. I was relieved, as I could envisage someone completing their journey in an ambulance!

All twenty-seven initial starters of the adventure some fifteen days earlier were taking to the road. At this stage I felt sorry for the seven who, although completing the journey, had not cycled, as planned, all the way.

Paul said he would like to cycle with Philip and me for the final miles. As we skirted Penzance the telephone rang; it was the Stephen Foster Show from BBC Radio Suffolk. There was a guest on the show and all three of us exchanged banter, with me reporting, that all being well, we would be at Lands End before midday. Stephen asked if I would telephone the station to let them know of our safe arrival.

In the studio after I had gone off-air the talk for some minutes apparently centred around me at sixty-five even entertaining what I had achieved. Stephen had been following the updates during the previous two weeks and, despite both he and his guest being much younger than me, neither could imagine even contemplating such a mad jaunt if they had only themselves to look after, let alone caring for a third party, day and night along the way. I didn't think of or see it that way!

Philip was now comfortable in Paul's company and respected what he said. As the exchange with Stephen had gone on for longer than expected the chase around Penzance to catch up with them certainly again took its toll on my already tired legs. Sensibly Paul, on seeing the distance I was adrift, suggested to Philip that they should stop for a drink.

Having rejoined them, after the break, Paul asked Philip if he would like to lead us. With no second bidding needed he was off like an express train, getting further and further ahead of us. Suddenly, it dawned on me what was going on in his mind. Just as in 1987, his mission was 'I'll get there first', despite having twelve miles still to go.

I chased after him and told him he was being unkind to Paul by cycling so fast, and as planned we joined the rest of the group, assembling a short way from Lands End to enable us to all arrive together.

As we cycled into the Lands End complex we were greeted by a beaming Mum, who had again passed us unnoticed out on the road soon after Penzance. She hadn't acknowledged us as, sensibly, she did not want to do anything which could break our concentration.

On our arrival folk within the group, who had hardly been able to acknowledge that Philip had been in their company for the past two weeks, started slapping him on the back, shaking him by the hand and congratulating him on his achievement. Quite incredibly, he knew everyone of them by name. Once again he had taken in so much more than given credit for.

With congratulations over I telephoned Radio Suffolk, asking that they let Stephen, who was on air, know we had arrived safely at Lands End. The noon news bulletin concluded by reporting our safe arrival at Lands End, and adding to the snippet the station's hearty congratulations.

When we started our epic journey I had not expected the ongoing level of interest we received from Radio Suffolk. What a chance to raise money went begging! Being too wrapped up in what we were doing, at no time did it occur to me to appeal for monetary support, and after 'signing off' none of the presenters appealed for support on our behalf. Sadly not a single penny was raised from the reports - what a missed opportunity! I had too many other things on my mind!

In retrospect, I still feel guilty that I was not able to respond to well-wishers at Lands End in the way that I should have done. Their enthusiasm and greetings were overwhelming but I was too exhausted to react and to give them the time they merited. I was still very much wound up with protecting Philip and being hustled by Outdoor Adventures to get to the signpost for their publicity photographs. What a feeling of triumph it was standing beside the arm pointing North to John O'Groats, some 874 miles away. It didn't seem five minutes since we had been looking at a similar sign pointing south toward Lands End. What a fortnight of experiences Philip and I had enjoyed!

When the back-slapping was over and the majority of the group had departed by coach for Bristol to catch their respective trains, it was time to finally relax with our bottle of champagne. It was a job well done and now I had time to feel exhausted. I was only too pleased we were staying put in the comfort of the Lands End Hotel for a couple of days.   As he sipped his glass of champagne Philip's face said it all.   Dad we've done it again!

Sitting quietly outside on the warm patio of the hotel, it was time for reflection.   Philip had done wonderfully well.   He could not have done better.   Out on the road he had not caused me a single moment of concern.   He had concentrated 100% and maintained his focus despite any distractions that may have been going on around him.

THE HIGH SPOT - our day together before the adventure started visiting Dunnett Head and Duncansby Head, coupled with those wheeling peewits in the sky at John O'Groats.

THE LOW SPOT - it still haunts me when I think about it. Bristol, when I momentarily feared for our safety when the tipper lorry passed me and I felt like an out of control feather as I was buffeted in its swirling slip stream.

Our cycling expertise had been put to the test in both 1987 and 2001, during which time we had between us, cycled some three thousand five hundred miles.   We did not over that vast distance, have a single puncture, buckle a wheel, bust a spoke, break a pedal or smash any gears.   What a credit to Philip's expertise!

Chapter 25 - Busy Times

With everyone from the group having departed the scene, our two days of relaxation at the Lands End Hotel was bliss. We just wandered about in the warm sunshine, taking in the coastal walks which gave Helen and me time to chat with Philip marching ahead, being still full of youthful energy. It was as if he had just been on casual cycle rides those past few days, not cycling up to seventy miles a day. The spring in his step emphasised how pleased he was with his endeavours over the previous two weeks - he was simply bouncing along!

Throughout the day Philip was intrigued by the noisy British Airways helicopters whirring overhead on their way from Penzance and out to sea via the Longships Lighthouse to the Wolf Rock beyond, and onward to the Isles of Scilly. We pointed out to Philip, on the map hanging on the hotel wall, where the helicopters had come from and where they were going to.

We asked if he would like to do that journey one day. Much to our surprise he thought he would. An idea for some time in the future!

Our one excursion from Lands End was to the nearby Minack Theatre. It was fascinating to visit this unique site, which was an amphitheatre hewn out of the rocky cliff edge. It was only with some difficulty we could appreciate how Rowena Cade and her gardener began this project as recently as 1932. Philip sat on the stone seats whilst Helen and I wandered around, marvelling at the now modern facilities and artefacts that graced the site.

Suddenly we were aware everyone had lost interest in the theatre. In the sea below a school of basking sharks was thrashing about, probably in play. As plankton-eating monsters, harmless though they are supposed to be, based on their vast size (which can be up to forty feet in length and weighing up to five tons) they are not a species I would wish to encounter in the water!

Unlike our 1987 'End to End', there were no bikes to collect from the railway station and despite my best endeavours at the laundry in Preston, Helen was still presented with a goodly pile of sweaty stale-smelling washing. What a homecoming treat for her!

Philip's return to Downley Grange was just as welcoming as fourteen years earlier. With the sun shining, tables were laid up on the patio laden with food and sparkling fruit juice. The fellow residents, who had cheered Philip off three weeks earlier, were waiting to cheer his return as we rounded the corner. He responded as heroes should, by being pleasantly overwhelmed at the fuss being made of him but nevertheless lapping up every minute of the adulation.

Photograph taking over, Helen and I bade everyone farewell, gave Philip lingering hugs and a further 'well done' and returned home to a more stable life.

It was not all tranquillity, however, as the committee of one still had plenty of tidying up to do by way of thanking our generous supporters. Money was still being received.

Thinking I was 'as fit as a flea,' on return home I bounced onto the tennis court full of misplaced confidence. Playing (or trying to), felt unreal. I had no hand/eye co-ordination, the former no doubt from gripping the handlebars of the bike so tightly over such a long period, and the latter through the constant wind pressure onto my eyes during the daily cycling. Within a week mother-nature had healed these problems and I was back to normal, making solid contact with the ball only for it to plop into the net or speed out of play beyond the base line. In my world nothing had really changed!

Philip said he would like to go to the annual Jogle Dinner at Newquay to collect a further certificate from the association which, we were advised, was ready for collection. Having attended the dinner a number of times since 1988 it was no big deal to be returning again. We always got a warm welcome and everyone was always pleased to see Philip.

On this occasion, having submitted a copy of our diary to Geoffrey, the editor of the association's magazine, we got a special welcome from members. Our adventure had been styled an epic journey, with Geoffrey adding his thoughts at the end of the diary which read:-

'There are always hazards for cyclists - any motor vehicle and traffic generally, especially on busy noisy roads when it's impossible to hear what's coming from behind, potholes, gravel, drains, manholes and debris, plus wind and rain. Excessive heat and cold don't help either, and I sometimes wonder whether those who don't cycle realise this. You had your fair share of most of these Andy, and you weren't even

riding your own bike.   There's also the sheer physical and mental effort that's needed - let's face it, unlike Philip, you no longer have youth on your side.   Above all, you had the added burden of your understandable concern for Philip's well-being and safety and special needs, which must have left you drained at times.   For me, this puts your Epic Journey up there with the best.   Well done to both of you; a fine achievement'.

On arrival at the hotel, our first port of call was to try to view the trophies so Philip could see his name on the Eagle Trophy alongside that of Ian Botham.   As he was still very much into his days at Lords it certainly made him feel good to find his name linked with such a famous one.   On this occasion, for security reasons, sadly the trophies were under lock and key away from the public's gaze.

As ever, resplendent in his new sports jacket, brown trousers and association tie Philip was obviously in good form and ready for his roast lamb dinner.   So that he could see what was going on I suggested to Philip he should sit facing the top table.

With the dinner over it was time for the presentation of the certificates and trophies covering the exploits of members, both old and new, in getting from one end of the country to the other by whatever means they saw fit during the previous twelve months.

Although the mode of transport was largely cycling there were plenty of others, motor bikes, of all sorts and sizes, walking, jogging (oh the sore feet!), motorised scooter, horseback and a return journey by car.

As in 1988 Dennis, as president of the association, was making the presentations.   Philip enthusiastically applauded each recipient knowing it would soon be his turn to be acknowledged when his certificate was presented.

It was time for the last trophy to be presented.   Dennis was a past master at building up the atmosphere prior to making his announcement of the winner of each award.   It was therefore no surprise that he was about to do the same again.

On this occasion he referred back to a young man who had touched everyone's heart fourteen years earlier and whom he was pleased to see was in the room again for the current dinner.   Autistic he may be, but Philip immediately knew to whom Dennis was referring and, with eyes sparkling, was anticipating being called up to get his certificate. As Philip was about to leap out of his chair Dennis continued his citation. "Not only is this young man in the room but, for the first time in the history of our association, the Eagle Trophy is being awarded to a previous holder. In cycling from John O'Groats to Lands End from 5th to 20th May and raising £23,880 in doing so, can I ask Philip Childs to come up and collect his trophy." Come up; no invitation was required! Hardly had his name left Dennis's lips before Philip's chair was flung back and in half-a-dozen loping strides he had reached the President, and was standing beside him ready once again to milk the acclaim of the assembled company.

As I furtively searched for a handkerchief to dab my eyes, with a beaming face, Philip posed for photographs clutching the large Eagle Trophy, with this time, a replica for him to keep. His spontaneity said it all. He was again an acknowledged hero with Dennis having reversed the Eagle Trophy presentation from first to last because of the significance of Philip being the first ever double holder!

As soon as we could, in a quiet corner of the room, we telephoned Helen for her to be excitedly told by Philip, "I've won the cup again," and with that he handed the telephone back to me to fill in the details. He was still a man of few words!

Shortly after this further momentous occasion in Philip's life, Helen received a telephone call from HFT's Head Office. "Would two members of your family be prepared to accept an invitation to a Buckingham Palace Garden Party?" It was decreed by both Helen and Alice that Philip and I, if he agreed, should attend. As Philip was not coming home for a further two weeks and there was some urgency for a reply, Helen telephoned Margaret and suggested it would be appropriate for her to ask him if he would like to go and to let us know his reaction.

Having asked Philip the question she telephoned, barely able to contain herself. "Does he want to go? He'd be on the next train it's such a great idea!" The important-looking envelopes containing the invitations duly arrived and the July date was set.

The March Review, in comparison with what had gone before, was a fairly routine affair. Emotionally, all was quiet and Philip was enjoying his cookery class at Hatfield College and the on-site gardening tuition courses conducted by tutors provided by the college.

Some residents had moved off-site into community houses but Philip had again refused to consider leaving his current accommodation. We also learned, for the first time, of future plans to redevelop the internal layout of Swallow Cottages, where he had lived for the previous thirteen years. It seemed incredible that, having been built so recently the cottages were already being considered inappropriate by the local authority to meet current guidelines.

A pattern had become established with the reviews that, rather than Philip sitting through the nitty-gritty discussion regarding his activities, some of which was not too complimentary, he would be called in at the end of the meeting and be given a summary of what had been discussed. Sarah, his new Reviewing Officer from Bucks, concurred with this arrangement.

Sarah's first report on the level of dependency Philip required concluded that he benefitted from a structured, predictable routine and that he needed support to manage his anxieties. She noted that Philip had many skills but that he needed support. This was a 'spot on' first assessment of Philip's needs.

At the end of the review, Philip was pleased to show Sarah where he lived and the gardens and kitchen where he worked.

When Helen had reached Lands End the previous May having seen the southern portion of the route she had expressed an interest in seeing the northern half. To concur with her wishes we decided that a spring holiday in Scotland with a few days on the Orkney Islands followed by retracing our route from John O'Groats to the Lake District, would be ideal. The two-week break was set up and everything, we thought, was set for 'go'.

The car was loaded and we set off to collect Philip from Downley Grange. On arrival we found him in a truculent frame of mind sitting out of sight in the garden and not at all ready to come on holiday. What was wrong? Had we taken it for granted he was coming - had we not talked enough about it with him - had we missed signals he was not keen on joining us? All of these queries suddenly flashed through our minds.

Shocked as we were at seeing him like this Helen sat on the seat in the garden chatting about what we intended to do during the holiday. Suddenly after twenty minutes she realised Philip thought we were flying to Scotland. On reassuring him that we were going by car his mood changed.   Almost immediately he was amicable, ready for a quick shower and change of clothes, and looking forward to seeing Uncle Malcolm and Aunty Diane at Leeds where we were scheduled to stay for the first two nights on our way to Scotland.

With the changed mood coupled with an air of relief and bewilderment, we departed.   We then realised we had taken it for granted that Philip would expect to go to Scotland by car, whereas in his mind it appeared he thought he would be going by air, just as he had done twelve months earlier.   What a break down in communication.   We should never take anything for granted!   The experience also showed how much he had wanted to do the second 'end to end' cycle ride - he had been prepared to fly to achieve that aim, but not so for a routine holiday.

Philip took the regular changes in our holiday accommodation in his stride, none more so than an unfortunate experience at Arrochar on our way south.   I had arranged, as I thought, two nights in the comfortable hotel overlooking Loch Long where we had stayed in 2001.   We confidently marched into the hotel without checking its name.   With Philip in tow with our cases, I made to check in.   After a thorough search we were told there was no reservation for us.   I duly produced my letter of confirmation only to be told we were at the wrong hotel.   Duly deflated we made our way to the right location.

Yet another shock was in store for us.   We checked into the correct hotel, behind a well known tour party.   By this time we were having misgivings.   The hotel had an uncomfortable feel about it which was reinforced as we were escorted to our rooms up dated dark staircases and into equally unattractive bedrooms.

The whole setting and ambience of the place was well suited to a Hitchcock movie.   A serious discussion took place.   We decided, as the place smelt and was damp, and not as clean as we would have wished, that we would rather not stay.

I returned to the original hotel.   They could accommodate us.   I went back to Helen and Philip and we decided for the first time in our lives to immediately check out, telling the staff why, as kindly as possible.   They were astonished.   As we left the foyer, our master of the English language added "It smells and it's dirty."   Our thoughts and earlier conversations had been very succinctly portrayed!

Despite this incident and after its uncertain start the holiday turned out to be an enjoyable break. Philip was able to recall every turning we had previously taken, including the wrong one in Kendal - all's well that ends well!

The spring edition of Today, HFT's magazine, had Philip emblazoned on the front cover holding the Eagle Trophy. It was a magnificently reproduced photograph showing one of the proudest moments of his life.

Philip's first reaction upon seeing himself on the cover of the magazine was, "That's me." He then hurried round the Downley Grange site plonking it in front of anyone he came across, taking a step back and excitedly awaiting their reaction. He was not disappointed with the responses; he was enjoying himself.

It was time for the Garden Party. For ease of transport we all stayed with Alice, who by this time had bought a terraced house near Beaconsfield.

Over the previous weeks Philip had looked forward to this day and was obviously very excited about it. Looking very smart and quite the 'city gent' in his new dark-blue suit complete with a maroon Jogle Association tie, Helen drove us to Beaconsfield station. There were ominous dark clouds gathering in the direction of London. Oh dear, were we going to get a soaking?

On the station platform, as we waited for the Marylebone bound train to arrive, I engaged in conversation with a lady and gent who were in equally smart attire, particularly the lady, who was peering out from below a large wide-brimmed hat; just right for a Buckingham Palace Garden Party I thought. I was correct; they had come from Penzance for the occasion and had stopped off nearby overnight.

For some reason which I never established, they were being treated like royalty by British Rail. They were seen off by a member of staff at Beaconsfield and welcomed by the Station Master at Marylebone.

During the journey from Beaconsfield the couple had been interested to learn of Philip's exploits and invited us to ride with them to Buckingham Palace. We were all shepherded into a waiting taxi by the welcoming Station Master. Philip thought this was all very grand, and it was.

Not knowing what to expect when we arrived at The Palace it was a surprise when the cab dropped us off in The Mall, some two hundred yards away, to join a snaking queue of other folk awaiting entry to the Party.

Once in the queue we were surrounded by all sorts of very important-looking people, some in dress uniform emblazoned with medals, some in national costume, some in morning suits and others, like ourselves, just very smartly turned out in new suits.

Philip was undoubtedly intrigued to be amongst such an assortment of people in their finery. I tried to tell him what the various dress codes meant and that the crowds behind the barriers on the other side of the road were onlookers who had not been invited to the party. He was taking in every last bit of the atmosphere and listening to every word I said.

As the queue shuffled towards the wrought iron entry gates to the Palace I told Philip we would walk very slowly so that once we got through the gates we would have time to look around and to take in the atmosphere. This strategy proved correct as Philip, once inside the Palace entrance doors, took stock of everything he saw.

We were soon ushered out into the by now sunlit gardens, and what a spectacular backdrop to the rear of the palace they provided. Keeping to the well-defined public areas we strolled around the gardens feeling very much part of the scene, along with thousands of others. The number attending was far greater than I ever expected – I had been expecting to join hundreds not thousands!

We wandered around the full extent of the gardens, listening to the bands and 'people watched'. How interesting that pastime was. Some were very pompous 'had to be seen' types as they strutted about, looking quite ridiculous, with their noses in the air as if they had walked in something left by misbehaving corgis! Others, like Philip and me, were just pleased and relaxed to be there.

When the royal party came out from the palace, we watched chosen guests being presented to The Queen and observed her majesty along with The Duke of Edinburgh, and the Princes Charles and Andrew, passing by. Philip was well aware of who he was seeing and recited their names and birthdays.

Realising the Royal Party was about to leave the marquee where they had had their tea I correctly assumed they would make their way back into the palace along the second defined walkway. Philip and I had a ringside view as we were first to the restraining rope. It crowned Philip's day as he could see the party approaching and could have touched them as they passed. With great satisfaction we wheeled away and departed for Beaconsfield to relate our experiences to Mum and Alice, who were eagerly awaiting us.

There was no doubting Philip was pleased to have been part of the afternoon and at no stage had he appeared overawed, rather he had loved every minute of it. Sadly he is not able to relate the experience to others, but it is all tucked safely away in his memory!

A routine blood test revealed Philip's Gamma GT levels were rising, having reached 101 against an expected norm of 10 - 50. As this could have been from the side effects of the Carbamazepine he was taking we asked to see the local practice doctor. He stated that he would not be concerned unless the level reached 200, but nevertheless agreed, taking into account the improvement in Philip's behaviour, that the drug level could be reduced. A 25% reduction to 300 mg per day was prescribed, with a further review in four months.

What a social year 2002 was turning out to be for Philip! As a family, we attended a service held at St. Martin's-in-the-Field to commemorate the 40th anniversary of HFT. Philip was pleased to see David, the manager at Downley Grange in the 1980's, who now managed a home in Yorkshire. We also renewed acquaintance with a number of folk from yesteryear.

After the service, a reception was held in Canada House. A short while after arriving we were conscious that Philip appeared to be the topic of conversation. One very intrigued, tall and imposing lady could no longer contain herself. She very purposefully strode over to Philip, grabbed his hand and congratulated him on his cycling achievements. He was completely taken aback by this sudden invasion of his privacy but, having digested the compliment said, "Thank you very much." Upon seeing this, the remainder of the group followed. By this time he was enjoying the adulation and thrust his hand out to accept their compliments. Other attendees suddenly realised what the fuss was about and followed suit in congratulating him on what he had done for HFT. He was again being treated like a hero and he loved it.

Somewhat puzzled by how Philip had been recognised by so many people, it did not dawn on us until, on returning home, we realised he was dressed exactly the same as in the A4 colour photograph emblazoned on the front cover of HFT's Today magazine depicting him happily holding the Eagle Trophy!

The time in London was concluded by queuing to ride on The London Eye. Philip enjoyed looking out over the city from the slowly moving wheel while the natural light faded and the vista twinkled as the artificial lights below became more prominent. It was another memorable day in his life.

The scheduled review of Philip's medication levels duly took place, as planned, after four months. The Gamma GT level had reduced to 75 and Margaret confirmed that there had been no noticeable deterioration in Philip's behaviour during the intervening period. She added that he now appeared more sociable and alert. It was agreed a further 25% reduction from the original dosage should be tried. This was welcome news.

It was also reported that Philip was making steady progress with his Basic Survival Cookery Course at Hatfield College. Although he was gaining in confidence and enjoying the experience of improving his expertise with a knife for peeling and cutting, I could never see him being self-sufficient in those skills. Under close supervision he could perform tasks but, in my opinion, on an independent basis it would be a non-starter.

It was holiday time again and Philip enthusiastically reaffirmed his interest, expressed some eighteen months earlier, in flying to the Isles of Scilly by helicopter. We wondered, could his initial reluctance to join us in Scotland the previous year have been his way of expressing his disappointment that we were not then going to the Isles of Scilly? As with many facets of Philip's life, we will never know the answer!

Using a helicopter as a mode of transport was not Helen's first choice but on hearing that the Scilly Isles were some twenty-eight miles from Lands End and that the crossing could be very uncomfortable she settled for the quicker option.

There were great expectations as we drove to Penzance where we met Mary from Netpack, the distributors of the Christmas Cards I sold on behalf of the Trust. For the previous five years (now increased to eleven years) I had been the top-selling agent and Mary, knowing we would be travelling to Penzance, wished to meet us and to offer parking facilities at Long Rock, not too far from the heliport, whilst we were on the Isles of Scilly.

No sooner had we arrived at the British Airways heliport than we learned that one of the two helicopters that usually made up the service was out of order. Our flight would not run and we would have to wait for the next one, which would fly via Tresco rather than straight to St. Mary's.

On a bright sunny evening it was no hardship whatsoever to fly past St. Mary's on our way to Tresco and to view parts of the archipelago from the air which we would otherwise not have seen. The waters below were crystal clear and unpolluted. As we touched down on Tresco we had our first glimpse of the famous Abbey Gardens - they looked inviting.

On leaving Tresco we flew over St. Mary's to the airport on the far side of the island. Just giving the house name was sufficient to be dropped off at the correct location in Old Town Bay, less than a mile from the airport. We were amused as both the transport and the driver appeared to be well past their sell by date!

The house we had rented was ideal. There was plenty of accommodation, including a self-contained conservatory so we would not have to be 'on top of ' Philip whilst in the house. He could watch television and go to bed when he was ready, but we would nevertheless still need to check that all the taps had been fully turned off before we could rest! This was a small price to pay for the use of a property which felt like home as soon as we had walked into it.

Philip agreed we should hire bikes for the week, but they were little used as the weather was very kind to us. We walked and caught boats from Hugh Town to the islands of St. Martin's, Tresco, Bryher and St. Agnes, all of which were relaxing in their different ways. Philip enjoyed being the first to spot which of the open boats was destined for our chosen island. The early morning was a hive of activity on the quay as prospective passengers converged from all directions complete with rucksacks and anoraks ready for their day out.

On our way to St. Agnes with the Bishop Rock lighthouse in the far distance we lingered in Smith Sound to watch the puffins on the water before they flitted off to their burrows with food for their young. Philip was incredible, he often spotted their movement before the trained eyes of the boatman who, much to the amusement of the other passengers commented "He must have 360 degree vision!"

Our seven active days seemed to have passed before they had begun, as we prepared for our flight back to Penzance. As we were going direct, the return route was slightly different. Instead of flying over Lands End as we had done on the outward journey we flew along the coast and saw the Minack Theatre from the air. What an imposing little complex it portrayed, nestling within the craggy cliff tops below.

The cricket outings in the summer, and in particular to Lords, still played an important part in Philip's life. I obtained the tickets and we would either travel to London together or he would be brought to the ground by a male member of staff from Downley Grange. It was a chance to give staff members a day out sitting in a stand reserved for members and their guests which they otherwise may not have had the chance to enjoy. There was certainly never any problem in finding a volunteer! Philip was always pleased to see me, being eager to write up the teams in his score book, and for play to start.

The highlight of his social calendar remained the receipt of an invitation from cousins Philip and Angela to stay with them for the weekend and to visit Lords with Philip on the Saturday. They always made him feel so welcome that cousin Philip was fast becoming, after Alice, the most important young family person in Philip's life.

His cousin makes the sympathetic effort to talk to him about things that are important in his life and does not fire off robotic-type questions, which would immediately put him on the defensive. John Parker, who escorted us on the 1987 cycle ride, has the same humane knack of addressing him: hence his continued close relationship with both of them. He is always at ease in their company due to their ability to empathise with him!

Philip and Angela were by this time the proud parents of twins. Henry and Amelia were a delight to be with and Philip responded most gently to their overtures and energetic games. It was a pleasure to catch them together on camera.

The cricket excursions extended away from Lords into another special weekend which incorporated the 20/20 finals at Edgbaston. Play consists of three matches commencing at 11.30 and concluding at 10 o'clock in the evening. It entails watching one hundred and twenty overs of play and general hub bub, including the zany entertainment that goes on between games. Despite a full day of activity Philip's day is not complete until the presentations have been made. He enjoys every minute and lives the drama of the musical build up to the umpire's 'referred decisions' culminating in the cheers or jeers depending on the decision. It is always a tired Dad and a contented Philip who make their way back to the hotel!

Philip's life at Downley Grange continued in an undramatic fashion but his one-to-one was becoming vitally important to him to the extent that he was becoming obsessive regarding the time and day of the week, so much so that if it clashed with a visit to us he would not come. To combat this, the previously static times had to become more flexible. He ultimately accepted this as long as he knew in advance what was planned.

During his one-to-one sessions Philip visited and joined the library. He borrowed mainly factual books which he could pore over. Coupled with this, his time at the library also included showing an interest in computers and the statistical information they contained.

A Review reported that the reduction in Philip's medication levels had helped his social awareness in that his disposition towards others had improved. He was now enjoying visits to the golf driving-range and was perceived as more outgoing and chatty. Additionally, he would attend the celebrations of other residents. In contrast to his adoption of new interests he had jettisoned gardening and, as there was now no central kitchen at Downley Grange, this occupation was sadly no longer available to him.

Other traits began to appear, causing temporary problems. He was seemingly deliberately picking up dirt or mud and soiling his clothes. He would, when asked, change into clean clothes. His key-worker dealt with this issue head on and the phase passed. Was he seeking attention?

Completely out of character he began to spend his money when he was out and, more seriously, created problems by being secretive concerning its whereabouts, saying that some of it was missing when it was getting low. Whilst his accusations were without foundation they could not be ignored, and it had to spelt out to him how unpleasant fabrications of this nature were for everyone. The incidents did not continue but he then decreed college, at £2 per session, was too expensive and declined to attend.

He was, however, still prepared to walk the two miles to buy his daily newspaper and to pay for a monthly subscription to receive his Sky Sport which had been set up. The latter had become important to him with the increasing year-round coverage of live cricket.

The lighter side of his fabrications came when we learned through Margaret who, in turn, had heard through her staff, that Helen and I were getting divorced. We concluded he must be watching too much television and was bringing into his world the dramas played out in East Enders and Coronation Street!

It felt peculiar that he should bring Helen and me into his fantasies in this way as, whilst Philip would never telephone us, it was always commented upon how important his contact with his family unit was to him and that he would regularly talk about Mum, Dad, Alice and cousin Philip. He went very sheepish when we tackled him for talking such nonsense.

We wished him to talk, especially as his meaningful ability was so limited but, not in this sad way. His comprehension was usually good but under pressure his language was still very stilted, and could easily turn into gobbledegoop. It is unlikely that it will ever be any different.

We assumed, as did those at Downley Grange, that the above episodes and changes in interests were directly related to the reduction in medication. An additional welcome effect was a reduction in the Gamma GT levels by fifty points to fifty-seven, which was a vast improvement.

After further reference to these incidents, the Review Report concluded that, on the whole, the medication reductions had proved successful and any subsequent behavioural problems were being managed effectively by the staff. It was further concluded that having management strategies in place was preferable, at that stage, to increasing the medication levels again to control behaviours. It was pertinent, and likely to remain so, that throughout his life Philip would still need close support with his day-to-day needs, such as a healthy diet, medication, hygiene and changing of clothes. Without prompting, these facets of his life were, sadly, largely non-existent.

After the build-up and excitement of the second 'end to end' jaunt, cycling still formed an important part of Philip's life, but by now only with me. The taking off by himself from Downley Grange had evaporated with his improved behaviour.

Whatever the season, we would go off on cycling trips when he came home. During the summer I would telephone Downley Grange to ask Philip if he would like me to visit him the next day to have a ride. The answer was always in the affirmative.

The concluding bonus of the day for Philip would be a quick dash up the motorway to a known vantage point near Stansted Airport where we were quite close to the main runway and could watch the aircraft taking off and landing. He would spot a Jumbo in the far distance by its shape well before I had even realised it was approaching. They were his favourite aircraft.

As only Jumbo jets carrying cargo came into Stansted it was always interesting to see them take off fully loaded. As they trundled along the runway looking very much as if they would run out of tarmac before lift-off, Philip would always say, with some tension in his voice as they became air-bourne, "Up she goes." Being a technical moron it never ceases to amaze me how such a weight can even get up into the sky, let alone fly for thousands of miles once it's there.

After such a busy social period in Philip's life, with the threat of the looming changes to his accommodation and routines, we could not help but wonder, and be concerned about, what might be in store. Would he understand what was going on and the likely timescales and the significance of the changes about to take place? Once again only time would tell!

Chapter 26 - Yet More Desperate Times

As we feared, the news of the impending redevelopment of the Downley Grange site, coupled with the reduction in Philip's medication levels, was leading to increased anxieties. Whether it was one more than the other we will never know. Out of the blue a kettle was unceremoniously thrown when a male member of staff asked him if he was speaking to him, after getting no reply from enquiring if he would like some tea. One can only assume he was already simmering about something and this innocent challenge tipped his anxiety over the edge.

For some weeks this was an isolated, but nevertheless worrying incident which we wished to discuss with Margaret before we left for a holiday in New Zealand. The discussion did not reveal anything conclusive except that the future reconfiguration of Swallow Cottages was now an open secret and it was felt likely, with his acute hearing, that he could have become anxious through not fully understanding something he had heard being discussed by members of staff. A snippet of information could so easily be misinterpreted and create anxieties.

We had to accept it was only natural that the staff would talk about the changes and in most cases it would not matter if they were overheard, but with Philip it was different. He would have a limited understanding of what was going on, but why when and how he would be affected would be beyond his comprehension. This was a sure recipe for trouble!

During our three week holiday, his cousin Philip, Aunty Lavy and Alice kept up weekly telephone contact. With us so far away, despite still making our weekly telephone call to him it was an uncertain time for Philip. He was, therefore, always pleased to get their calls and especially an outing to the Imperial War Museum at Duxford with Alice. These three, plus Uncle Robert, additionally always sent him cards whenever they were away from home.

Our holiday over, it was time for me to become involved in the appeal to raise £2.3m to redevelop the Downley Grange site. As part of the launch I had been asked if I would speak on behalf of the Downley Grange parents immediately after The Princess Royal had formally launched the appeal. Having said, "Yes" it was becoming a frightening prospect.

During the early part of the appeal proceedings, Philip had carried out a Powerpoint presentation which covered his life with HFT and that of his family. He looked very smart and obviously felt very important with a scarf, which he refused to take off, casually slung around his neck.

Having decided, as part of the parent's appeal, that I would need to make a pledge, and on seeing Philip earlier 'doing his stuff' my emotions got the better of me. Relating to everyone that The Princess had earlier told me I was mad for taking on the exploits I had on behalf of HFT, I tore up my prepared notes and spoke from the heart. This was certainly appreciated by the assembled 'potential' donors. It told them how a parent viewed the outstanding work of the Trust and how much it meant for this to continue.

After his moment of glory, Philip's life was getting ever more confused and his anxieties increasing just by being on site and hearing the tittle-tattle. His attendance throughout the appeal launch would not have helped, as he would have heard and seen things he did not understand, except that where he had lived for the past thirteen years was, in a matter of a few months, going to be empty and temporarily closed down. Time scales, plans and reassurances of events some eighteen months hence, however many times they were repeated, were not comprehensible to Philip. Furthermore, with his lack of the conversational ability needed to ask any questions which were bothering him, his anxieties increased!

Knowing the problems he was facing in those circumstances, we could only refer back to the words of Dr. Hughes, who had tried to describe how, due to the utter bewilderment in Philip's mind, his unpredictable actions could seriously impair both his quality of life and the confidence of those dealing with him.

At the April Review it was reported Philip had returned to his earlier traits of self-inflicted accidents. He was dropping or throwing coffee mugs, leaving taps turned on and flooding the bathroom, running off site and, more worryingly, physically abusing staff.

From the comments made it was becoming ever more evident that Philip wanted to do more with computers. He was using the facility in the Resource Centre at Downley Grange, but finding an off-site happy medium was difficult.   He didn't want to go to Welwyn College but to Hatfield, where the course included other aspects of living which he did not wish to pursue.   It would have been a pointless exercise to send him somewhere he didn't want to go and a sure-fire recipe for disaster.

At the conclusion of the review we were handed a copy of the proposed plans for Philip's section of Swallow Cottages.   He would continue to live within the same area of the cottages and be part of the Autistic unit, which would house four residents.

Once we had had time to digest the proposals we considered the suggested layout to be quite inappropriate.   The area of the ground floor where Philip had lived for thirteen years had been allocated within the revamped building to someone else and to make matters worse he had been allocated accommodation on the first floor.   In our opinion it was another recipe for disaster.

After aligning the new plans with the existing layout we made our observations.   Bearing in mind the earlier problems Philip had created with water, when he was agitated, we thought a first floor room was asking for future problems.   Water on the ground floor can be controlled but not on the first floor.   Overall we thought the architect employed had little empathy with those who would be using the revamped accommodation.   We were on the one hand desperately worried by Philip's worsening behaviour and on the other hand fighting for his future.

In May our world plummeted to new depths of despair and with no prior warning.   We were staying in Kent with our friends Terry and Dee.   As per normal, on the Sunday evening we telephoned Downley Grange to speak to Philip.   Much to our amazement he wouldn't come to the telephone and no amount of coaxing from the staff would change his stance.   On future Sunday evenings he would take himself off into the grounds to avoid our calls.

As we could not let this continue we tried a different tack. Midweek, on our way from Beaconsfield, we telephoned and again tried to talk to him with the offer of taking him out to lunch.   Despite being in the room he again declined to talk.

In some desperation on another occasion we called unannounced and were relieved when he was pleased to see us, and quickly changed ready to go out to lunch.   What was now going on in his mind was a mystery as, for the first time his family had been given the cold shoulder. This unusual attitude continued.

Alice was rebuffed when she telephoned, offering to pick him up for onward transmission to us for a Father's Day lunch. To combat this we reversed the invitation and visited Downley Grange, where Alice joined us and we took him out. He was quite happy and relaxed once he got over his initial reticence on our arrival. The bewildering series of events continued throughout the summer.

8th July – We arranged to collect Philip to spend the weekend with Alice. This would incorporate Saturday on the Thames, cruising from Maidenhead to Windsor, and on the Sunday a visit to Lords. In his previous disposition it would have been a weekend of enjoyable activities!

On arrival at Downley Grange, Philip was missing. I found him in a very agitated state in the grounds and he was reluctant to come with me, claiming he was due to have his one-to-one with Kerry. Thankfully Paul, who was on duty, hearing what was going on, came quickly to the rescue, saying Kerry was involved in holidays with other residents and there would be no one-to-one. Philip reluctantly condescended to come with me and on the face of it, had a thoroughly enjoyable time.

18th July - The staff at Downley Grange were surprised as Philip, most unusually, had expressed a wish to attend the Duxford Air Show. As nobody was available to take him we were asked if we could help out rather than let one of the first times he had ever suggested doing something, fall by the wayside. He was not at all enamoured with that suggestion so we did not go and nor did he.

29th July - I collected Philip for the weekend. On my arrival at Downley Grange he had spilt coffee in a computer, knowing full well that neither food nor drink, were allowed near the keyboard. The staff gave him the benefit of the doubt, accepting that it was an accident, but I was not so forgiving, neither did I believe that other residents were moving his ground based, satellite television dish. In my opinion he was the culprit, either seeking attention or indulging a masochistic perversion by harming things which were important to him.

Once again, having got over the collection nonsense he had an enjoyable weekend attending the 20/20 finals at The Oval along with

Uncle Robert.   As the cricket did not conclude until 10 o'clock, on our return to Liverpool Street Station Philip was highly amused to be able to get his early edition of the Sunday Times on a Saturday!

A further treat on the Sunday was an enjoyable visit to Aldeburgh where we ate their renowned fish and chips out of the paper sitting on the beach.

On this occasion his time with us was no different from normal. He would spend more time in his bedroom than we would have liked but it was his decision and, in his own private space, he could watch the television programmes of his choice, play musical tapes or watch cricket videos.   He would eat properly at meal times and whilst he had to be prompted to shave, shower, and clean his teeth these tasks were carried out without undue fuss. He was still a pleasure to have at home.

August - Our usual plan to see Philip, either at home or visiting others every four weeks, was in tatters.   For no reason that we could fathom, suddenly a 'home' visit was unacceptable.   Hard as it was we had to accept this as his wish, but we asked ourselves why.   What was happening to him?

2nd September – The annual social event not to be missed - spending the weekend with his cousin Philip, Angela and the twins. Saturday was spent at Lords and we called to have a barbecue with Alice on the Sunday. He was ready and waiting to be collected, there was no nonsense for this visit!

8th September - As Philip and I were scheduled to take part in HFT's fifty mile sponsored cycle ride in early October I wished to make sure he was fit enough to do so. I telephoned as usual to make sure I was not conflicting with any other arrangements, and drove to Downley Grange. He was pleased to see me and, after the cycling, we took a trip along the M11 to have a picnic watching the aeroplanes at Stansted Airport.   This was all very much along the lines of our normal procedure. "Thank goodness for cycling" I thought!

17th September - I set out to achieve a repeat of the outing on the 8th by telephoning Downley Grange to make sure Philip was free the next day. Although on the premises, he would not talk to me. The next morning, as the sun was shining, I again telephoned and asked Barbara, the lady covering the night care duty, to tell Philip I would be arriving at 10 o'clock.

Within minutes a somewhat distraught Barbara telephoned to tell me how, on hearing of the arrangements, Philip had immediately stormed out of his flat and run off site. As I could not leave the problem unresolved, and Barbara thought it would be a good idea, I said I would nevertheless make a visit. I duly arrived on time at Downley Grange not knowing what to expect. Philip was missing, with a tepid, half-drunk mug of coffee on his windowsill. After searching the grounds to no avail I found him dawdling back from the shop after buying his newspaper. This was despite my having said that I would collect one for him on my way.

He said he would cycle, but I was not happy with his disposition. Whilst this would probably have changed once we were out on the road I was not prepared to expose him to danger. In his state of mind at that time, he may have done something erratic and caused an accident. What was the point in taking that risk? It immediately crossed my mind that we had come to the end of an era as cycling had been his emotional safety valve for so many years!

There had always been a risk factor in taking Philip out on his bike. Until now it had been at an acceptable level, but not anymore. In quieter moments we would try to talk to Philip about what was bugging him and the changes we were seeing, but it made no difference. Our Sunday phone-call was again rebuffed, so we decided to try to put our feelings over to him in a simple letter. When he chose to he could read and understand simple messages. It was worth a try.

We arranged that the letter would be sent via Norma, his current Key Worker, so that she could hand it to him and casually observe any reaction. The letter was sent, fully addressed, reading as follows:-

Dearest Philip,

Sadly Mum and Dad have to write to you as you will not talk to us on the telephone. We do not know why. It makes us very sad and unhappy as we do love you lots and lots and always will.

It seems you have become tired of cycling so we will not do it any more this year and will only start again in 2006 if you wish. This means when you come to see us we can go on the long walks at Orford/Aldeburgh/Felixstowe or Bawdsey which you so enjoy.

As you do not want to cycle Dad will go on Hilary's ride on 2nd October by himself and see you when he gets back. He would like to start at 9 o'clock so he is back by 2 o'clock. To save too much driving of the car in one day Dad is going to stay in Ware on Saturday 1st October. If you like, Dad will take you to the local Chinese or Pub on Saturday evening.

A change of plan as John will not be at home on 4th November. He and Chris have now asked if we would go and see them on 11th November for the weekend which we hope you are happy to do. We will collect you after college on the Friday and return to Downley Grange on Sunday afternoon, before it gets dark. (a phobia had arisen about travelling at night)

Perhaps you can talk to Norma about this letter and she can let us know what you think.

Lots of Love.

The letter was duly read without any obvious reaction. We had to console ourselves that, apart from the occasional upset his life at Downley Grange was seemingly happy enough. It seemed affairs relating to us were his problem. This was hard to accept, but his life with HFT had to be the number one priority. We were still fearful of further upsets as the move from Swallow Cottages back into the old core house at Downley Grange had yet to be negotiated. He had not enjoyed living there during his early days with HFT, and we could not see this being any different.

The weird chain of events continued, with Philip pleased to talk to anyone in the family who telephoned except ourselves. He reacted to them as if nothing in his complex brain was amiss. He was prepared to visit and stay with others but did not wish to come to visit us. What had we done wrong to set off this eerie state of affairs?

With Christmas looming, there was every indication that Philip was not going to grace us with his presence, refusing to put rings on his calendar around the dates of his homecoming. Norma, his ever-faithful key worker, and Karen, who usually took him out on his one-to-one, ultimately won the day for us, stressing that nothing goes on at Swallow Cottages at Christmas and it would therefore be very lonely. We could have left him to get on with it but it was not our style. Philip was part of our family and come what may, we still had every intention it should remain so and that, as far as possible, he should be involved in our family and the affairs of the extended family. Christmas without him was to us unthinkable.

In dire times such as these Alice, as ever, was a tower of strength and never waned in her supportive efforts to understand how Philip's mind was working. How lucky we and Philip were to have her, after thirty-five years in which our attention had been largely focused on her brother, still willingly doing whatever she could to help him. Considering what she had had to put up with throughout her life she could easily have had a different attitude towards him.

The catalogued events make for bewildering reading but with a thread becoming apparent. Open contact was in order with everyone except Mum, Dad and Alice. Margaret tried to reassure us that it was a passing phase and circumstances such as those we were suffering were not unusual. She also added that, in times of stress, those most loved by the offending party are those most severely tried. It was no reflection on how we treated Philip, just some odd hang-up going on in his mind. In those circumstances who does one feel most sorry for? Philip's reviews had always commented upon our sensible support for him and in turn how much his family meant to him. We now wondered if this was still the case in his befuddled mind.

As for the scheduled reconfiguration of Swallow Cottages which would take place after the completion of a nearby new high care unit we could not let the first plans proceed without a protest for change. It was grudgingly accepted that the points we were making about the initial plans had some merit, and through the District Executive the negotiations regarding the future layout of the Autistic Unit were brought to a satisfactory conclusion.

Eventually, Philip was allocated a ground floor unit which was scheduled to be ready by Christmas 2006, a seventy-one week build, if all went according to plan. We could now talk to Philip about where he fitted into the new plans but we had no idea what was going on in his increasingly muddled mind.

On seeing the footings of the new builds being excavated we realised just how much the noise and close proximity would intrude, for the next ten months, on Philip's need for peace and quiet. It was all going on just outside his lounge window. Wirelesses blaring, cement mixers whirring, coupled with the general crashing and banging about for a minimum of five days a week was not a happy prospect for anyone, let alone someone with such acute hearing, who by his very nature needs a fairly organised, stress-free type of environment. Even without this mayhem it was already plain that just talking about the proposed changes over the previous nine months or so had already had a detrimental effect on his well-being.

To say Philip's peace and quiet was being shattered was an understatement. Within days of starting the new build Swallow Cottages were deemed unsafe by the local fire officer. The contractors had managed to impact a mains power cable and smoke was seen coming out of the power points throughout the cottages. This in turn ruined all the plugged in appliances. With modern technology how do contractors manage to consistently do such things?

As a direct result of this disaster the occupants of Swallow Cottages were billeted for seven nights at a nearby Travel Lodge. Some residents thought it was a great adventure but Philip who was more knowing was awkward and stressed by the whole affair. His television, radio and video recorder were useless and he was being shunted around day and night!

This is the worst type of upset an autistic person could have. It was no adventure to Philip to be returning to Downley Grange during the day only to be shipped off back into bewildering circumstances again each afternoon. Had we been called we could easily have taken a good deal of the stress out of this calamity for Philip. Extracted, even reluctantly, from those chaotic conditions, his already frail equilibrium could have been protected and who knows it may have restored his faith in us. Like so many things in Philip's life we will never know the answer.

Through this incident nearly every electrical appliance at Swallow Cottages was condemned. This added to the confusion and stress as the most important tools in Philip's life needed replacing and this was not done immediately.

Although he looked rather dishevelled and his bedroom was a mess when I collected him, despite a strained beginning the Christmas holiday went well, with Alice joining us for a few days. Philip was pleased to see her. He and I made our usual visit to Burgh church for the Christmas Eve Carol Service. On our departure, the rector, Norman Davis, always had a cricket snippet to exchange with Philip, who responded as best he could and referred to Norman as, "A very nice man."

Despite 2006 being the year Philip would reach the big four zero, which was expected to be an important event in his plan of things, trying to talk him about celebrating it was another matter. A family party and one at the local village hall with the other forty residents was a taboo subject. However, ignoring it was not an option. With his phenomenal memory he was still very much into logging everyone else's birthday, so we could not ignore his own milestone. We were certain, despite his ongoing traumas, that he would expect a celebration. We decided that, on a low key basis, in the New Year we would make preliminary arrangements for the April parties. If we got it wrong it would have cost us a few pounds, but so what.

In contrast to the indecision regarding his birthday celebrations it was quite a different matter when planning the forthcoming cricket season. Visits to his cousins Philip and Angela, with Alice as an interim resting place for Lords, and a trip to Nottingham to stay with friends Mike and Judy for the 20/20 finals, were all immediately given the green light.

On three occasions during the Christmas break, and in particular when we were opening the presents, we noticed Philip momentarily appeared to stop what he was doing, wince and then carry on. Both Helen and I saw it happen. On his return to Downley Grange we reported these incidents so that it was logged on his medical records, just in case there was a health problem brewing.

At the conclusion of having spent a very pleasant ten days with us, on his return after New Year to Downley Grange, we could have cried when he opened the door to his bedroom. Not only was it still a tip, but it now had a far from pleasant odour about it. Suddenly Philip was gone having taken off into the darkness of the site. Was he ashamed of the state his bedroom or did he not want confrontation when the subject of his next visit to see us would be broached?

Having tracked him down and brought him back to Swallow Cottages all was calm. In the meantime Helen had complained to Angela, the senior person on duty, about the bedroom conditions he had returned to. During Philip's absence nobody had even peeked inside his bedroom to see that all was well.

Angela was aghast at what she saw and made what seemed to us to be a tell-tale remark. "Will Philip flip if I go into his bedroom?"

"Will he flip!" we said, "He can't live like this and we would think everything is in such a state he can't even start to think straight." Contrary to Angela's misgivings about encroaching into his room Philip was thrilled that she was prepared to help, and as we left was giving her a hug. Messrs. Jekyll and Hyde were still very much alive!

Whatever the circumstances leading up to it were we could not let this issue pass without for the first time in twenty years making a formal complaint. Even in an era of Political Correctness surely it had to be applied with an element of common sense. This was especially so with a vulnerable person such as Philip whose past history had indicated that close supervision would always be required.

On formally querying the state of his bedroom we immediately received a telephone call from Margaret, the manager, and for the first time we heard of the marked deterioration in Philip's behaviour during the weeks leading up to Christmas. The uncertainties and complexities we were experiencing with him were also now spilling over into his life at Downley Grange, so much so that outbursts and agitation were regular occurrences, to the extent that the staff lacked confidence in trying to deal with him.

Margaret hastily arranged an urgent Review. At such short notice it was only attended by in-house staff. It was soon revealed to us just how much Philip's behaviour had deteriorated. His moods swung from being an absolute delight one minute to a demon the next, for no apparent reason. He would appear calm and peaceful and then suddenly start shouting out loud. Something was happening to him which he could not control. He had become so unpredictable that some of the staff, in particular the younger ones, were losing their confidence in dealing with him and most certainly would do anything they could to avoid confrontation, hence the marked deterioration in the state of his living quarters and personal hygiene.

Of the current staff nobody remained who had experienced Philip in his fractious moods of the 1980's. It was a sad fact that despite his considerable earlier achievements and the passing of some twenty years since he was first accepted into HFT's care, from the sequence of events now occurring, it was plain to see that nothing had really changed or matured in his make-up during the intervening years. On the face of it they had, but under pressure, his anxieties soon returned and were still expressed in a most unfortunate manner. The cumulative effect of the alterations, and the uncertainties of life, were certainly getting to him in a most unpleasant way.

During his previous periods of extreme anxiety Philip broke things, but objects were not used as missiles as maliciously as they were now. Previously he was a danger to himself but not to others. The former still applied to his forays, unannounced, into the darkness of the unlit site, where even with the protective fencing there were still areas in which he could hide. Despite searching, it was never known where he went for an hour at a time, often without being adequately clothed. He simply vanished into thin air and returned when he was ready. He must have had the constitution of an ox as incredibly he suffered no ill effects from these lengthy periods exposed to the elements.

Margaret suggested she assemble a group of professional people associated with Downley Grange and that we should all meet in a further six weeks. What was going to happen in the meantime only time would tell! What was certain was that it would be a further five months before Philip would move back into the old core house of Downley Grange. When that happened he might be able to start understanding future plans and the likely time scales, but there was no guarantee of this.

The next meeting opened with the report of four serious incidents since the previous assembly.

5th February - Threw a plate of food in the kitchen.

8th February - Threw a cup of coffee and attempted to overturn a dining room table.

10th February - Threw a frying pan containing hot oil and food to the floor.

28th February - Threw a plastic bottle of milk at a college tutor. This last action had not been witnessed by any escorting staff from HFT and a college report was awaited, with the likely sanction against his further college attendance. What was he doing destroying the things which appeared so important to him?

It was reported that when Philip was individually supported his behaviour greatly improved. In other words his one-to-one was becoming, obsessionally, ever more important to him. A solution it may be but the cost of the extra support needed would be impossible for HFT to fund alone. Sarah, the Bucks Reviewing Officer, had made an application for increased monetary support from the council but a decision was still awaited.

Charts were being maintained to monitor behaviour, both good and bad, to see if any significant patterns emerged. A dietician assessed the types of food he ate and went through his likes and dislikes. Evening rotas of individual staff support were being established and a new medication, Paroxetine, had been introduced to see if this would reduce the intensity of the outbursts. We were to receive a telephone call each Friday from Norma, Philip's Key Worker, to let us know how the previous week had gone. We knew we would dread the Friday build-up to each call but we had to know what was currently going on regarding his behaviour.

These were desperate times, and Margaret re-emphasised the effect Philip's behaviour was having, not only on the staff but also on other residents. He could not go on upsetting almost everyone he came into contact with. We fearfully asked ourselves whether HFT were set up to cope with Philip's current levels of anxiety-induced outbursts. At this point we feared they were not and he would have to be placed elsewhere. If this happened it could only have been in a restrained, secure environment. How he, or we, could cope in those circumstances just did not bear thinking about – would his place with HFT be lost for ever?

Though we had listened with sympathy to the accounts of the problems Philip was creating, there seemed little we could do to help! He wouldn't come home so we could do nothing to give the staff a few days respite from him.

In discussing solutions, Margaret thought a forcible removal by us would do more long-term harm than good, despite agreement that a few days away from Downley Grange could have served to break up the pattern of increasingly intense outbursts. We could see he was in a vicious spiral and, try as we may, we could see no solution. We were all in a helpless predicament!

We were able, quite legitimately, to keep in touch with Philip through the regular reviews and quarterly meetings of the Friends Staff Association. Philip accepted this low level of contact, where he obviously did not feel threatened that we would be trying to coerce him to have a break with us.

It was certainly more difficult, now we were older, to cope with the traumas being thrust upon us. When younger we seemed able to respond to the adversity so much more easily. This did not mean we were other than fully committed to helping Philip but we felt the circumstances were certainly stacked against us. At this point we were distraught with worry. In short, we were powerless, and could help neither Philip nor HFT!

The plans for the fortieth birthday celebrations continued and we were pleased that they did, as suddenly in late March they were acceptable and interesting to Philip. Once the O.K. had been given he looked forward to the event and was prepared to visit us, no doubt encouraged by the fact that his favourite family members would be present.

I wrote to The Times, explaining what he had done in his life and asked that they put his birthday amongst other well known figures as a Charity Cyclist and to my delight they did as I asked. We also put a notice in the East Anglian Daily Times.

Having collected the daily newspapers as he sat on our sunlit patio looking through the Hatched Matched and Despatched columns, without prompting, the announcements concerning himself were triumphantly pointed out to us. He had that old look of satisfaction written all over his face! Oh for it to continue, but we knew that it wouldn't.

The close family party was a great success, with Philip taking on the role of host. This was followed by a further party, complete with Downley Grange's own disco at the local village hall which was splendidly decked out for the occasion. The caterers arrived and again it was very much Philip's function for the other residents and staff. It was a joy to see him suddenly so full of vitality and so obviously out to enjoy his celebrations.

With the music blaring we discreetly left the party as soon as we could to let an uninhibited Philip enjoy himself, which we understand he did for a further two hours. As we drove home we were pleased with our efforts on his behalf, though whether it would change anything in his current make up 'only time would tell'.

We were very soon to find out if anything had changed. Despite, at long last, the medication levels being increased back to their former dosage, at the next six weekly Review meeting it was very evident the anxieties had intensified. In addition to his disruptive behaviour being more pronounced, we were faced with hearing how he had physically assaulted a visiting college tutor, and had assaulted and hurt Margaret when she, as a voice of authority, had tried to reason with him about his behaviour in an attempt to get some rationality into his troubled mind. She was also trying to explain, and to reassure him about the future.

In destroying people's trust in him he was not now able do what he wanted to - he had been banned from the college course he now so desperately wished to attend. Most worryingly, Bucks County Council, through the requests for ever more increased finance for his one-to-one support, were asking ominous questions. Was Philip now in the most suitable environment for his needs? Did he need to be moved elsewhere to a specialised autistic unit? They had provided an extra £300 for the previous months one-to-one but, as we knew, with money short they could not commit to repeating it.

On hearing these comments we were again struck with terror but we could not defend his corner against whatever was decreed to be necessary. Philip's emotions were largely out of control and we also feared this could be an easy reason for HFT and Margaret to jettison a whole load of trouble. It could conveniently have been passed off as the decree of Bucks, their third-party paymaster.

Many times over the previous twenty years we had realised how fortunate we were to have chosen HFT as Philip's long term carers and despite everything now occurring they again came up trumps in his favour. Margaret stoutly resisted B.C.C.'s comments that he was in the wrong place and needed change. What a relief to hear her words, "The Trust still wishes to support Philip and a move at this crucial time would do more harm than good." These were the same words of wisdom she had used when we were suggesting forcible removal for a period with ourselves. Margaret, on behalf of the Trust, was showing the same level of fortitude and support for Philip as had her predecessors Bill and David.

It was now a matter of weeks before the move out of Swallow Cottages into the old Downley Grange house would take place. In the meantime, Philip was getting ever more agitated about everything in his life without being able to explain his intense frustrations and fears. He didn't need to explain as we all knew the uncertaintes of his life at

Downley Grange were incomprehensible to him. They were winding him up and the poor chap just could not cope with everything that was going on around him. The only thing he still valued was his one-to-one care, which included his time off-site shopping or swimming.

Even those times, however, were not drama free. In a fit of awkwardness, just as he had done with me some twenty years earlier when cycling, he set out to lose Karen, his one-to-one carer, in Epping. He achieved his goal, ultimately to the consternation of both of them, Karen as she had lost her charge, and Philip because he got lost in the town's backstreets. Having realised this, and that he had no support, when found he was in a complete panic. It never happened again!

Philip was a good swimmer but did not relish children splashing about in the water as he swam up and down the pool. Previously, he had not rebuked offenders but now he chose to do so, giving them a stilted lecture on behaving themselves. The children were left open mouthed as he swam off. It made for uncomfortable, but thankfully non-confrontational moments with accompanying parents. After so many years of using the same pool perhaps those affected, with good grace had become aware of Philip's limitations.

One day, we received a dramatic call from Downley Grange. Philip was acting intolerably and they wished to sedate him, but before telephoning the local surgery felt we should be advised. We were not against whatever action they felt was necessary, but said we would cancel everything we were committed to and would drive to Downley Grange. This was, in our opinion, an emergency and we had to do all we could to support Angela, who was the Team Leader in charge. From the previous Christmas we had every confidence in her ability to do what was necessary for Philip, and in turn for the other residents. She was very appreciative that we were on our way.

By the time of our arrival Philip had calmed down from his peak of anxiety but he looked a sorry, dishevelled, pathetic young man. Angela and I left to collect the prescription and to then find the late night chemist.

Trying to get some balance into the problem Angela agreed if, after sedation, we could get Philip into the car we should take him home. We were prepared to face whatever consequences were forthcoming the next morning but we were confident once with us at home he would calm down. With the sedative taken we waited as Philip became drowsier and drowsier. He walked falteringly towards the car, with Angela in attendance as if we were about to depart. The plan was that once there we would ask him to get into the car. All seemed to be going according to plan but, drowsy as he was, he steadfastly refused our invitation to get into the front seat of the car. Angela shrugged her shoulders. We all knew we were beaten.

For a draining four hours, despite the drugs having taken effect, we had done all we could but had to admit failure. We made to leave, watching Philip stagger back down the path on Angela's arm. Our anguish at this sight was excruciating and, with tears in our eyes and Helen crying out, "Whatever will become of him," we left for home.

He was still 'our boy,' and this was undoubtedly one of the lowest points in our lives.

Chapter 27 - The Mist Finally Lifts

The journey home from Downley Grange was not unlike our journey some forty years earlier from Hammersmith Hospital when we were handed our little bundle, with Professor Tizzard's comment that what we made of Philip would be up to us. The significant difference was now we were now largely powerless to shape his future. He had a mind of his own and from this we were now excluded. However we were still seeking to help him in any way we could, and the first hurdle to surmount would be the passing of the next eight weeks, after which when he would move from Swallow Cottages back into the old core house.

Thankfully Philip's agitation never again reached the fever pitch of the previous chapter and it was only necessary to administer the one sedative. It had been heartrending to witness, while at the same time feeling utterly helpless as we watched our dear son turning into a zombie before our very eyes.

Although over the following weeks there were still distraught and challenging times, life took on a slightly more balanced pattern, no doubt as a result of the Risperdal medication which had also been prescribed. Philip's demeanour was certainly quieter but it did not change his attitude towards us, Alice, or coming home. Thus our agony continued.

It was a relief when the day of the move back into Downley Grange finally arrived. Philip helped to pack up his belongings and seemed quite relaxed about his move into a quiet, spacious area of the old house, which had previously been used as the administrative hub of the home. He was pleased to be given his own key to the area. Within the limitations of the available accommodation it was an ideal temporary unit which was well away from the building site and also separate from the other residential areas.

A final quirk, or was it a last word? On the day of the move Philip decreed he would stay one more night in Swallow Cottages. Margaret saw this as a small price to pay if it satisfied his whim. The next morning he moved quite happily. "What was that all about?" we asked ourselves.

At the August Friends Staff Association meeting, we were pleased to see his allocated space for the first time. It included a bathroom, with a shower room not too far away. Although the shower room was outside the immediate confines of his living space it was adopted and his personal hygiene improved overnight.

On viewing his accommodation and sensing he was showing small signs of being more settled, I hit on the idea of creating a large wall chart running from mid-July until the arbitrary date of 5th January, when his flat would be ready, and his nightmare over. My time scale was dishonest, as I could see even at this early stage that Swallow Cottages would not be handed back to HFT by the developers on time. I reasoned it was preferable to choose an optimistic goal which could be moved to a firm date later rather than make the chart vast, with squares covering some eight months. By Christmas the accommodation areas would be clearly defined, enabling us to talk realistically about the future.

Philip immediately appreciated the chart's purpose when I explained it to him. He replied it was a 'good idea,' and so the chart was born. Margaret also thought it would help Philip, and others who would be staying on site, to see the days ticked off. Some of the current residents would be moving off-site into the community before the end of the year.

One could only feel sympathy for Margaret, with her workload. She was acting as 'clerk of works' for the builders, trying to find community accommodation for the soon to be displaced residents, recruiting staff and trying to ensure that the care of some forty residents was ongoing, and last but not least, acting as the focal point for parental concerns. With her assistant manager on maternity leave it was, in our opinion, an impossible burden to carry, hence if we had something to say which required action 'from above', we took a direct route with our queries. It saved Margaret acting as a Post Office and us then finding that her subservient superiors to Head Office were being dilatory and kicking issues into the long grass, hoping they would go away!

Weekends away for the purpose of watching cricket were still very acceptable even in Philip's distorted world. I arranged to deliver the chart when I called to collect him for our weekend in Nottingham, when the 2006 finals of the 20/20 would be played at Trent Bridge.

The arrival of the chart was greeted with great enthusiasm and immediately taken by Philip to be hung in the main hall of the house.

It was his chart and he wanted everyone to see him monitoring progress. By this time, over four weeks had elapsed since his initial occupation of his new accommodation. It was, therefore, with great aplomb that he gleefully scored out the first thirty days of the chart with his red felt-tipped pen. There was an immediate feeling that the next goal was now well within his comprehension. It didn't necessarily mean that during the intervening period he would always behave himself, but it did give him a topic which he could refer to and also act as a visual reminder that progress was being made.

Although Philip had never misbehaved with third parties, in view of what had gone before I explained to Mike and Judy, our hosts in Nottingham, that Philip was having a few behavioural problems at Downley Grange. Mike, who had known Philip for twenty years, was confident all would be well, and when we left they commented on the 'perfect gentleman' they had hosted.

The 20/20 finals were immediately followed by the annual cricket weekend with his cousin Philip, Angela and the twins. I provided the supper which always consisted of a selection of smoked and fresh delights from the sea. Alice would join us for the evening and transport Helen to Beaconsfield. Philip and I would join them for Sunday lunch when we collected Helen. It was a perfect family arrangement.

When cricket was in the offing, and Helen was about, Philip never fully relaxed until he could see she was ready to depart. Any teasing suggestion that she might join us at the cricket was always greeted with "No, just me and dad." Helen knew her place. In Philip's eyes it was a man's game!

There was never any nonsense on these weekends. Philip was always 'topped and tailed' and ready to have lunch out on our way to Reigate. This was followed on the Saturday by a day at Lords with his cousin Philip, a fitting climax to the well-established annual highlight of his social calendar.

During the day at Lords I had observed that his overall mood was noticeably down compared to three weeks earlier in Nottingham. At first I put this down to the cumulative effect of the drugs. At times, with his eyes closed, he appeared close to tears and he was obviously deep in thought. What was he thinking about? What was brewing?

On the Saturday evening I found out.   Suddenly he blurted out, "I don't want to go back to Downley Grange."   Obviously under the most intense emotional pressure, he had communicated his feelings. It was the first time in over twenty years he had made such an utterance.   In the past he may have gone quiet when the time to return had come, dilly-dallying around to delay his departure but never previously, given his limited language, had he made such a declaration.

Gathering my breath on the shock of hearing this I replied that we had to call at Downley Grange on our way back from Alice's on the Sunday and he could then come back with us to Woodbridge, if he chose to.   The issue was apparently resolved in his mind on the Sunday as he declined to continue home with us but agreed we could visit him on the following Saturday, on our way back from staying with Derek and Shirley near Marlow.   As we departed for home Helen gave him two options for the coming visit.   We could have a picnic lunch and visit Stansted Airport or he could return with us to Woodbridge, either after completing the first option or even not doing it.   Was there at last a gentle thaw in process, that we could even make these suggestions?

We duly arrived on the Saturday to be greeted by the news that Philip had been rather truculent during the morning but there had not been an incident.   We were thankful for small mercies!   Helen repeated her options of the previous week but he wasn't disposed to answer.

To defuse the issue she suggested he went to the shower room and had a shave.   On his return she asked him if he had decided what he wanted to do.   To our utter amazement, and with a big grin on his face, he said he would come to Woodbridge.   With complete spontaneity Helen threw her arms around his neck, gave him a big kiss and said, "Darling I am thrilled to hear that.   Now let's get the medication from Karen."

The relief on hearing those few words was indescribable.   It had been over four months since we had had him under our roof and now it was happening with no planning whatsoever.   Had we got him back from the brink?   Had we turned the corner?   We certainly hoped so, but these were early days.

As we left for Woodbridge, Philip asked when he would be coming back. To remove any pressure we answered that if he wished it could be the next day, so that he wouldn't miss his one-to-one on the Monday, but it was up to him to let us know.

There was an air of all round relief as the car left Downley Grange with an unexpected but most welcome additional passenger. Philip soon settled into working the indicators and flashing my lights as if nothing had been amiss for such a long, long period. He willingly helped Helen to make up his bed - he was totally relaxed to be back in our company.

The decision on whether Philip's return would be the next day was removed before it became an issue. Walking along the river wall at Woodbridge we met Aunty Mary and Uncle Ed (Philip's godfather) who were surprised and delighted to see him. They asked Philip how long he was staying, to which he immediately replied "a few days." Our problem was solved.

The 'few days' were extended to a week and then two weeks after we were again faced with a blurted out statement at breakfast on the third day that he did not want to return to Downley Grange. Helen countered this by saying she would have a word with Margaret to see if it was alright for him to stay a further week and then we could organise further regular visits for the diary. This placated him, at least for the time being.

As the end of the second week approached Philip became noticeably more reticent, culminating in our finding him in his bedroom sobbing his heart out that he had to go back to Downley Grange. Which was more distressing, him not wanting to come home or now to be faced with him not wanting to return? Our worlds had turned a full circle in a matter of days. Whilst we agreed it would be convenient for him to stay a further week we decided it may not be in the long term interests of any of us for this to happen. Distressed as we were we decided, after contacting Margaret, to abide by the two week arrangement.

In an attempt to defuse the problem we went through the family's ongoing commitments which included our trip to South Africa four weeks ahead. We built into the future a further four visits before the end of the year, culminating in accepting Alice's invitation to spend

Christmas with her in Beaconsfield followed by the New Year with us at Woodbridge.

Socially, with Philip around we had many years previously given up celebrating New Year with friends. It was a price we were prepared to pay to give him a long festive break. He in turn looked forward to enjoying a glass of champagne to welcome in the New Year. In general, Philip enjoyed the good things of life. An eating quirk in our eyes, and probably a further trait of his autism, is that each category of food on the plate is eaten separately but not in any particular order. The peas may go followed by the meat and then the beans. They are never mixed on the fork!

The setting out of the ongoing arrangements certainly helped to ease us over the immediate problems, but they intensified again on the day he was due to return to Downley Grange. He was weepy in bed and, on getting up, bravely tried to be grown up, although a tear was never far from his eyes. Thankfully there was no further outburst by way of protest. Throughout the $1\frac{1}{4}$ hour journey he dabbed his eyes and turned away from any eye contact with us. Who was most upset by the current emotions was impossible to tell. We had never previously had to cope with such an outpouring of emotion but knew that we had to stand firm. At times it would have been easier to have given in, but what then?

Back at Downley Grange, having unlocked his bedroom, it was business as normal with the first job to obliterate a further fifteen days from his wall chart. Thankfully, nobody had interfered with it in his absence. We left, rather bemused by the happenings over the previous two weeks but nevertheless heartened that our family bond had been re-established. However other issues were rearing their ugly heads.

As we had noted, the short periods of blankness which were reported to HFT some nine months earlier were, under stress, still happening, so we had asked for an EEG scan. The answer to this, from the Department of Neurology at the local hospital, had been simply to increase the current level of medication. In frustration at the remedy of pushing more pills down Philip's throat without any investigation, we offered to pay for the scan. We battled with the Clinical Assistant, who ultimately, but very reluctantly, conceded to our request. Surprise, surprise, the EEG showed 'abnormalities compatible with a seizure disorder with a left parietal temporal focus'. What this meant was that he was having mini-fits!

The detailed builder's drawings of Philip's proposed flat were provided. At first glance they immediately appeared unsuitable and impractical which led to me seeking permission to discuss our suggested amendments direct with the architect. With Derek's help realistic solutions were found and the District Executive was only too pleased for me to deal direct as it took the decision-making away from her.

The architect agreed that every point being suggested was valid and that the solutions were practical and, more to the point, the changes would not add to the sacrosanct budget! Thank you Derek, for your professional help!

Despite the battles and emotional upsets, we bade the year good-bye in better shape than when we had welcomed it in, twelve months earlier. Lots of water, both clean and dirty, had flowed under the bridge, but we were now looking forward to 2007 with an element of guarded optimism.

As expected, the handing back of Swallow Cottages to HFT drifted on to March. A few extra squares on Philip's chart were acceptable as the reconfiguration of the cottages took shape. We managed to have an unscheduled peek inside. Despite the rough interior I could identify Philip's future living-area for him. It certainly helped to reassure him that in a matter of weeks he would have his own private rooms, with his privacy restored, and his nightmare of uncertainty over.

Whilst he was still not 100% committed to Downley Grange, the vibes were improving and his behaviour more stable. One could not sense any excess level of excitement from Philip about moving back into Swallow Cottages but he was certainly looking forward to it even if it did mean another upheaval. We also looked forward to the move, hoping against hope that this would restore him to some semblance of what we perceived as his normal self. At present he was being suppressed by drugs and we didn't like that.

Come the day; come his sister! As Helen had previously had a serious operation, Alice had said she would like to help Philip move into his new accommodation. What a joy to behold and to hear their voices as they unpacked boxes together in his bedroom. They conversed and reached decisions about what should happen to various belongings. Alice quietly made the suggestions and Philip equally quietly acquiesced. It was simply magic to hear them.

Unpacking complete, Alice took Philip off into Epping to get shades, a throw for the settee and oddments for his shower room. Everyone who graced his flat with their presence during the day was greeted with the words, "This is my sister Alice. She is helping me to move into my new flat." This turned out to be a most important day in his life and he was purring with appreciation at the support his sister was giving him. With everyone whacked, but very satisfied, we left an exhausted Philip sitting on his settee just staring into space. Could he really believe his nightmare was over?

Another world was evolving. Gone were the constant agitated moods. Gone at least for the time being, was the fighting of officialdom. Gone were the uncertainties of our family life. Gone was the dropping of his eyes to avoid visual contact as his self esteem returned. What a traumatic two years for Philip, all in the quest of progress! Nobody could have foretold the agonies he'd had to endure – he was very close to going over the edge!!!

As we had earlier agitated for action we were invited to attend the six month follow-up meeting subsequent to Philip's EEG. Dr Roy, the Neurologist at the local hospital, was a much more positive person than we had imagined and we had a clear and concise two way exchange. She readily accepted and appreciated our earlier concerns, and was pleased to hear that Philip was now more settled. She agreed to reduce the levels of Risperdal, with the added proviso that if he remained stable it could be stopped altogether. Tegretol would remain, as already prescribed, and was likely to continue at the current levels. We bade her farewell in the knowledge that Philip had now been properly assessed. In conclusion, she expressed a willingness to see us again if it became necessary.

After six months back in Swallow Cottages, and various changes of staff, it was again Review time. Philip's new Key Worker, Ann, was good for him and tried to organise him into an acceptable way of life. Whilst we had had to endure "I don't want to return to Swallow Cottages," and the tearful sessions when weekend breaks were over, we had not expected to hear, during the report, that Philip said he didn't like living where he did, but that he used to. We were of the opinion that he was feeling settled and liked his new environment.

He was in some respects his own worst enemy, in that he interacted well with staff but only occasionally mingled with the three other residents in his unit, despite having known them all for many years. Whilst he looked forward to and enjoyed his one-to-one outings with Karen he did not relish going on group outings. He was still a loner, preferring his own company and watching his television.

At meal times he would often eat in his own room and his choice of food, namely pies, sausage rolls and bacon consumed late at night was a far from ideal diet. He still needed close supervision and constant cajoling to keep his weight down and to look after his personal hygiene.

Philip now had two very different worlds and it was a case of 'never the twain shall meet.' At Swallow Cottages he was erratic in his social and domestic behaviour but 'at home', with reminding, he shaved, showered, ate his three meals a day, and was generally very particular about changing his clothes. As pointed out by Dr. Hughes some years previously, he found it impossible to transfer disciplines from one location to another. Thankfully we were in receipt of the more predictable Philip, no doubt influenced by over forty years of being organised by his Mum!

On-site his priorities had changed in that he now paid scant attention to the Garden Centre and was more interested in having time on the computer, where he could seek out the personal details of various celebrities. Once seen, these facts were never forgotten and could be effortlessly recalled.

Philip has always been adept at recalling birth dates to which he now also adds, sometimes embarrassingly, a person's age. This gets updated in his brain as the years pass. His ability to store and retain this information amazes outsiders who do not realise it is an autistic trait which sadly in today's world produces lots of useless facts. In his low periods the one sure way of getting him to react is to start talking about birthdays and ages. It immediately ignites a spark!

After an inglorious start Philip had learnt to operate the unit's laundry room. He would watch the digital clock on the washer or dryer count down to zero and then sort the clothes into their respective piles and duly leave them outside the rooms of the other residents.

Aggressive incidents had reduced to just one in the past six months, but he no longer cycled, walked to get his newspaper or showed any interest in visiting Stansted Airport, all of which had formed part of his earlier regular routines.

It was confirmed that the family relationships had been fully healed, and visits, either to Alice or ourselves, were eagerly awaited events. What happened within his mind in those lost months we will never know but they were still painful memories which we hoped would never be repeated.

All in all a fair amount of spiky progress was reported and with the aggression having subsided, other more manageable traits which were occurring could be accepted. There was now no talk from Bucks C.C. suggesting he was in the wrong location but with the improved living conditions and increased staffing ratios in the dedicated Autistic Unit, the care costs requested by HFT were sure to increase, and ultimately become another battle for us to get involved in.

As time passed, old routines returned. He walked to get his newspaper and became a well-known figure as he strode up and down the road. There was a wide path for the entire length of the mile journey. This was just as well, as to avoid a dog he could easily have side-stepped into the road, such is his ongoing discomfort near them. He was again regularly swimming and, once in the pool, was minding his own business!

Cycling, which had been so important to him over some thirty-five years, has not been taken up again. It is only likely to be back on his agenda via my encouragement when at Woodbridge. I made the decision to let 'sleeping dogs lie.' For thousands of miles both of us had enjoyed the good fortune of not having had any serious problems on the roads, either mechanically or accident-wise. Would our luck one day run out? I was still fit, but now in my seventies, whilst Philip had put on weight and was far from fit for arduous journeys. An era was thus finally put to bed.

Some three years after the Downley Grange appeal was launched, it was time for The Princess Royal to formally open the new facilities. With all credit to HFT, despite the serious emotional problems suffered by Philip, what had been achieved looked splendid and made for a very attractive complex.

As part of the ongoing arrangements, Margaret telephoned advising that Philip's flat, out of the eighteen created, was the one that had been selected for use as an example of the development. There was just one problem: Philip had indicated that The Princess would not be welcome to look round his flat! Could we help him to change his mind? The earlier battles and cosmetic changes which were initially resisted had now made his unit into something the Trust was proud of, and rightly so. Additionally, Philip, if on top form, would be a marvellous ambassador for HFT.

We agreed to bring Philip home to try to persuade him to change his mind. Achieving a change of heart was easier said than done, added to which he had indicated that he did not want to be at Downley Grange when The Princess came. Was he taking after his father and being just plain difficult? We reported to Margaret that we were having problems, but that as a last resort we would try to bribe him.

For the first time ever, in our endeavour to support Margaret, we sat him down and said we had a proposition we wanted him to think over. Helen was the spokes-person saying, "Philip, we know you have said you do not want to see Princess Anne when she comes to Downley Grange, but she has specifically asked to see your flat after the Powerpoint presentation you gave her in 2005 when she was fifty-five. She also remembers you from 1986, when she was thirty-six and you were twenty. She would now like to meet you again and to see where you live. If you agree to meet her, the next time you are home we will go out for dinner at your favourite restaurant, the Bistro on the Quay."

The result of this heavy sales pitch was simply, "I'll let you know," which in Philip's language really means NO.

He then duly left the table. At a discreet distance we followed him and we listened at his bedroom door. We could hear him chuntering to himself about the proposition but, try as we may, we could not get the gist of his reactions. Talking to himself in solitude about ticklish issues helped him to sort them out, or to at least give the problem an airing.

Twenty-four hours later, Helen started to lay his smartest clothes out on his bed, with the 'throw away' comment that he would look 'the bee's knees' in his blazer on Friday. As there was no adverse reaction to this we let Margaret know we thought we were winning and would arrive early for him to rehearse a welcome. There was a chuckle, coupled with an air of relief in Margaret's voice, as Philip had been chosen as the initial star turn to start off The Princess's visit, and his decline would have caused a hurried rethink. We kept our fingers crossed that there would be no last minute hiccups.

It would be wrong to report that the next two days were full of enthusiasm for the task in question but come the Friday morning a very smart, six foot, upright young man, adorned in blazer and light trousers, strode out to the waiting car. It was obvious he was 'going to do the business' and a message was left at Downley Grange that he was on his way and in good spirits.

In view of the earlier reticence there had been no rehearsals of how Philip should welcome The Princess to his flat. Of course there was a protocol to be followed and Philip was duly briefed. The Princess would knock on his door and he should open it, bow, and greet her with "Good morning ma'am, please come in." The rehearsals went well and everyone relaxed, including Helen, who Philip indicated was not needed. She duly left to attend the main reception. In the event protocol went ever so slightly awry. The Princess had to knock not once as planned but twice before the door was flung open and, without any pretence of a bow she was greeted with a bright and breezy, "Morning, Hello Princess Anne, come in." For good measure she could have had her birth date added to the greeting but it didn't happen, on this occasion!

As The Princess accepted Philip's invitation she smiled and asked him to show her round. As she stood talking in the lounge she spied his miniature framed cricket bats hanging on the wall. I had selectively bought the bats, each with a photograph of the star player involved, adorning the top of the blade. They were not any old stars; they were the ones important in Philip's following of cricket. Having sent the bats off to each player, they had all responded magnificently.

The six bats, three in each of two wooden frames and all personally- autographed to Philip, in Pop Larkin's language looked 'purrfik'. The greetings were plain to see:-

1. *To Philip, Happy Christmas and Best Wishes 2005 Graham Hick* – It was a marvellous statistic for Philip to devour when Graham reached 100 centuries and with every subsequent 100 he duly reported the event to me at the time of our next Sunday evening telephone call.

2. *To Philip, Happy 40th, Ian Botham (Beefy)* - Ian had won the Jogle Association Eagle Trophy previously to Philip - his cricketing exploits are legendary.

3. *To Philip, Best Wishes Graham Gooch* – Philip's video of Graham's 333 run Test Innings against India must be nearly worn out!

4. *To Philip, Best Wishes Darren Gough* - A larger than life character who had joined Essex after a long Test Match career.

5. *To Philip 40 n.o., Brian Lara 400 n.o.* - The prize possession. What a star, holder of the Test Match record of an innings of 375 runs which he lost to Matthew Hayden, when he scored 380 runs. He then won it back with an innings of 400 against England. Without any research, or prior knowledge of the question, Philip supplied this statistic.

To my shame I checked the facts he gave me. Of course they were correct. I cannot recall a time when, having doubted something Philip has said, he has not been proved 100% correct - oh ye of little faith - and we still do it!

6. *Brian Lara* - With Brian having retired and only occasionally visiting this country, so desperate was I to get this signature that I had two options going. The first bat had been autographed through the co-operation of Warwickshire C.C. but the second one, simply emblazoned with a vast signature, was obtained via 'The Home of Cricket', the secretariat at Lords.

Having seen and referred to the bats, The Princess was then bombarded with a load of facts, which to her credit, she tried to assimilate. She was intrigued with the personalisation of the Brian Lara bat. When she met Helen later she immediately linked her with Philip and, with a beaming face, related the story of the information which had been imparted to her with such enthusiasm. The animation had been such that she had even been in receipt of a wagging pointing finger – all very much against protocol!

The remainder of the day went like clockwork. Philip was HFT's ambassador throughout. He was ready to welcome all and sundry to look round his flat. He was proud of it, and rightly so.

When Margaret met Helen at the formal reception she could not contain herself and related the saga of the unscheduled reception received by The Princess, adding that for one scary moment she'd feared he had changed his mind about her admission. Was this brinkmanship at its best?

Another emergency was soon upon us. Christmas was over and we were looking forward to New Years Eve, when suddenly Philip's slightly protruding front tooth erupts and has to be removed. Our local dentist was superb. Even late on New Years Eve he took an emergency appointment. As he concluded the treatment he said to Philip, "Now no alcohol this evening young man." "Ah, ah, ah my champagne," exclaimed Philip through his still numb mouth. Helen related the ritual of the evening and a single glass was permitted and enjoyed.

The tooth, which had been loose for some time, had obviously been the cause of both breath and body odour problems. Food was accumulating around the gums. Both odours disappeared with the tooth!

On speaking to Geoffrey of the Jogle Association, he asked if Philip would make the presentation of the Eagle Trophy at the forthcoming January dinner. Richard Barber, the Chairman of HFT, a man I admire for his hard-working no nonsense approach to life, had cycled from Lands End to John O'Groats and was the winner of the trophy. In view of Philip's history in winning the trophy twice, and as Richard was also supporting HFT, the committee felt it would add a personal touch if one of Richard's minions was able to present him with his trophy.

Having not wished to attend the dinner for five years I was not sure how Philip would respond to the invitation. As he was to be in the limelight this would no doubt have had some bearing on his agreement to attend. He would be returning into the company of people who had witnessed his two greatest triumphs. It would be just like old times making the long journey back to the West Country.

Having briefed Philip on what he was expected to do, and on being beckoned by the Jogle Chairman to join him at the top table, he stood motionless but obviously feeling very important, listening to the citation before being handed the cup to pass to Richard. In passing over the cup he said, "Well done Richard." He was an old hand at such ceremonies! Richard, gentleman that he is, showed his pleasure on being able to receive the trophy from Philip.

Even as I approach the conclusion of my story, events are still unfolding. Philip has still not resumed his cycling but now enjoys the freedom of long walks. He always walks ahead but will stop at a point where paths converge if he is unsure which direction to take.

One beautiful sunny morning, however, just before I'd completed writing this book, Philip and I were having a relaxing walk between two of his favourite places, Flatford and Dedham on the Essex/Suffolk border, in the area known as Constable Country. We expected our chosen circular route to be a pleasant two-hour jaunt; great exercise for Philip, and his Dad!

As usual Philip strode on ahead and then waited patiently as I leaned over a bridge on the River Stour to take some photographs of baby coots who were chasing insects on the top of a large pad of flowering water-lilies. They were a sheer delight to watch, although not something to interest Philip.

We climbed a long open-meadow gradient and as I observed the timeless view below I saw Philip a little way off tying up his shoelaces at the forthcoming stile. Without taking too much notice I walked on and arrived at the stile, although I had some difficulty climbing it due to having injured my knee in a game of tennis a few days earlier. In climbing the stile I somehow managed to drop the lens cap of my camera and was forced to climb back over the stile as I could not recover it through the animal proof wire mesh. A tiresome task considering my troublesome knee!

Having regained my equilibrium I looked ahead to find Philip had mounted the next stile and was out of sight. Not a problem, I thought to myself as I hurried the hundred or so yards to catch up with him. In my haste, however, I managed to take the wrong fork on the cart track which bisected the path and it was only after walking for another hundred yards that I realised I should have taken the other fork which led through the woods. I retraced my steps confident that, with his phenomenal memory, Philip would have remembered to take the correct path out of the three choices available to him.

Realising that Philip, with his long loping strides, would be some distance ahead of me at this point, and with no chance of glimpsing him through the wooded area through which I now walked, I hurried through the ascending, overgrown pathway and met a young couple with a bounding dog coming in the opposite direction. I asked if they had seen a young man in blue jeans, a blue and white check shirt and a white sun hat. I was dumbfounded when they told me they had not seen Philip, however they offered me the use of their mobile phone to call him.

"He doesn't have a mobile," I emotionally replied, "and if he did he wouldn't be able to use it, or tell me where he was." By now feeling helpless, but trying to keep calm, I set out to retrace my steps over half a mile. Getting more and more hot and bothered, with a raging headache to go with my rising blood pressure and the temperature, already in the eighties I raced along the difficult pathways, calling out to him in the hope that he would reply. Along the way I met another couple who'd not seen anybody matching Philip's description. It was a nightmare situation, as there were so many footpath options in the area that if he had gone wrong I would have had no idea where he could be, and he would not be visible through the many hedgerows.

As I got to within a hundred yards of the three-way junction, still calling out, to my enormous relief a voice answered, "Dad!" It was Philip, who had mistakenly taken a wrong turning himself and had walked on oblivious that I was not following. Fortuitously after eight hundred yards he had correctly interpreted a 'Private no entry' sign and retraced his steps. To ease my distress, we laughed about being silly and losing ourselves. All was well that ended well and we enjoyed the remainder of our walk! I did not calm down until we reached Flatford and had a strong coffee, once again realising that, even at forty-four, Philip is still very vulnerable. Under supervision he may have ridden the length of England and Scotland but in a distressed state, on his own, he could have been in big trouble.

Where better could I reflect on the contents of this book than St. Edmundsbury Cathedral at Bury St. Edmunds. As a family we were still in harmony and with Philip we were listening to a concert being performed by the Grimethorpe Colliery Band. My mind turned to Tuba-playing Bill, the manager of Downley Grange some twenty-five years earlier, and Margaret and her staff, who have supported Philip for the past fifteen years. The band incidentally had starred as the fictional Brass Band Grimley in the entertaining British film "Brassed Off."

Despite our problems over the years we had no reason to link the film title to our affairs. Together we have enjoyed our lives. Challenges and low spots there may have been but we must not forget the happy times, the achievements and the high points, the latter, in hindsight, far outweighing the former. May this continue for many years to come!

In writing this book to catalogue the ups and downs, achievements and flat spots in Philip's life, the book's title is also intended to encapsulate the plight of many thousands of families similarly affected and hopefully to inspire them to both enjoy and cherish the shafts of light and joy as they appear. Rest assured that you are truly 'not alone' during the many ensuing struggles. Life is never a 'bowl of cherries,' there will always be obstacles along the way. The skill is to make the best of one's lot and to remember that life is not a rehearsal for anything else. We all need to make the most of it!!!!

Appendix

INVITATION

If you have enjoyed the contents of this book and would like to make a donation to assist with the sterling work of HFT please send it to 21 Ipswich Road, Woodbridge, Suffolk IP12 4BS - All donations will be acknowledged.

I wish to donate £   to assist with the work of HFT - Registered Charity No. 313069

I am a UK Tax payer and want HF Trust Ltd to treat all gifts of money I have made in the past 4 years and all future gifts of money that I make from the date of this declaration as Gift Aid donations. I understand that I must pay an amount of income tax or capital gains tax each year (6 April one year to 5 April the next) that is at least equal to the amount of tax that HFT will reclaim on my gifts for that tax year.

Signature ....

Date ....

Full Name ....

Address ....

....

Post Code ....

THANK YOU FOR YOUR SUPPORT - IT IS VERY MUCH APPRECIATED